Rudolf Otto and the Foundation of the History of Religions

Also Available from Bloomsbury

All Religion Is Inter-Religion
Edited by Kambiz GhaneaBassiri and Paul Robertson

Community and Worldview among Paraiyars of South India
Anderson H. M. Jeremiah

Narratives of Disenchantment
Edited by Robert A. Yelle and Lorenz Trein

Rudolf Otto and the Foundation of the History of Religions

Yoshitsugu Sawai

BLOOMSBURY ACADEMIC
LONDON • NEW YORK • OXFORD • NEW DELHI • SYDNEY

BLOOMSBURY ACADEMIC
Bloomsbury Publishing Plc
50 Bedford Square, London, WC1B 3DP, UK
1385 Broadway, New York, NY 10018, USA
29 Earlsfort Terrace, Dublin 2, Ireland

BLOOMSBURY, BLOOMSBURY ACADEMIC and the Diana logo are trademarks of Bloomsbury Publishing Plc

First published in Great Britain 2022
Paperback edition published 2023

A catalogue record for this book is available from the British Library.

Library of Congress Control Number: 2021950373

ISBN: HB: 978-1-3502-5944-7
PB: 978-1-3502-5947-8
ePDF: 978-1-3502-5945-4
eBook: 978-1-3502-5943-0

Typeset by RefineCatch Limited, Bungay, Suffolk

Contents

Preface vi
Acknowledgments xi

Introduction The History of Religions and Otto's Perspectives on Religion 1

1 Otto's Lifetime as a Christian Theologian 13
2 Journeys to the East: India as the Foundation of Otto's Comparative Religion 29
3 Comparative Religious Perspectives on *the Holy* 51
4 Influences of the History-of-Religions School on Otto's Religious Theory 71
5 Parallelism of Mysticism in Religions East and West 85
6 The Concept of the "Wholly Other" and the Experience of the Depth 103
7 Vedānta Philosophy as the Discourse of Mystic Experience 115
8 Toward the Semantic Understanding of Religions 127

Conclusion 147
Notes 151
Bibliography 177
Index 189

Preface

The discipline of the History of Religions or *Religionswissenschaft* came into existence in Europe from the latter part of the nineteenth to the beginning of the twentieth centuries, freeing itself from Christian theology, and Protestant theology in particular. In this regard, however, one should keep in mind that there was not one single uniform development of the History of Religions in Europe, but a rather pluralistic development. For the History of Religions was known differently in each language area, and was tied to different academic disciplines (e.g., sociology in France). Against the traditional background of Western Christian cultures, the religious concepts and their framework in the study of the History of Religions were constructed. Thus, the religious concepts and their implications, influenced by Western religions and cultures, reflect these cultural aspects. In other words, the conceptual frameworks of the History of Religions were constructed under the influence of religious traditions in modern Europe, especially Protestant faith and culture. In the modern academic world of religious studies, particularly since the 1990s, on the basis of such an understanding of the conceptual frameworks of the History of Religions, international historians of religions have been globally reexamining the religious concepts used in their studies. In Germany, this started much earlier, in the 1970s. This meant a reexamination of older conceptual frameworks of the History of Religions that were based on Christian theology.

Rudolf Otto (September 25, 1869–March 6, 1937) was one of the scholars in religious studies who contributed to the establishment of the History of Religions. His significant works left an impact on the development of the contemporary study of religion. Many historians of religion were influenced by his works, including Gustav Mensching (1901–78), Friedrich Heiler (1892–1967), Joachim Wach (1898–1955), and Mircea Eliade (1907–86). Gustav Mensching who was a student of Otto, cooperated with him in developing new types of liturgical matters in Christian services. Friedrich Heiler was an ardent admirer of Otto after he met him personally when he was appointed to a professorship in Marburg University. Moreover, in their original ways of dealing with Otto, Joachim Wach and Mircea Eliade included Otto's ideas in their religious theories respectively. Before Otto's death, there were arguments for and against his works on religion. According to the American historian of religions Robert A. Orsi, Christian theologians found Otto "insufficiently Christian," while other scholars accused him of "imposing a Christian construct on other religions." Liberal Protestants faulted Otto for "overemphasizing the emotional dimension of religion at the expense of the ethical and the rational," while conservative Protestants did not like "his openness to other religions."[1] Thus, his works had opposing critiques, but it is obvious that his research has played an important role in the development of the History of Religions.

Otto was a Lutheran theologian who served as professor of Systematic Theology at Marburg University in Germany. In 1928, when he delivered his final lecture before resigning from Marburg, he is said to have described himself to his students as "a pious Lutheran adherent" (*pietistischer Lutheraner*). After he was called to Marburg in the summer of 1917, he remained there for the last twenty years of his life. He was fully active for the first ten years, and continued to conduct research and limited teaching for the last ten years.[2] As Otto himself suggests, Luther's theological perspective and faith were at the core of all of his own lifelong works. Like Luther's Christian faith, Otto's perspective was not derived from his theological reflection, but an interpretation of his deep and living religious experiences. As I shall argue later, Luther's theological framework obviously supports Otto's interpretations of *the numinous* in his religious theory.

In constructing the concept of *the numinous,* Otto "recalled Luther's expressions, and borrowed them from his *divina majestas* and *metuenda voluntas*," which had rung in his ears from the time of his earliest study of Luther. Moreover, he understood *the numinous* and its difference from the rational in Luther's *De Servo Arbitrio* long before he identified it in the *qādosch* of the Old Testament and in the elements of "religious awe" in the history of religions.[3] His statement suggests why in his final lecture at Marburg University, Otto called himself "a pious Lutheran adherent." During his life, Otto worked on Christian theology, philosophy of religion, and comparative religion, all of which are organically interrelated in his unique Christian theology. As his calling himself "a pious Lutheran adherent" suggests, his Lutheran faith penetrates his life and works. In later life, he influenced both Christian theology and the History of Religions. Even today, his works are still influential among scholars of religious studies. In the contemporary field of the History of Religions as well, such religious concepts as *the holy* (*das Heilige*), *the numinous* (*das Numinose*), and *the wholly other* (*das ganz Andere*) are critically used as key terms.

Moreover, Otto's religious thought is known to have asserted a certain influence on the Eranos Conference, a meeting of minds in which such scholars as the psychologist Carl Gustav Jung, the historian of religions Mircea Eliade, the Islamic philosopher Henry Corbin, the Jewish philosopher Gershom Scholem, the Islamic and Oriental philosopher Toshihiko Izutsu, and the clinical psychologist James Hillman participated. The Eranos Conference was conceived as "a meeting place for the minds of the East and West" by Olga Fröbe-Kapteyn (1881–1962). Fröbe-Kapteyn was interested in philosophy, religions (especially Indian religions), and depth psychology. She was born of Dutch parents in London and received a large inheritance from her father. She founded the Eranos Conference in 1933; it was named *Eranos* (ἔρανος) at the suggestion of Rudolf Otto when she consulted with him about the conference. This international conference was annually held in late August at Ascona on the shores of Lake Maggiore in Switzerland from 1933 until 1988.[4]

While keeping close contacts with Christian theology, though simultaneously gradually separating from it, the academic field of the History of Religions was established in Europe from the second half of the nineteenth century to the first half of the twentieth century. The period of Otto's activity was indeed transitional, a time in which the History of Religions became independent of Christian theology. In such an academic environment, Otto developed his Christian theology, conscious of being a Lutheran theologian. At the same time, his study of comparative religion, focusing on Indian religious thought, constituted an important academic field in his Christian theological studies. In Europe, where Christianity had been the basis of religion and culture, he developed his understanding of Indian thought as "religion," while taking "other religions" in the East seriously. In reinterpreting Otto's works in the contemporary academic polemics of the History of Religions, one can regard his religious theory as foundational to "the History of Religions."

For a contemporary perspective of the History of Religions, it is important to examine the adequacy of Otto's various religious concepts. When the independent discipline of *Religionswissenschaft* arose and developed from the latter half of the nineteenth to the beginning of the twentieth centuries, his concepts of religion were widely employed in the academic world of religious studies. But an important question remains: are these concepts effective in understanding not only Western religions but also non-Western ones? Reconsidering Otto's concepts may help answer that question. For the contemporary study of religions, Otto's research on religions includes some noteworthy facts. As suggested above, while conscious of himself as a Protestant theologian, he pursued significant studies of Indian religious thought. He thought he could more deeply understand the truth of Christianity in which he had placed his faith. An indication that he was deeply interested in studying Indian religious thought was his trip to the East from 1911–12. On this trip, he first visited North India, where he found Indian religions and philosophy deeply fascinating. At first, Otto planned to visit South India, but he cancelled that trip in order to stay longer in North India.

Since the Age of Discovery, through cultural exchanges with such non-Western societies as Africa, India, China, and Japan, European societies have gained a great deal of information about the religions and languages of various areas. In the latter half of the eighteenth century, Indology was born in Europe. Prompted by Western scholars' discovery of Sanskrit, the academic field of comparative linguistics was also established. The foundation of Indology was laid by officials of the East India Company of that era, such as William Jones (1746–94), Charles Wilkins (1749–1836), and Henry Thomas Colebrooke (1765–1837). In classical Indian studies, Western scholars learned Sanskrit from the Brahmin paṇḍits (in Sanskrit, *paṇḍita* meaning "a learned or wise man"), who for millennia memorized the scriptures and transmitted the oral tradition of the "spoken scriptures." These scriptures, later published as "books," became precisely "written scriptures." The earliest full translation into European languages was of the *Bhagavadgītā*, which was translated into English by Charles Wilkins, Secretary of the East India Company, and published in London in 1785.

On February 2, 1786, on the third anniversary of the Asiatic Society of Bengal in Calcutta, William Jones, the first president of this Society and an orientalist, delivered a commemorative discourse, "On the Hindus." In this lecture, Jones argued that Sanskrit is "of a wonderful structure; more perfect than Greek, more copious than Latin, and more exquisitely refined than either," and that Sanskrit and European languages could "have sprung from some common source, which, perhaps, no longer exists." He called attention to the fact that Sanskrit's vocabulary and grammar are significantly similar to Greek and Latin.[5] This lecture prompted subsequent research into the Indo-European languages and later paved the way for the formation of such disciplines as comparative linguistics, comparative religion, and comparative mythology. From the middle of the nineteenth century, many Indian classical documents, especially those in Sanskrit, translated into English and German, were introduced to European societies. In this way, knowledge of Indian culture spread broadly throughout Europe. With such a background, Otto conducted research on Indian religious thought, which he placed in the field of Christian theological studies.

In this book, I discuss the totality of Otto's religious perspective at a time when other scholars were separating the History of Religions from Christian theology. Otto had three "faces": the first was his "face" as a German Protestant theologian. His second "face" was that of a neo-Kantian philosopher of religion, attending to both the rational and non-rational aspects of religion. He attempted to illuminate the theoretical basis for the understanding of religion and to elucidate its nature with such concepts as *the numinous*. Otto's third "face" was that of a scholar of comparative religious studies. To reiterate, he studied not only Christian thought and faith, but was also interested in Eastern religions, especially Indian religion. Thus, he was a Christian theologian, a philosopher of religion, and a scholar of religious studies. In previous studies of Otto, these three "faces" have been interpreted separately, presenting a one-sided view of him as a scholar and human being. This book attempts to redress that imbalance by presenting a more rounded view.

By gathering and re-evaluating previous studies of Otto, this book tries to clarify all of his perspectives on religion. It will be possible to gain a deeper understanding of the significance and effect of his work in the contemporary field of the History of Religions. The purpose of the book is to elucidate the totality of his perspectives on religion from a semantic viewpoint. Thus, the book might have been entitled "A Semantic Understanding of Rudolf Otto," suggesting that it consists primarily of applying semantic analysis to Otto's religious theory. In the words of the Japanese philosopher Toshihiko Izutsu (1914–93), what I call "semantics" here means "an analytical study of the key-terms of a language with a view to arriving eventually at a conceptual grasp of the *Weltanschauung* or world-view of the people who use that language as a tool not only of speaking and thinking, but, more important still, of conceptualizing and interpreting the world that surrounds them."[6] Thus, the semantic understanding of religion in this book is a study of the nature and structure of the worldview in Otto's theory of religion, characterized by such key terms as *the holy*, *the numinous*, and *the wholly other*. In other words, it is a study of the "meaning" of religion, argued in Otto's works.

Before ending this preface, I would like to note that the book is based on my research on Otto's religious theory, on which I have continued for more than thirty years, especially on my Japanese book *Rudolf Otto: The Origin of the History of Religions* (in Japanese, *Rudorufu ottō: shūkyō-gaku no genten*), published by Keio University Press, Tokyo, in 2019. Thus, this book is the culmination of my Otto studies so far. Nothing would give me more joy than for the book to contribute even a little to future research on Rudolf Otto's religious theory and to religious studies in general.

Acknowledgments

Otto's book *Das Heilige* (1917) has been called a classic masterpiece in the History of Religions. His study of religion has contributed significantly to the development of religious studies and still arouses various discussions among scholars of religion today. Such religious concepts as the "numinous" and the "wholly other," which Otto emphasized, have been helpful in examining the methods and theories of contemporary religious studies.

Over the years, Otto's work has been studied and referenced by not only scholars of his theory of religion, but also among many scholars of the History of Religions. He made a great contribution to the development of religious studies, but evaluation varied among the critics and depending on which aspect of his research was under consideration.

As repeatedly discussed in this book, Otto had three "faces." The three "faces" are those of a Lutheran theologian as well as a professor of Christian systematic theology at Marburg University, a philosopher of religion who wrote such books as *Kantisch-Fries'sche Religionsphilosophie und ihre Anwendung auf die Theologie* (1909), and a scholar of comparative religion, focusing on Indian religious thought. In this book, I have attempted to clarify his view of religious studies by unifying these three "faces" as much as possible. Of particular interest is his study of Indian religious thought, hitherto underplayed by scholars. As I delved into his theory of religion, I became more and more aware of his breadth and depth and, one after another, new issues emerged. Unfortunately, my research is still far from a complete understanding of Otto's theory of religion. However, I am glad to be able to publish my research so far, based on my understanding of Otto.

Before starting my book, I would like to touch on the moment when I initially became interested in Otto's theory of religion. It dates back to the time of my study at Harvard University. At that time, Professor John B. Carman, who was the Director of the Center for the Study of World Religions at Harvard University, was also my academic advisor. Dr. Carman is a well-known historian of religion, who is familiar with such phenomenological theories of religion as those of Rudolf Otto and William Brede Kristensen (1867–1953), as well as Rāmānuja's Vedānta philosophy. Moreover, during my time at Harvard, Professor Wilfred C.

Smith, who contributed greatly to religious studies in the latter half of the twentieth century, directed the core seminar of the doctoral program. Professor Smith taught me the importance of maintaining a sympathetic understanding of religion.

One day in the summer of 1984, when I had completed my doctoral dissertation for submission to Harvard University, Professor Carman gave me the following advice: "Otto as a Protestant theologian studied Indian religious thought. Through his study of Indian religious thought, he sought to gain a deeper understanding of Christian teaching and faith. Yoshi [meaning me], you have been studying Indian religious thought while having faith in Tenrikyo. In a sense, you are in a position very similar to Otto. So if you work on Otto's theory of religion, I think that you can conduct a very interesting study. Following Otto's example, you can ground your History of Religion in your own Tenrikyo theology, even if that means a different kind of scholarship than that of many Japanese and Western scholars, who do not want to be considered 'theologians.'" After finishing my studies in the United States, and even after I returned to Japan, Professor Carman's words left a deep impression and I found opportunities for research on Otto. For many years now, I have been giving presentations on Otto at conferences such as the annual meetings of the Japanese Association for Religious Studies (JARS) and other academic meetings.

Tenri University, where I have taught the study of religion, has a sister university relationship with Marburg University, where Otto taught Christian theology. Academic exchanges between the two universities have been actively carried out over the years. Dr. Martin Kraatz (former Director of the Marburger Religionskundliche Sammlung), known for his research on Otto, visited Tenri University several times with Mrs. Margot Kraatz. I myself had the opportunity to visit Marburg University several times to participate in conferences. In my research on Otto's religious theory, Dr. Kraatz helped me immensely at Marburg University and also provided me with a lot of valuable advice and comments on the manuscript of this book. Moreover, Professors Toshimaro Hanazono and Tsuyoshi Maeda, my seniors at Tohoku University, also provided help on my research on Otto's theory of religion. Before the publication of this book, Professor John B. Carman and Mrs. Ann Carman gave me thoughtful advice and comments.

Moreover, in developing the presentation of Otto's religious theory, I received valuable comments and advice from such scholars of religious studies as Professor Gavin Flood of Oxford University, Professor Gergory D. Alles of McDaniel College, Professor Francis X. Clooney S.J. of Harvard University, and

Dr. Katja Triplett of Leipzig University. Many other scholars and colleagues also helped me in advancing my Otto studies. I would like to express my heartfelt gratitude to all of them. Moreover, my thanks go to my old colleague, Professor Matthew Eynon, formerly of Tenri University, who offered stylistic suggestions for my manuscript and to Bloomsbury Academic and in particular, Lalle Pursglove and Lily McMahon, who kindly assisted with the publication of this book. It is thanks to the efforts of all of these people that this manuscript finally reached the publication stage. I would like to express my heartfelt gratitude to all, including those not mentioned here, who offered their generous help leading to the publication of this book. Finally, I would like to express my sincere gratitude to my parents and family.

June 30, 2021

Yoshitsugu Sawai
Tenri, Japan

Introduction

The History of Religions and Otto's Perspectives on Religion

In the first half of the twentieth century, liberal Christian theologians such as Rudolf Otto (1869–1937), Nathan Söderblom (1866–1931), and Friedrich Heiler (1892–1967) placed the experiences of *the numinous* and *the holy* in the center of Christian thought and faith from the viewpoint of the comparative study of world religions. They placed experiences of *the holy* not only at the center of Christianity, but also at the center of all other religions.

Even today, Otto is known as the author of a classic in religious studies, *Das Heilige: Über das Irrationale in der Idee des Göttlichen und sein Verhältnis zum Rationalen*. Otto, a Lutheran theologian who was a professor of Systematic Theology at Marburg University, focused on Christian theology as well as on the study of religions, including Indian religious thought. Consequently, there have been many academic attempts to elucidate Otto's work in its entirety. Considering his religious studies as foundational in the field of the History of Religions, it is essential to grasp his comparative religious viewpoint. In this Introduction, I will review the history and theoretical background of the History of Religions, noting its development in nineteenth-century Europe. Moreover, I will review previous studies of Otto.

1 Origin of the History of Religions

Before Otto's work, considerable research had already been done in Europe on Indian religious thought. After the fifteenth century, a considerable amount of information became available on non-Western countries. Some European merchants and Christian missionaries became interested in studying Sanskrit and Indian thought. In Europe, Indology as a discipline was established in the eighteenth century. Scholars and others in England especially worked to gain an understanding of Indian culture, religion, and thought in order to govern India as a colonial country. Europeans were attracted to an unknown and mysterious Oriental wisdom, which influenced the establishment of Indology. William Jones (1747–94) founded the Asiatic Society of Bengal in Calcutta in 1784, and Charles Wilkins (1749–1836), a secretary of the East India Company, learned Sanskrit and translated the Hindu scripture, the *Bhagavad-gītā*, into English in 1785. This was the first book translated from Sanskrit into a European language in the modern period. Later, when interest in Indian culture and thought spread throughout Europe, the study of Indian classics began in earnest. As a result, studies were published by William Jones, Henry Thomas Colebrooke (1765–1837), and the Schlegel brothers, i.e., August Wilhelm von Schlegel (1767–1845) and Karl Wilhelm Friedrich von Schlegel (1772–1829).

History of Religions as a discipline was established by Friedrich Max Müller (1823–1900), a German-born Orientalist, who lived in England for most of his life and worked in Sanskrit studies and comparative philology. In his four lectures, *Introduction to the Science of Religion*, delivered at the Royal Institution in London in 1870, Müller coined the term "the Science of Religion" (*Religionswissenschaft*) for the discipline of the comparative study of religions. Earlier, in 1850, as deputy professor of modern European languages, he worked on Vedic Sanskrit at Oxford University. Later in 1868, he became the first professor of comparative philology at Oxford. Moreover, Müller was the editor of the *Sacred Books of the East* (1879–1910) that consisted of a fifty-volume English translation of Eastern scriptures. This publication stands as concrete proof that the academic foundation of the History of Religions was firmly established. In comparing Western religions with Eastern from the viewpoint of comparative philology, Max Müller studied the mythical thought of ancient India. In so doing, he established "the Science of Religion" as an independent discipline. He is regarded as one of the founders of the fields of comparative philology, comparative mythology, and comparative religion; his book *Introduction to the Science of Religion* (1873) was the first to include "the Science of Religion" in a title. He is known for applying Goethe's words to religion: "He who knows one religion, knows none" (*Wer eine Religion kennt, kennt keine*). What Müller implied is that a scholar who knows only Christian teachings knows nothing of religion; he emphasized the significance of comparative studies involving non-Christian religions.

Since the mid-nineteenth century, scholars have researched the origin of Indo-European language groups; many Indian classics were introduced to Western countries. Therefore, knowledge about Indian culture expanded throughout European societies, and Western Indology was related to comparative philology. The nineteenth-century interest in the origin of religions became less important in the twentieth century. Many Christian scholars implicitly or explicitly regarded Christianity as the highest form of religion.[1] Otto also considered the field of comparative studies as part of Christian theology. Otto thus committed himself to the study of Indian religious thought as well as to the study of Christian theology and the philosophy of religion. Although various Otto studies have been undertaken, no serious research on his understanding of Indian religious thought has been conducted. Still a Christian theologian, Otto broadened his study to include Indian religious tradition after his first journey to India and Japan. In India, he became very interested in the Hindu Vaiṣṇava faith that emphasized *bhakti* (devotion) as a means of salvation. Witnessing the faith of Vaiṣṇava followers, Otto called it "India's religion of grace" (*die Gnadenreligion Indiens*) and regarded it as a parallel to Christianity.[2] By learning more about Indian religion, he felt he could more deeply understand the truth of Christianity.

At that time, European scholars of Indian philosophy knew a great deal about the Vedānta philosophy, especially the philosophy of Śaṅkara (*c.* 700–750), the leading proponent of Advaita (non-dual) Vedānta. Otto was also interested in Rāmānuja (1017–1137), the chief proponent of Viśiṣṭādvaita (qualified non-dual) Vedānta philosophy. In fact, in *West-östliche Mystik: Vergleich und Unterscheidung zur Wesensdeutung* (1926), Otto compares Śaṅkara's philosophy with that of Meister Eckhart (*c.* 1260–1328). In contrast to Śaṅkara's philosophy, well-known to European scholars, Rāmānuja's Viśiṣṭādvaita (qualified non-dual) Vedānta philosophy that emphasized faith in a personal God (*bhakti*), was not as well known in Europe at that time. It was Otto who first brought Rāmānuja's thought to the European academic world, as pointed out by the historian of religions Philip C. Almond.[3]

Following his journey, Otto writes in the first section of *Vischnu-Nārāyana: Texte zur indischen Gottesmystik* (1917) about his "first encounter with Viṣṇu" (*Erste Begegnung mit Vischnu*).[4] As the historian of religions Hans Rollmann says, "It fell to Rudolf Otto to introduce Vaiṣṇavism and Rāmānuja to Germany, at a time when Deussen's previous publications on Advaitavedānta had left theologians and historians of religion with the impression that this philosophical tradition was the only authoritative expression of India's philosophy."[5] As Rollmann points out, Paul Deussen (1845–1919), a German Orientalist and philosopher, had previously published works on Indian philosophy, with a special interest in Śaṅkara's Advaita Vedānta philosophy. Thus, especially in the 1930s, Otto attracted attention in the European academic world.

Like Otto, Ernst Troeltsch (1865–1923), a Protestant theologian, also recognized the significance of including the study of other religions in Christian theology. As seen in his works such as "Die Dogmatik der 'religionsgeschichtlichen Schule'" (1913), Troeltsch emphasized the significance of Christian theological studies from a comparative viewpoint. However, as a historian of religions, Joachim Wach argues that, unlike Otto, Troeltsch lacked knowledge of the philosophy of non-Christian religions. When the History of Religions was established as a discipline, many scholars separated it from normative Christian theology. At the same time, however, as Troeltsch points out, the History of Religions came to include Christian theology of different denominations. But differences among various Protestant denominations "turned off" more secular scholars.[6] In such an academic environment, Otto deepened his understanding of other religions, especially through his translations of Hindu texts. It is noteworthy that Otto's research on Indian religious thought constituted a part of his Christian theological studies. His important book, *Das Heilige*, is evaluated by some scholars of religion as a classic in the History of Religions. From the perspectives of the contemporary study of religion, this implies that Otto's Christian theological studies were closely linked with his religious studies.

2 The History of Religions and Otto's Religious Theory

From the late nineteenth to the early twentieth century in the European academic world, interest in the origin and history of religions increased with the discovery of religions among various non-Western cultures. Philosophers David Hume (1711–76) and Friedrich Hegel (1770–1831) argued for the historical development of religions. On the basis of much data about non-Western religions, historians of religions tended to base their understandings on a comparative perspective, from a viewpoint of religious "evolution" culminating in monotheism. Christianity was located at the highest pinnacle. Under the influence of the Age of Enlightenment (seventeenth and eighteenth centuries), the interpretation of the History of Religions was influenced in various ways by the modern views of history, including the theory of evolution, which prevailed in the Western world after the Enlightenment and the Romantic movement. Post-1920s, however, more and more scholars denied that monotheism evolved from polytheism. Therefore, the theory of the evolutionary history of religion gradually disappeared.

Descriptions of religious development by historians of religion were influenced by their historical perspectives. The contents changed somewhat as the viewpoints changed. This is the limited validity to the much-quoted criticism of Jonathan Z. Smith (1938–2017): "There is no data for religion. Religion is solely the creation of the scholar's study. It is created for the scholar's analytic purposes by his imaginative acts of comparison and generalization."[7] This criticism goes too far, however, for the material that scholars interpret does exist. When this material is interpreted in a way that deviates from a religious and cultural context, it may run the danger of being the "creation of the scholar's study," to which Smith refers. It is noteworthy, however, that even though it might be the "creation of the scholar's study," a description of religion is still a "narrative" in which one captures the things and events of religion, that is, religious reality, from a particular perspective. That is because the History of Religions consists of the linguistic acts describing the religious history. This description is modified according to new discourse concerning the historical development of religion. In order to understand other religions, in his world journeys, Otto collected the material objects that represented the "data for religion." These are contained in the Religionskundliche Sammlung (Museum of Religions) of Marburg University. His academic interest was in understanding how they presented the feelings of *the holy* and *the wholly other.*

Otto's research on comparative religion with special interest in Indian mystical thoughts resulted in several books including: *Vischnu-Nārāyana* (1917), *Siddhānta des Rāmānuja: Ein Text zur indischen Gottesmystik* (1917), *West-östliche Mystik* (1926), and *Die Gnadenreligion Indiens und das Christentum: Vergleich und Unterscheidung* (1930). Details of these books will be discussed in following chapters. Otto later translated the *Bhagavadgītā* into German. Starting as a Lutheran theologian, he incorporated comparative religion into his Christian theological studies.

Otto studied Hindu and Buddhist traditions through his encounter with religions and cultures in India and Japan. Thereby, he became conscious of parallels in the historical development of Eastern and Western religions. Moreover, he concluded that humankind shares a "common religious feeling." As the American historian of religion John B. Carman points out, it is important to recognize that "Otto himself thinks that his philosophical analysis of religion does not depend on his Christian theology." Moreover, Carman says:

> He [Otto] believes that the experience of ultimate reality as holy—that is, as a mysterious combination of the terrifying and the fascinating, the awesome and

> the attractive—is a possibility for all human beings and is at the heart of all genuine religion. Each particular religion, according to Otto, combines this common non-rational core of awesome awareness of the ultimate mystery with a rational apprehension of that same reality's moral character.[8]

From Otto's perspectives of religion, as Carman rightly argues, the "experience of ultimate reality as holy," which is "at the heart of all genuine religion," can be shared beyond religions and cultures among all human beings.

In his book, *West-östliche Mystik*, Otto argues that the two main patterns of "mysticism" in the East and West are represented by the thoughts of Śaṅkara and Eckhart. By regarding mysticism as "the essence of a strange spiritual phenomenon" (*das Wesen der seltsamen geistigen Erscheinung*), Otto holds that Śaṅkara's Advaita (non-dual) Vedānta philosophy, a school of Indian philosophy that argues the identity of *brahman* and *ātman*, is one of the main patterns of Eastern mystical thought. Central to his study of mysticism is the religious concept of "the wholly other" (*das ganz Andere*), the *a priori* and non-rational nature of the holy, an aspect that constitutes the experience of *the numinous*. In the Upaniṣad texts, Otto says, the supreme reality *brahman* as the "wholly other" is an "[unspeakable] marvel" (*āścaryam*); it is expressed with a negative formula that "it is not thus, not thus" (*neti neti)*. Moreover, Otto argues that this reality is implicit in the words of the *Chāndogya Upaniṣad*, i.e., "one only, without the second" (*ekam eva advitīyam*). According to Otto, these terms in the *Upaniṣad* throw light on certain speculations about the "simplicity of God" (*simplicitas Dei*). In this text, however, there is no relation between the supreme God and human reality, as premised in Christian theology. The *Upaniṣads* affirm the identity of *ātman* (the self) as the nature of an individual existence with *brahman* as the supreme reality, as Śaṅkara emphasizes in his Vedānta philosophy. This fact provides us with the insight that Otto attempted to "read" the monotheistic meanings of Christian thought in the *Upaniṣad* texts.

As seen in his interpretation of these texts, Otto interprets the Hindu idea in "parallel" with a Christian one. He proposes his theistic interpretation of understanding the world and human reality in the *Upaniṣad* texts, in which he regards *nirguṇa-brahman* or the non-qualified Brahman, which Śaṅkara emphasized, as transcending the *saguṇa-brahman* (the qualified Brahman), i.e., the personal God (*īśvara*). Moreover, what especially interested him in Indian religious thought was not only Śaṅkara's philosophy, but also the faith in the supreme God Viṣṇu or Rāmānuja's thought, in which the significance of *bhakti* was emphasized. Otto regarded Rāmānuja's Vedānta thought as similar to his own Christian doctrine of God. Thus, his perspectives on Christian theology and the philosophy of religion are clearly reflected in his understanding of Indian religious thought. It is necessary to grasp the issues of Otto's study within the contexts of religion and culture in the East.

3 Otto's Religious Theory and Its Reception

Since the 1990s, historians of religions have reexamined the previous conceptual framework of religions. Otto's religious theory has also been reexamined from a new viewpoint of religious studies. Stressing that religious experience cannot be reduced to such factors as society, culture, and the human mind, Otto emphasized the uniqueness of religion. Otto attempted to capture the essence of religion from the dimension of experiences that underpins religion. This dimension constitutes a non-rational aspect of religion which conceptual cognition does not reach. Otto attempted to express this non-rational aspect by coining the term "das Numinöse" from the Latin *numen*. This concept is still often used in the contemporary field of religious studies. Marburg University, where he taught, was founded in 1527 as the first Protestant university in the world. Since then, this university has been the driving force of Christian theology as the center of Protestant theological studies in Europe. Moreover, Marburg University has also been a center of the History of Religions in the academic field of comparative religious studies, which was incorporated into Christian theological studies.

Otto's influence on contemporary scholars of religious studies is still great. In September, 1969, at one of the lectures commemorating the 100th anniversary of Otto's birth, the German historian of religions Gustav Mensching mentioned that he owed his own academic life and work to Otto.[9] After his encounter with Otto, Mensching adopted Otto's viewpoint and subsequently argued that Christianity as the "complete" form of religion is superior to other religions. Moreover, he acknowledged himself as a disciple of Otto and promoter of the "Religious Studies of Understanding" (*Religionswissenschaft des Verstehens*). Friedrich Heiler, author of the book *Prayer* (*Das Gebet*), taught the "Comparative History of Religions" (*vergleichende Religionsgeschichte*) as a colleague of Otto at Marburg University; he held views similar to Otto's. In 1920, a course on the "Comparative History of Religions and Philosophy of Religion" was started in Marburg's Faculty of Theology. On Otto's recommendation, Heiler was put in charge of this course. Just as Otto incorporated the idea of "holiness" into the core of his teaching, Heiler put "prayer" into the core of world religions. Like

Otto, he also attempted to demonstrate the superiority of Christianity over other religions.[10]

In the University of Chicago Divinity School, Joachim Wach, who studied with Heiler in Munich, taught the History of Religions from 1945 to 1955 and is known as the founder of the "Chicago School." Wach relied on Otto in constructing his analysis of the experiences of *the holy*. Although in his later years, Wach was invited to succeed Otto as professor of Systematic Theology at Marburg; he declined this invitation just several days before he passed away.[11] Soon after Wach's death, Mircea Eliade succeeded him at Chicago. In *Das Heilige und das Profane* (1957), influenced by Otto, Eliade constructed his own framework of the History of Religions. His understanding of "the sacred" is indebted to Otto's view of *the holy*. Eliade attempted to explore "the sacred" in its variety by attending to both the sacred and the profane. While "the sacred" is the realm of extraordinary things and events, "the profane" is that of ordinary ones. The reality of "the sacred" is unique; it is *the wholly other* to which Otto refers.[12]

Now, let us look at the recent research on Otto. In October 2012, a four-day international conference, "Rudolf Otto: Theologie-Religionsphilosophie-Religionsgeschichte," was held at Marburg University, in which forty-six international scholars presented papers on various aspects of Otto's religious theory.[13] Agreeing that Otto's theory of *the holy* was widely accepted, the participants shared their understanding of Otto's work. All the participants felt that, in order to clarify his religious theory, it was indispensable to try to understand it not only from the standpoints of previous Christian theology and the philosophy of religion, but also from that of the History of Religions. I was also invited to present a paper on Otto's study of Indian religious thought and was in attendance at this conference. At that conference, I read a paper entitled "Rudolf Otto's View of Indian Religious Thought."[14] In late November 2013, the annual meeting of the American Academy of Religion was held in Baltimore, Maryland. At that meeting, a panel discussion was organized on "Genealogies of the Numinous," in which the main scholars in the USA of Otto's religious theory gathered together. This project was set up to continue consideration of Otto's religious theory, developing the results of the international conference on Otto at Marburg. I presented a paper, "Rudolf Otto's Perspective of Indian Religious Thought as a Type of Mysticism."[15] Due to the growing interest in Otto's religious theory among the historians of religions, another international conference, "The Holy in a Pluralistic World: Rudolf Otto's Legacy in the 21st Century," was held at the University of Wisconsin in November 2014. This conference was organized to examine Otto's theoretical and practical legacy with regard to religious pluralism, reconsidering Otto's potential significance for interreligious relations as well as the academic understanding of religions. The conference was organized by Gregory Alles from McDaniel College, and Ulrich Rosenhagen from the University of Wisconsin–Madison. As mentioned above, many scholars of religion have recently come to be interested in Otto's views. This renewed interest in Otto has come to be referred to by some scholars as the "Otto Renaissance."

In 2017, a collection of articles, *100 Jahre "Das Heilige": Beiträge zu Rudolf Ottos Grundlagenwerk*, was published as the 32nd volume of *Theion: Studien zur Religionskultur*.[16] Already, in 2014, the centennial edition of *Das Heilige* had been published. The editor was Jörg Lauster (1966–), Professor of München University, who was then a professor of Systematic Theology at Marburg University, and his disciple Peter Schüz (1983–). In the "Epilogue" (*Nachwort*) of this centennial edition of *Das Heilige*, the German sociologist Hans Joas (1948–) included his essay, "Secular Holiness: How Current is Rudolf Otto?" (Säkulare Heiligkeit: Wie aktuell ist Rudolf Otto?). Joas emphasizes an understanding of Otto's theory of holiness through its "historical contextualization" (*historische Kontextualisierung*). This means understanding how Otto's view was influenced by the theories of holiness, developed by his older contemporaries, Émile Durkheim (1858–1917) and William James (1842–1910).[17] Moreover, Martin Kraatz, former Director of the Marburger Religionskundliche Sammlung, is compiling Otto's letters, which may deepen the understanding of Otto's religious theory.

In regard to Otto studies, there are the works of such scholars as Martin Kraatz, Philip C. Almond, Gregory D. Alles, Melissa Raphael, Todd A. Gooch, and S.P. Dubey. Before introducing their works on Otto's religious theory, it is noteworthy that by helping many scholars of religious studies work on Otto, Martin Kraatz has contributed to the development of specific Otto studies. In *Rudolf Otto: An Introduction to His Philosophical Theology*, Philip C. Almond intends to "provide a framework upon which a fuller understanding of Otto's thought can be constructed." As Almond points out, "There have been surprisingly few studies in English of the full extent of his [Otto's] thought, the last and only full-scale account having been published in 1947." By the "last and only full-scale account," Almond is referring to the detailed research on Otto's religious theory, *Rudolf Otto's Interpretation of Religion*, published by Robert F. Davidson from Princeton University Press (1947). Almond maintains that the dearth of Otto studies was mainly derived from over-emphasis on *Das Heilige* and also that historians of religions could not easily access many of Otto's other works. Thus, among Otto studies works, Davidson's book is still valuable as an understanding of Otto's religious theory. In order to construct "a fuller understanding of Otto's thought," Almond himself attempted to "present a detailed introduction to his thought" and to "set it in the religious and philosophical context out of which it arose."[18]

In *Rudolf Otto: Autobiographical and Social Essays* (1996), in which he collects and edits Otto's various essays by translating them from German into English for English-speaking readers, Gregory D. Alles argues that "Otto's heart was decidedly in politics" and that "it was in many other social and ecclesiastical projects, too." As a result, Alles says, "His [Otto's] comparative study of religions encapsulated the political loyalties of a religiously committed, politically active, moderate left-liberal."[19] As Alles points out, Otto founded an international league called the "Religious League of Humanity" (*Religiöser Menschheitsbund*) in 1920 in order to work for righteousness, justice, and peace in the world despite religious differences. This organization continued for thirteen years until it was dissolved by the Nazis in 1933. It is noteworthy that Otto's concern with this league was fundamentally non-political.

Todd A. Gooch, in his book, *The Numinous and Modernity: An Interpretation of Rudolf Otto's Philosophy of Religion* (2000), attempts to clarify the significance of Otto's philosophy of religion, emphasizing the concept of *the numinous*. This book is a revised version of his Ph.D. dissertation, submitted to the faculty of the Department of Religion at Claremont Graduate University in 1999. Through his research, he intends to "present the most complete and sympathetic account possible of the development of Otto's approach to religion, and of his argument in *Das Heilige*."[20] Another work on Otto's religious theory, Melissa Raphael's book, *Rudolf Otto and the Concept of Holiness* (1997), is also noteworthy. From contemporary theological viewpoints interpreting Otto's concept of holiness as "a form of philosophical theology," Raphael attempts to convince the readers that "the numinous experience is a useful category of theological analysis."[21] In her book, she discusses the contemporary significance of Otto's concept of holiness, focusing on the relationship of *the numinous* and *the holy* to the divine personality, personal morality, religious experience and liberation. By presenting her "freer reading" of *Das Heilige*, she demonstrates that Otto's model of holiness is adaptable to "theological discourses," that is, the emancipatory, feminist theological discourses developed in the second half of the twentieth century. I also wish to mention *Rudolf Otto and Hinduism* (1969), written by S.P. Dubey, who taught the philosophy of religion at the University of Jabalpur in India. According to Dubey, the purpose of his work is "to examine Otto's treatment of Hinduism from an Indian's standpoint."[22] Dubey criticizes Otto's religious theory, especially the autonomy of religion, the "mystic monotheism" argued by Śaṅkara, the Bhakti religion as "religion of grace" emphasized by Rāmānuja, and his interpretation of the *Bhagavadgītā*. Dubey remarks that Otto, while comparing India's "religion of grace" with Christianity, argues for the maturity and superiority of Christianity, because it is grounded in his concept of *the holy*. Dubey sharply criticizes Otto's interpretation of Hindu religious tradition as inadequate and incomplete.

Finally, let me briefly introduce the recent works on Otto by such Japanese scholars as Toshimaro Hanazono, Tsuyoshi Maeda, Toshihiko Kimura, Satoko Fujiwara, Chie Warashina, and myself.[23] From the phenomenological or anthropological viewpoint of religion, Hanazono, who translated Otto's *Das Heilige* and *West-östliche Mystik* into Japanese, has been working on Otto's religious theory for a number of years. In *Introduction to the Phenomenology of Religion* [in Japanese, *Shūkyō-genshōgaku nyūmon*, 2016], which contains the chapter, "An Anthropological Understanding of Otto's Study of Religion," Hanazono examines Otto's main concepts such as "the numinous," "emotion," and "debt." Maintaining that Otto's experiences on his trips to different cultures became the foundation of his religious theory, Maeda published his work *The Ground of Holiness: Traveling Otto* [in Japanese, *Sei no daichi: tabisuru Otto*, 2016]. Here, he carefully investigated Otto's letters and diary in the Rudolf-Otto-Archives of Marburg University. Kimura, in his book, *Rudolf Otto and Zen* [in Japanese, *Rudorufu ottō to zen*, 2011], discusses Otto's understanding of Zen in relation to mysticism. In her book *The Concept of 'Holiness' and Modernity: Toward a Critical Study of Comparative Religion* [in Japanese, *'Sei'-gainen to kindai: hihanteki hikaku-shūkyōgaku ni mukete*, 2005], focusing on the concepts of "holiness" in Otto and Durkheim, Fujiwara explored which perspectives appropriate to modernity were constructed in the earliest period of the study of religion. Moreover, in her doctoral thesis, "Between Theology and the History of Religions: on R. Otto, *Das Heilige*" [in Japanese, *Shingaku to shūkyōgaku no hazama de: R. Ottō, Seinarumono o megutte*, 2017], Warashina attempted to clarify the religious and spiritual conditions at the time when Otto wrote his work *Das Heilige*, locating this book in its historical context. Finally, focusing on Otto's views of Indian religious thoughts, I have explored Otto's religious theory.

As discussed above, various works have been published on Otto by Christian theologians, philosophers of religion, and historians of religions. In the present scholarly world of religious studies where the previous concepts of religion are being continually reexamined, Otto's religious theory could lead to further investigation into the meaning and structure of religion.

1

Otto's Lifetime as a Christian Theologian

In regard to the religious theory expounded by Otto as a Lutheran theologian, various critiques and arguments for the pros and cons of his religious theory existed during his lifetime. Although Otto published many works, only his main work *Das Heilige* attracted widespread attention. Various critiques of his religious studies may have been due to the fact that discussions were held centered only on the content of his main book *Das Heilige*. As the historian of religions Eric Sharpe points out, Otto's work suffered "a more than usually severe vilification" from scholars in religious studies.[1] In his lifetime and after his death, according to the historian of religion Robert A. Orsi, criticism came both from Christian theologians and from the historians of religions. Christian theologians found Otto "insufficiently Christian," while the historians of religions accused him of "imposing a Christian construct on other religions." Liberal Protestants faulted him for "overemphasizing the emotional dimension of religion at the expense of the ethical and the rational," while conservative Protestants disliked his "openness to other religions."[2] Up to the present, the book has been considered either a tome of Christian theology or of the phenomenology of religion. I will discuss that topic in detail in Chapter 3. In this chapter, I will argue that Otto's religious theory essentially represents a Christian theological perspective even when he discusses other religious positions.

I would like to call attention to the following two facts: first, as a Lutheran theologian, Otto was interested in the study of Indian religious thought. He had already done research in the philosophical study of religion influenced by Neo-Kantian philosophy. Secondly, I will discuss his influence from Friedrich Daniel Ernst Schleiermacher (1768–1834); his interaction with the Protestant theologian Ernst Troeltsch (1865–1923) and the phenomenologist Edmund Gustav Albrecht Husserl (1859–1938), who lived during the same era as Otto; and Otto's relationship with the "Religionsgeschichtliche Schule" (the History-of-Religions School).

1 Otto as a Lutheran Theologian

Rudolf Otto was born in the town of Peine, Hanover Province, Germany on September 25, 1869. His father Wilhelm Otto was the owner of a malt-factory, first in Peine, then in Hildesheim. His family members were Lutheran Christians. Otto was born as the twelfth among thirteen brothers and sisters, and received confirmation in the Lutheran church in 1884. Lutheran doctrine and faith greatly influenced Otto's personality formation. On the curriculum vitae that he submitted to Göttingen University, Otto wrote, "While still in school I had already developed a desire to become a 'pastor.' Along with that desire came an interest, lively but hardly theological, in everything ecclesiastical and theological that managed to appear within my narrow horizons."[3] For Otto, who was raised in a strict Lutheran family, Lutheran faith was the foundation of his understanding of religion.

In May of 1888, Otto joined the Department of Theology of the Friedrich-Alexander University at Erlangen, a stronghold of the conservative Lutheran theology at that time. As Philip Almond points out, he intentionally "avoided the University of Göttingen for fear of being forced into too liberal a theological position." At Erlangen, he wanted to learn the "means to defend the conservative orthodoxy to which he was committed." In the spring of 1889, however, when he was ready to begin his formal Christian theological studies, he was faced with "a choice: either to follow his friends to Göttingen, or to remain at Erlangen alone." He chose to go to Göttingen in the summer of 1889. In regard to his study of religion there, Otto says:

> My older friends, from whom I wanted to learn this, had gone to Göttingen. So I decided that I would spend a semester with them in order to learn methodology. This decision was a somewhat bitter one, for it ran contrary to my plan first to become quite certain and steady in traditional theology before I exposed myself to the "modern." But it seemed to me unavoidable: so I went with the intention of protecting myself as much as possible from the "other approach," of working chiefly with my friends, and then returning quickly to Erlangen the following winter. With this semester in Göttingen began a new period, not only of my theological outlook, but of my entire life.[4]

In the world of Christian theology at that time, historical studies became prominent, and the influence of the *Religionsgeschichtliche Schule* (the History-of-Religions School), was increasing. After studying at the University of Göttingen, Otto gradually became interested in the historical studies of Christian theology. As a result, his views of religion changed subtly from the previous traditional and Biblical theological perspective, which emphasized the Biblical Christianity as the only truth, to the liberal approach that employed historical-critical methods of research.

After he returned to the Friedrich-Alexander University at Erlangen, from the winter semester in 1889–90 to the winter semester in 1890–1, Otto studied under the Systematic Theologian Franz Reinhold von Frank (1827–1894), founder of the Erlangen School of Neo-Lutheran Theology. Frank focused not only on the inner dimensions of faith, but also on the outer. After studying under Frank, Otto began to pay attention to the objective as well as the subjective side of religion. Otto's conservative view of the Bible was also shaken by Frank's liberal interpretation. It can be said that the root of Otto's religious perspective rests in Frank's point of view. It is especially noteworthy that Otto studied Schleiermacher under Frank. All of the German liberal Christian theologians were more or less influenced by Schleiermacher, but his influence on Otto was particularly pronounced. As will be mentioned later, Otto edited and published the 100th anniversary edition of Schleiermacher's *Über die Religion: Reden an die Gebildeten unter ihren Verächtern* (in English, *On Religion: Speeches to its Cultured Despisers*) in 1899. Schleiermacher regarded religion as *sui generis*: it cannot be reduced to metaphysics or ethics. He argued that the essence of religion is "not thought or action, but intuition and emotion." Schleiermacher's view came to be the basis of Otto's subsequent study of religion. His encounter with Schleiermacher's theology had a crucial impact on his own theological formation.[5]

In the summer of 1891, Otto enrolled in the Department of Theology at the University of Göttingen, where he studied until 1899. While studying Systematic Theology mainly under Theodor von Häring (1848–1928), Otto was inspired by Häring's academic attitude and personality. Häring was professor of Systematic Theology at the University of Göttingen as the successor to Albrecht B. Ritschl (1822–89), a leading German theologian at that time. Otto's dedication of *Das Heilige* to Häring suggests how much Otto respected him. He received deep scholarly stimulation from him.

In 1898, Otto submitted his doctoral dissertation *Geist und Wort bei Luther* (in English, "The Holy Spirit and Word in Luther") to the University of Göttingen. On July 9 in 1898, he received the Doctor of Theology (*Licentiatus theologiae*) degree. In the same year, he published his dissertation as the book *Die Anschauung vom heiligen Geiste bei Luther* (in English, *Luther's View of the Holy Spirit*). His interest in the concept of the "Holy Spirit" is important for his religious theory throughout his life, not only in *Das Heilige* (Chapter 14, "Das Numinose bei Luther"), but also in such later books as *West-östliche Mystik*. Nurtured in the Lutheran tradition in which he was born and raised, Lutheran faith had a great influence on the construction of his religious theory. Nurtured in the Lutheran tradition and in Luther's theology, he took the position that religion is fundamentally a matter of inner experience. In Wach's words, Otto was not "one of the conventional traditionalists among the latter-day Lutherans;" he remained a disciple of Luther as long as he lived. It is noteworthy that the doctrine of the Holy Spirit, which Otto emphasized, was "a field neglected by the official theologians of the day," as Wach points out.[6] During his years at the University of Göttingen, where he became a lecturer in 1899, Otto was influenced by the so-called *Religionsgeschichtliche Schule*, which became increasingly influential there. As research on the background of the New Testament progressed and the existence of neighboring religions became clear, Otto recognized that Christianity could not be separated from its historical context.

In 1902, Otto published his book *Leben und Wirken Jesu nach historisch-kritische Auffassung* (in English, *The Life and Ministry of Jesus, According to the Historical and Critical Method*, 1908). In the beginning of this book, Otto writes, there are two images of Jesus's life and ministry; one represents "the Church tradition" (*die kirchliche Tradition*) and the other is based on "the critical study of history" (*die kritische Geschichtsforschung*). From the latter perspective, he attempted to understand the human Jesus from a historically critical standpoint.[7] For several years, the Lutheran Church blocked him from a full professorial position because of his liberal theological approach. In 1915 after being cleared by the Lutheran Church, he became a professor at Breslau University. As Almond notes, when Otto was a private lecturer (*Privatdozent*), he thought of giving up Christian teaching and study. He considered becoming a church minister in Paris or a missionary in China. However, with the encouragement of the Christian theologian Ernst Troeltsch, he decided to stay in Christian theological studies.[8] Later in 1934, Otto revisited Jesus's life and ministry in his book *Reich Gottes und Menschensohn: Ein religionsgeschichtlicher Versuch* (in English, *The Kingdom of God and the Son of Man: A Study in the History of Religion*, 1943). This book amends his view of primitive Christianity by revealing unique aspects of Jesus's preaching about the kingdom of God.

At the University of Göttingen, Otto concentrated on the philosophy of religion during his period of exclusion from a full-time professorship. In particular, he was interested in the philosophies of Schleiermacher and Immanuel Kant (1724–1804) and made their framework his theoretical basis for understanding religion. In 1904, Otto's encounter with Leonald Nelson (1882–1927), a professor of philosophy at the University of Göttingen, became an opportunity to study the philosophy of Kant's successor, Jacob Friedrich Fries (1773–1843). According to Fries, adequate knowledge is acquired not only by reason and rational experience, but also by "feeling" (*Gefühl*) or "intuitive apprehension" (*Ahndung; Ahnung*). The validity of rational and empirical knowledge is based on the "feeling of truth" (*Wahrheitsgefühl*). In 1904, Otto published his first book on the philosophy of religion, *Naturalistische und religiöse Weltansicht* (*Naturalism and Religion*, 1907), in which, relying on Kant-Fries's philosophy of religion, he argued the autonomy of religion from the natural sciences. In this year, he became an associate professor at the University of Göttingen and remained in this position until 1914. In 1909, he published *Kantisch-Fries'sche Religionsphilosophie und ihre Anwendung auf die Theologie* (*The Philosophy of Religion Based on Kant and Fries*, 1931). For Otto, Fries's Neo-Kantian philosophy provided a sufficient philosophical basis for his own Protestant theological studies. Otto's notions of "religious *a priori*" (*Religiöses Apriori*) and "divination" (*Divination*) were influenced by Fries's philosophy. Otto wrote *Das Heilige* largely in Fries's philosophical framework. While relying on Fries's religious interpretation, Otto modified it in order to construct his own religious views and concepts. As Davidson points out, perspectives in Fries's philosophy provided the theoretical basis for Otto's Christian theology.[9]

In 1933, Otto was invited to give the renowned Gifford Lectures in Great Britain. Just before participating, however, he declined the invitation for health reasons. If he had participated, the theme of his lectures would most likely have been "Moral Law and the Will of God" (*Sittengesetz und Gottesville*). He was also invited by the University of Calcutta, India, to deliver a lecture on "Comparative Religions." But he declined this invitation also because of poor health.[10] The last ten years in which he was able to write, Otto focused his research on religious ethics. As a politician, he belonged to the Prussian Landtag (State Legislature) as a member of the National Liberal Party from 1913 to 1918. He represented Göttingen in the Abgeordnetenhaus (House of Representatives).[11] As a Christian, he was passionate about establishing the "Religious League of Humanity" (*Religiöser Menschheitsbund*) to promote mutual understanding among religions. In addition, based on his understanding of the holy, he worked to reform the Protestant service and published a book for improving public prayer, *Zur Erneuerung und Ausgestaltung des Gottesdienstes* (in English, *For the Renewal and Reformation of Divine Service*, 1925). Otto also collaborated for many years in the publication of orders of service for special occasions, prayers for use in church, school and home, and general liturgical aids for ministers. For example, in his article entitled, "Towards the Reform of Divine Service," Otto says:

> I follow my Lutheran tradition, which in Hanover, the land of my birth, still recognises the old, beautiful custom of the Altar, the Altar-lights and the kneeling position for prayer. I here take these forms for granted, but it is manifest that such externals are not essential to the matter. Where they are felt to be strange and intrusive they may be left out.[12]

On this basis, he proposed the reform of worship in "Liturgy for the Chief Service on the Sunday after Trinity." According to Otto, the Reformation of Luther and Calvin brought about a considerable change in the form of worship: Calvin gave up entirely the order of the Mass, while Luther conformed at first to its actual order, but changed its significance. As Davidson points out, "the breadth of Otto's interest and the depth of his spiritual insight is well evidenced by his important contribution to the reformation of divine service in the Lutheran Church."[13]

When Otto passed away on March 6, 1937, he was sixty-seven years old. As Almond points out, the direct cause of his death was pneumonia, which he contracted some eight days after entering a psychiatric hospital in Marburg. However, severe arteriosclerosis, which he suffered for twenty years, also contributed to his death. In 1936, he seemed to be depressed all year long. According to Almond, in early October, 1936, Otto hiked alone to Staufenberg near Marburg and climbed to the top of a manor-house tower. He fell some sixty feet and broke his leg and foot. The cause of this accident was "unclear," but Almond believes, "the evidence points to a suicide attempt."

In December, 1936, his sister Johanne Ottmer wrote to his close friend Birger Forell, "Rudolf complains much about his head, so that he cannot often think coherently; also depressions have set in again . . . He cries more often."[14] According to the same sister, while he was in a psychiatric hospital, Otto tried to leave, planning to throw himself under a train. His close Jewish friend Hermann Jacobsohn had thrown himself under a train in April 1933, for fear of being placed in a concentration camp. According to Johanne, Otto was dreadfully distressed by Jacobsohn's death.[15] In late April, 1936, Otto wrote to Birger Forell, "I have had a bad attack of influenza for ten weeks and was so weak that I could scarcely function. I can still do no work and lie down almost the whole day." On May 31 of the same year, he wrote another letter to Forell, "We have been having a very difficult time. Johanne had an accident in March, I myself was so ill for a quarter of a year with influenza that I didn't know what was going to come of it."[16] Otto's letters suggest deep depression because of his sickness.

Otto was buried in the Marburg Friedhof. The tombstone is engraved with the inscription, "The Book of Isaiah" (6, 3), "Holy, holy, holy, is the Lord of hosts" (*Heilig, Heilig, Heilig, ist der Herr Zabaoth*). As suggested above, in his last lecture at Marburg University, he called himself a "pious Lutheran adherent" (pietistischer Lutheraner). He intended to clarify the essence of human existence from universal religious experience, rooted in his self-awareness as a Lutheran. It is important to note that Otto's Christian theological analysis has been confirmed by later historians of religions.

2 The Study of Religion as "Christian Theology"

Although much of Otto's work concerned religion in general, he was not conscious of his own academic position as a proponent of the "History of Religions." Rather, he considered himself chiefly as a "Christian theologian." His main book *Das Heilige* belonged to his work on Christian theology. For Otto, the aim of his study of religion was not research on religion in itself, but on the truth of Christianity based on the divine revelation. Otto stated in 1909, in *Kantisch-Fries'sche Religionsphilosophie und ihre Anwendung auf die Theologie*:

> The task of Christian theology will then be this: on the foundation described to conceive and present the real nature and spirit of Christianity, and in the form of doctrine, which is to be assayed critically, brought into shape, and developed, to expound it and to impart it, so that it may be practiced and fostered. The latter part can only be performed by one who is a Christian himself, i.e. whose "free power of judgment" affirms the truth of Christianity that is felt, but cannot be proved. This, in the very case when Christianity is acknowledged to be the one form of religion which is superior to all others, can only be effected in a truly scientific manner if Christianity is understood in its natural affinity and connection with religion in general, i.e. against a background of comparative religion and the history of religion, to which the right approach is once more given by the philosophy of religion.[17]

Furthermore, in his book *Religious Essays: A Supplement to "The Idea of the Holy"* (1931), the following is clearly stated:

> Our line of inquiry in *The Idea of the Holy* was directed towards Christian theology and not towards religious history or the psychology of religion. We sought, by means of an investigation of the Holy, and its irrational as well as its rational content with their mutual interactions, to prepare ourselves for a better

> and more definite understanding of the experience of God revealed in the Bible and especially in the New Testament.[18]

As Otto clearly states above, *Das Heilige* concerns Christian theology. Today, however, this book is known as a masterpiece of the History of Religions. Furthermore, in *Kantisch-Fries'sche Religionsphilosophie und ihre Anwendung auf die Theologie,* he states: "Modern 'theology' (*Theologie*) is 'the study of religions' (*Religionswissenschaft*); 'Christian theology is the Christian study of religions'" (*die christliche Theologie christliche Religionswissenschaft*).[19] In other words, the "Christian theology" to which Otto refers means "Christliche Religionswissenschaft", or the study of religions in which Christianity is treated as a subject of religious studies. Therefore, from Otto's standpoint, Christian theology is a study of religion that includes Christianity. For him, the study of religion was based on the absoluteness of Christianity. Therefore, he considered *Das Heilige* as a contribution to Christian theology, aimed at "a better and clearer understanding" of "the experiences of God" revealed in the Bible and especially in the New Testament, through the "exploration of the holy" and also through the "exploration of the interactions between the rational and the non-rational."

In the preface of his book, *Vischnu-Nārāyana* (1917), Otto states:

> You should notice that the purpose of this book is neither "Indological" nor "for the history of religions," but "for religious studies" and theological. It is as a *theologian* that I am interested in these religious forms.[20]

Thus, Otto emphasizes that his study of religion is intended for Christian theology. For him, the study of other religions is not only an important introduction to Christian theology, but also an essential research area for Christian understanding. For Otto, the comparative study of religions is a part of Christian theological studies. Ernst Troeltsch, a Christian systematic theologian, who lived in the same period as Otto, was a leading member of the so-called "Religionsgeschichtliche Schule." In 1902, Troeltsch published *Die Absolutheit des Christentums und die Religionsgeschichte* (in English, *The Absoluteness of Christianity and the History of Religions*). In this work, by locating the absoluteness of Christianity at the core of his argument, Troeltsch included the relationship of Christianity with other religions. It is noteworthy that Otto was interested in the study of non-Christian religions earlier than Troeltsch. The Religionsgeschichtliche Schule was established and developed in Germany about 1900. A group of German Protestant theologians, including the New Testament scholar W. Wrede (1859–1906), applied the methods of the history of religions to the interpretation of the Bible. It is known for its rapid development of liberal theology, centered on the University of Göttingen. Otto also had contact with the theologians of this Schule (school). As Kurt Rudolph points out, according to the Religionsgeschichtliche Schule, "Theology is only one side of religion—the rational, conceptual, and systematic side;" thus, the "essence of religion" is "nonrational experience."[21] The concept of "religion" in this Schule originated in Schleiermacher's thought. The aim of this Schule was not to describe the history of Christian doctrine, but to describe Christianity as a religion. Although this Schule began as a movement within Christian theology, its method was so radical that it eventually transcended the framework of traditional Christian theology.

The Religionsgeschichtliche Schule had two main characteristics.[22] The first is represented by the method of understanding "history." The scholars belonging to this Schule attempted to clarify the "historical facts" beyond written data. They were dissatisfied with traditional philological research, confined only to the philological and historical criticism of the Biblical documents. Therefore, they used the methods of history and related disciplines at that time; they shared the academic standpoint of "comparative" research on various religions. The second characteristic of the Religionsgeschichtliche Schule was that it emphasized the clear differences between "religion" and "theology." The term "religion" as used by this Schule did not mean "theology" as a result of speculative reflection or its consequences, but "the totality of 'popular religiousness' and 'ritual' as sociological facts."[23] It was characteristic of this Schule to treat religion as a non-mediate psychological phenomenon from the viewpoint of "popular religiousness." After he became a lecturer at the University of Göttingen in 1899, Otto amended the traditional Christian theological framework; by incorporating the methodology of the "comparative" study of religions used by the Religionsgeschichtliche Schule, he began to pursue his own Christian theological research. Against this background, Otto published *Leben und Wirken Jesu nach historisch-kritische Auffassung* (1902, *Life and Ministry of Jesus, According to the Historical and Critical Method*, 1908).

In *Die Gnadenreligion Indiens und das Christentum: Vergleich und Unterscheidung* (1930, *India's Religion of Grace and Christianity Compared and Contrasted*, 1930), Otto draws a distinction between "theology" (*Theologie*) and "the history of religions" (*Religionsgeschichte*).[24] According to Otto, the fundamental difference between "Christian theology" and "the history of religions" lies in the former's acceptance of the concept of "revelation" (Offenbarung). Theology based on "revelation" includes narratives based on faith. On the other hand, "the history of religions" attempts to interpret religions as unique to the human spirit. Otto's comparative religious method, adopted under the influence of the Religionsgeschichtliche Schule, was one of his methods of understanding Christian truth, based on divine revelation, in comparison with the teachings of other religions.

3 The Meaning of "Theology" in Otto's Study of Religion

In order to understand the academic situation in German society at the time when Otto lived, I refer to a lecture by Adolf von Harnack (1851–1930). Otto wanted to distinguish his position from that of Harnack and therefore claimed to be a Christian theologian in his works, and not a scholar of the history of religions. When there are discussions about the formation of the German "Religionswissenschaft," Adolf von Harnack's lecture is often talked about. The lecture delivered by Harnack in 1901 as the Dean of the Faculty of Theology at the University of Berlin was entitled, "The Task of the Faculty of Theology and the General History of Religions" (Die Aufgabe der theologischen Fakultäten und die allgemeine Religionsgeschichte). In his lecture, the Lutheran theologian Harnack said: "Those who do not know this religion (Christianity) do not know religion. Those who know this religion along with its history know all religions." In contrast to the words of Max Müller, referred to as the ancestor of the History of Religions, who preached the significance of the "comparative study of religions," Harnack completely denied the *raison d'être* of the "History of Religions." Moreover, in his lecture, Harnack said, "What is the importance of Homer, the Vedas, and even the Koran other than the Bible?"[25] When considering the academic context of the early twentieth century, it is no wonder that Harnack's argument was raised from the standpoint of "theology," which advocated itself as the "discipline" of "religion."[26] In fact, it has been said that Harnack's lecture became the biggest cause of delay in the institutional establishment of "Religionswissenschaft" in Germany.

However, in his lecture "The Significance of the Faculty of Theology" ("Die Bedeutung der theologischen Fakultäten") in 1919, Harnack acknowledged the significance of "Religionswissenschaft" for university studies.[27] The driving force behind Harnack's change of position may be that he came to understand "Religionswissenschaft" as an academically based field which was capable of dealing with the innermost religious dimension of human beings. At the same time, however, this 1919 lecture was delivered at the time when the abolition of the Faculty of Theology at the universities was discussed. This lecture also shows that from the perspective of orthodox Christian theology, the implication of "academically neutral Religionswissenschaft" was invoked as a strategy for the survival of the faculty of theology.[28] In any case, the first course of "Religionswissenschaft" in Germany was "Allgemeine Religionsgeschichte und Religionsphilosophie" (the General History of Religions and Philosophy of Religion) at the Faculty of Protestant Theology, University of Berlin, established in 1910. Furthermore, in 1920 the course of "Religionsgeschichte" (the History of Religions) was established in the Faculty of Protestant Theology at Marburg University, where Otto taught. The professor invited from the Catholic Church for this course was Friedrich Heiler (1862–1967), who was born and raised in a very traditional Roman Catholic family. At first, the Protestant theologians in Marburg refused to invite him to their Faculty. Finally, however, they agreed after they were convinced by the Swedish Archbishop Nathan Söderblom that Heiler in Sweden had taken the communion "in both forms" (in beiderlei Gestalt), not only the bread but also the wine, in the very special Swedish church the act of conversion to a Protestant denomination. Thus, in 1920, he became a member of the Faculty of Protestant Theology at Marburg University.

As the Japanese historian of religions Noriyoshi Tamaru points out, Otto's understanding of "theology," which he inherited from the Lutheran Christian tradition, was unique. From Otto's point of view, theological studies comprise a way of thinking of "religion considering itself, using categories derived from religion itself."[29] When we consider Otto's religious theory, the term "theology" to which he refers is broad and implies at least two main concerns. In Tamaru's words, one is the "relationship of religion with other fields (metaphysics, morality, scientific worldview, etc.)" and the other is the "relationship of Christianity with other religions." Needless to say, Otto continued to be interested in these topics throughout his life, but in the first half of his life, the first was in the forefront of his research, whereas his interest in the second gradually increased in the latter half of his life after he published *Das Heilige* (1917).[30]

In Otto's Christian theological studies, what was closely related to his comparative religious perspectives is that he was interested in religions in non-Western cultures, especially Indian religious thought, and that he conducted a comparison of Christianity with other religions. During his travel to the East (1911–12), he first stopped in India and began learning Sanskrit. This trip provided impetus for Otto to enter a new phase of his comparative religious studies. His trip to the East set the direction for his religious studies in later academic life. As Friedrich Heiler points out, the preparation for Otto's "most complicated and most valuable task" for the History of Religions was "facilitated by his congenial and keen psychological intuition as well as by a knowledge of the languages in which each of the religious texts was written." Moreover, Heiler continues describing Otto's study of religion:

> In his study and ever available stood the great Petersburg Sanskrit Glossary; his remarkable knowledge of ancient Sanskrit enabled him to translate many Indian philosophical and theological books.[31]

Heiler's description illustrates how important Otto's comparative studies, especially with Indian religious thought, was for his Christian theological studies.

In commemoration of the hundred years since the publication of the first edition of Schleiermacher's *Über die Religion* (1799), Otto, who became a lecturer (*Privatdozent*) at the University of Göttingen in 1899, edited this book, providing a preface and a postscript in 1899. In his article, "How Schleiermacher rediscovered religion" ("Wie Schleiermacher die Religion wiederentdeckte"), published in the journal *Die christliche Welt* in 1903, Otto argued in support of the essence of Schleiermacher's religious theory. Schleiermacher had posited that the unique realm of religion lay in "feeling" (*Gefühl*); against the rationalistic tendency of thought at that time, he developed a theological theory centered on "feeling" as an experience beyond rational perception: God and the absolute. Otto praised Schleiermacher for such insights. Fries's neo-Kantian philosophy provided the philosophical basis for Otto's understanding of religion; it supported Schleiermacher's religious theory. In *Kantisch-Fries'sche Religionsphilosophie und ihre Anwendung auf die Theologie*, Otto explains that religion, which is different from metaphysics, has as its life "emotion and will" (*Gemüt und Willen*). Moreover, in discussing Fries's philosophy, he states:

> It [the infinite] for us is still the incomprehensible. But we may achieve in the feeling (*Gefühl*) what the comprehension cannot achieve. Feeling, with knowledge (*Wissen*) and faith (*Glaube*), gives a third kind of recognition (*Erkenntnis*), one which combines and unifies both of these: "intuitive apprehension (*Ahnen*)."[32]

In short, Otto argues that although human beings cannot understand the infinite, they can obtain "intuitive apprehension" (*Ahnen, Ahnung, Ahndung*) of it. The "intuitive apprehension," to which Fries refers, is a vague premonition of what occurs in "feeling" (*Gefühl*), which is not based on rational grounds; it is grasping by just feeling. In *Wissen, Glaube, und Ahnung* (1805), Fries describes "the recognition by pure feeling" (*die Erkenntnis durch reines Gefühl*) as "the apprehension of the infinite in the finite."[33] In Fries's words, *Ahnung* means the "recognition by pure feeling." According to Fries, "Concepts belong to knowledge

(*Wissen*), ideas to faith (*Glaube*), and pure feeling to intuitive apprehension (*Ahnung*)."[34] Moreover, in regard to the significance of feeling, Fries continues:

> We cannot understand the relationship of the finite with the eternal with the concept of knowledge or with the idea of faith. In this regard, only the inexpressible feeling remains for us.[35]

Otto points out that both Fries and Schleiermacher share a common view in regard to the recognition of religion by its aspect of feeling. In *Wissen, Glaube, und Ahnung,* quoting Schleiermacher's *Über die Religion*, Fries points out that he agrees with Schleiermacher in regard to the importance of feeling for religion. Otto maintains that Fries's theory of "intuitive apprehension" (*Ahnung*) is closely related to Schleiermacher's "intuition and feeling of the universe" (*Anschauung und Gefühl der Universums*). But while Fries's primary concern is to clarify the relation of religion as feeling to aesthetic judgment, moral conduct, and knowledge, Schleiermacher's intention is to establish the independence of religion from morality and metaphysics. Thus, although the two philosophers tend to be in sharp opposition, they are united in their understanding of religion. According to Otto, Fries's "feeling" is philosophically based on Kant's criticism of judgment, whereas Schleiermacher's "intuition and emotion" is a "divination" by "inspiration" (*Einfälle*). Otto finds difference in the understanding of conceptual meanings between them.[36] Here, Fries does not limit the range of "recognition" to the understanding (*Verstand*) to which Kant refers, but extending it to "knowledge" (*Wissen*), "faith" (*Glaube*), and "feeling" (*Ahnung*), gives all these functions values and validities equal to spirit. In other words, "intuitive apprehension" bridges the "disconnection between the sensitive and the supersensitive," that is, between knowledge and faith.[37]

Formal metaphysics and speculative theology which purely pursue ideas can never express religion which has its essence in "heart and will." To summarize Otto's argument, although an idea is different from experience, religion is based on experience. Therefore, the idea itself does not reach the reality of religion; it can acquire the concrete reality of religion by intuitive feeling alone.[38] Thus, in Fries's philosophy, Otto finds a philosophical basis for understanding the concrete substance of religion. For several years before his publication of *Das Heilige*, Otto represented "Neo-Friesianism" (*Neufriesianismus*), the school to which his friend Wilhelm Bousset (1865–1920), a prominent scholar in the Religionsgeschichtliche Schule, also belonged.[39] To understand the concept of "holiness," it is important to note that Otto was acquainted with Nathan Söderblom, a Swedish Christian theologian as well as a historian of religions. In fact, Otto often exchanged letters with him even though they had no contact over the years during which Otto wrote *Das Heilige*. Otto's interaction with Söderblom had a great influence on his theological perspective. Söderblom published his article "Holiness" in the *Encyclopaedia of Religion and Ethics* in 1913, before the publication of Otto's *Das Heilige* in 1917. It is noteworthy that although Otto's *Das Heilige* is generally regarded as the pioneer study of "holiness," Söderblom's article was published first.

In his article "Holiness," Söderblom argues that the concept of holiness is "even more essential than the notion of God," and that "real religion may exist without a definite conception of deity, but there is no real religion without a distinction between holy and profane." Moreover, Söderblom says that throughout the Christian church, *the holy* is not merely an ethical word, but primarily suggests the divine and supernatural powers; "religious is the man to whom something is holy."[40] Söderblom's view of holiness was based on his own experiences of the holiness of God. Both Söderblom and Otto were influenced by Schleiermacher, but Otto inherited the concept of holiness which I will discuss in detail in Chapter 3. In the next chapter, I will focus on Otto's journey to the East, which inspired him to build his religious theory.

As a Lutheran theologian, Otto explored the truth of Christianity based on God's revelation. In Wach's words, "the numinous experience of Luther, the personality of the mighty prophet-like promulgator of the notion of the hidden and yet mercifully revealing God, fascinated and deeply influenced Otto throughout his life."[41] At the same time, from the perspective of comparative religion, Otto attempted to find the essence of human existence in the experiences of *the holy*, shared by all humankind. The American historian of religion Hugh Nicholson, who uses Otto's book *Mysticism East and West* as "a point of reference for comparative theological exercises," emphasizes that it is certainly reasonable to understand Otto as a "precursor" or an "exemplar" of "the kind of theologically sensitive and philologically rigorous comparative work," currently practiced by such contemporary comparative theologians as Francis Clooney. According to Nicholson, the field of "comparative theology" has its goal of "fostering relations of mutual respect and understanding among the religions," accompanied by "its underlying theological conviction that the knowledge of other traditions enlarges our understanding and awareness of God's presence in the world."[42] From the perspective of comparative theology, Nicholson says that the aim and method of Otto's "apologetic" in his book *Mysticism East and West*, that is, "the vindication of Eckhart and the use of Śaṅkara as a foil" respectively, recapitulate "a history of modern scholarship." In Nicholson's words, "Otto's interest in vindicating Eckhart reflects a preoccupation with the issue of pantheism in the modern reception of Eckhart, and his use of Śaṅkara as a foil reflects a long orientalist tradition of lifting up Śaṅkara's school of Non-Dualist Vedānta as the epitome or essence of Hinduism."[43] Thus when reinterpreting Otto's view of religion, it may certainly be possible to understand that Otto was a "precursor" in the field of "comparative theology." In any case, there is no doubt that Otto was convinced that by studying non-Christian religions, one could gain a deeper understanding of the truth of Christianity.

2

Journeys to the East: India as the Foundation of Otto's Comparative Religion

From the autumn of 1911 to the summer of 1912, Otto traveled to the East. On his journey, he visited various Asian countries starting with India, Burma, Japan, and China and then crossed Siberia on his way back to Germany. In India, which he visited for the first time, he was greatly attracted to Indian religious thought. Thus, it may be said that a foundation of Otto's religious theory was his experience in India at that time. In this chapter, I would like to clarify what his experiences in India and his interests in Indian religious thought meant for his theory of religion and Christian theology.

1 Otto and His Journeys

Throughout his life, Otto was a Lutheran theologian, who taught at Göttingen University (1899–1915), Breslau University (1915–17), and Marburg University (1917–29). At the same time, he traveled to various parts of the world to observe non-Christian religions directly in the lands where those religions were practiced and believed. Otto's journeys are related to the introduction of comparative religious perspectives within his framework of Christian theology.

His main trips were as follows. First, in 1889 he traveled to England for the term-end holidays. In 1891 he traveled to Greece for the term-end holidays, and in the spring of 1895 to Egypt, Jerusalem, and Mount Athos. He traveled also to Russia during the term-end holidays of 1900. Moreover, in 1911, he traveled to the Canary Islands, including Tenerife, and to North Africa, and in 1911–12, to the East including India and Japan. In 1923, he was invited to deliver the Haskell Lectures on "Mysticism East and West" at Oberlin University in the United States of America. In 1926, he traveled to Uppsala, Sweden, to deliver the Olaus Petri Lectures on "India's Religion of Grace and Christianity." Both his lectures were later published as books after his revision of the lecture contents. Then, on his last trip to the East from 1927 to 1928, he traveled to the Balkans, Asia Minor, Ceylon, India, and Palestine. The main purpose of this last trip to the East was to visit India.[1]

"It would not be wrong to say that Otto became the first world traveler among the theologians," says Reinhard Schinzer, who has sketched Otto's life.[2] At that time, Otto was the only scholar among Christian theologians to travel many times, often for several months at a time, around the world. Throughout his journeys, while observing religions in various regions, Otto became aware of the importance of dynamic religious feelings in different cultures. The Japanese historian of religions Tsuyoshi Maeda explores the primordial images of Otto's religious theory by investigating the contents of letters and travel diaries that he sent from his travel destinations. Maeda suggests the significance of these journeys for Otto:

> The significance of these trips for the construction of Otto's religious theory and for the cultivation of his religious ideas was great. Otto, who began his religious studies as a Lutheran theological student, turned into a historian of religions by abandoning the ideas of the philosophy of religion in his heart-shaking encounter with the world of different religions. A number of journey signs, spelled at the invitation of the other world, vividly narrate the radical transformation of his religious understanding. In any case, the image of traveling Otto is noted as a means of reading the primordial images of Otto's religious studies; it is valuable as a key to deciphering the original images of his religious ideas.[3]

As Maeda suggests, Otto's journeys to different cultures provided new material for his comparison of Christianity with other religions. In his encounter with different religions and cultures, comparative religious perspectives were gradually introduced into his Christian theological framework. In his journeys, he vividly observed other religions in different cultures with his own eyes and sensed the dynamics of living religions. Thus, he gained a deeper understanding of Christian teachings and faith and confirmed his belief in the absoluteness of Christianity. His description of the religions that he observed throughout his journeys is essential to understanding the nature of Otto's religious theory.

It may be said that Otto's encounter with other religions on his journeys transformed his perspectives on religion from Lutheran theologian to historian of religions. By encountering non-Christian religions, his self-consciousness as a Christian theologian was further strengthened. This view of other religions provided an opportunity for Otto to understand Lutheran faith more deeply. Maintaining the framework of Christian theology, Otto deepened his understanding of religions, rooted in the concept of "holiness," through what he learned about various religions during his journeys to various parts of the world. In 1912, when Otto was in the East, he conceived the idea of the "Marburger Religionskundliche Sammlung" (Museum of Religions), which was founded in 1927 at Marburg University. This fact also points to some of the influences of his travel experiences on his comparative religious perspectives.

2 Indian Experiences on Otto's Journeys to the East

Before discussing Otto's journeys to the East, it is necessary first to touch upon his "journey to Tenerife and North Africa" from March 1911 to the summer of the same year. For on this journey, Otto came to recognize the significance of *the holy* in religions. Otto's concept of *the holy* may have begun with his experience of worship at a synagogue in the coastal city of Morocco, Mogador (now Essaouira). There in May, 1911, he was deeply moved by hearing in Hebrew the familiar "Holy, holy, holy Lord God . . . ." He later sent a travel letter, entitled "On the Sabbath," to Martin Rade, professor in Marburg, for *Die christliche Welt*, Rade's weekly magazine for liberal Protestants in which he describes the experience:

> It is Sabbath, and already in the dark and inconceivably grimy passage of the house we hear that sing-song of prayers and reading of scripture, that nasal half-singing half-speaking sound which Church and Mosque have taken over from the Synagogue. The sound is pleasant, one can soon distinguish certain modulations and cadences that follow one another at regular intervals like *Leitmotive*. The ear tries to grasp individual words but it is scarcely possible and one has almost given up the attempt when suddenly out of the babel of voices, causing a thrill of fear, there it begins, unified, clear and unmistakable: *Kadosh, Kadosh, Kadosh Elohim Adonai Zebaoth Male'u hashamayim wahaarets kebodo!* (Holy, Holy, Holy, Lord God of Hosts, the heavens and the earth are full of thy glory).
>
> I have heard the *Sanctus Sanctus Sanctus* of the cardinals in St. Peter's, the *Swiat Swiat Swiat* in the Cathedral of the Kremlin and the Holy Holy Holy of the Patriarch in Jerusalem. In whatever language they resound, these most exalted words that have ever come from human lips always grip one in the depths of the soul, with a mighty shudder exciting and calling into play the mystery of the

> other world latent therein. And this more than anywhere else here in this modest place, where they resound in the same tongue in which Isaiah first received them and from the lips of the people whose first inheritance they were.[4]

It is very difficult to determine whether this experience of hearing the chanting in Morocco laid a background for Otto's concept of "holiness," but it is obvious that his later journey to the East provided the breadth and depth for the subsequent development of his religious theory incorporating *the holy*. After his encounter with Eastern religions, his works consisted not only of the Christian theological view, or specifically the Lutheran one, but also added a comparative religious perspective. Otto's first journey to the East lasted from October 1911 to June 1912. While visiting India, Burma, Japan, and China, he encountered various Eastern religions. Through this trip, he became aware of such Indian religious thoughts as Śaṅkara's Advaita (non-dual) Vedānta, Yoga, and Buddhism. This trip became the foundation of Otto's religious studies, especially his Indian religious studies.

Otto embarked on his journey from Trieste to the East on October 12, 1911. After three weeks, he arrived in Karachi on November 2. Initially, he planned to go to South India as well as North India, but he changed his itinerary and decided to stay longer in North India. In regard to this change, Otto wrote a letter to his sister Johanne Ottmer five days after arriving in Karachi on Monday, November 7, 1911. Otto wrote:

> In Karachi, Monday, November 7 [November 6], 1911
>
> Tomorrow, on Tuesday, November 7, I will depart for Lahore. I gave up the whole [trip] to South India. If I want to see something fairly carefully, it's simply impossible to go to South India. My travel plan looks like this. I will visit Lahore, Agra, Delhi, Banaras, Cooch Behar, Darjeeling and a part of Tibet, Calcutta, Jagannath and Baripada. After that, I am heading to Rangoon and then, *probably* going to Japan from there. Dr. Hübbe will give you a map of where I am going. (Italics by Otto himself.)[5]

In his travel, he was obliged to "act as a kind of cultural envoy" at the various destinations, for his trip was financed through the German government by the Kahn Foundation, founded by Albert Kahn, a cosmopolitan French banker, for the purpose of his academic works. Therefore, he may have had various restrictions on his travel activities. In his "Report," Otto wrote:

> In order to escape the distracting observational fate of the world tour and gain deeper insight, at the expense of all visits to the South, I limited India travel to the Indus and Ganges, the easy-to-go Himalayas of Sikkim, the Teesta gorges,

> Kalimpong, and in the southern, limited it to just Puri and set foot on the small city Balipada in Mayurbandi.[6]

Otto limited his trip to places he felt important to the understanding of Indian religion. While in North India, he spoke with Hindus, Muslims, Sikhs, and Parsis. The experience was significant for Otto, both in his study of Indian religious thought and in his comparative religious studies. What was most important for him was to discover the "parallelism of development" of religions in the East and West, even though there was limited cultural exchange between them.

In Japan, he delivered a lecture at the Asiatic Society of Japan on April 11, 1912, entitled "Parallelisms in the Development of Religion East and West." The lecture reveals Otto's comparative religious approach. In the fall of 1923, he was invited to give the Haskell Lectures at Oberlin College, Ohio, USA. In his lectures, he compared Eckhart's Christian thought with Śaṅkara's Vedānta philosophy in Hindu religious tradition. The content of his lectures was later revised and published as *West-östliche Mystik: Vergleich und Unterscheidung zur Wesensdeutung* in 1926. In this comparative philosophical work, Otto developed a comparative religious perspective, based on the law of "parallelism of development" of religions in the East and the West.

From October 18, 1927 to February 3, 1928, Otto made his second and last visit to India. The journey was made possible by a grant from the Emergency Association of German Science (die Notgemeinschaft der deutschen Wissenschaft), founded after World War I in order to support scholars in Germany. On the occasion of this second trip, he traveled to South India, accompanied by his disciple, the Swedish minister Birger Forell. After visiting India, he continued on to Egypt, Palestine, and Turkey traveling until May 14, 1928. After returning to Germany, he described the events of his long trip in a report entitled "Report on the Research Trip for the Purposes of Religious Studies to India, Egypt, Palestine, Asia Minor and Constantinople, from October 18, 1927 to May 14, 1928" (Bericht über eine Studienreise zu religionskundlichen Zwecken vom 18 Oktober bis 14 Mai 1927/28 nach Indien, Ägypten, Palästina, Kleinasien und Konstantinopel).

3 Otto's Research on Indian Religions

Otto's areas of research can be divided into three categories: (1) Christian theological studies, (2) research on the philosophy of religion, and (3) studies of

Eastern religions, especially Indian religious thought. These three are organically linked to each other, based on Christian theological research. They constitute the whole of Otto's religious theory.

In addition to Otto's *Das Heilige*, his works include such books as *Die Anschauung vom heiligen Geiste bei Luther: Eine historisch-dogmatische Untersuchung* (1898) and *Kantisch-Fries'sche Religionsphilosophie und ihre Anwendung auf die Theologie* (1909). In the 1930s, his interests turned to the relationship between religion and ethics. Moreover, in regard to his religious studies focused on Indian religious thought, Otto wrote many works. The following is a list of books and articles (excluding book reviews) in order of publication year.

1912

a "Parallelisms in the Development of Religion East and West." *The Transactions of the Asiatic Society of Japan*, 40.

1913

a "Parallelen der Religionsentwicklung." *Frankfurter Zeitung*, April 1.

1916

a *Dīpikā des Nivāsa: Eine indische Heilslehre.* Tübingen: J.C.B. Mohr.
b "Aller Meister Lehren, aus dem Sanskrit." *Zeitschrift für Missionskunde und Religionswissenschaft* 31.
c "Artha-pañcaka oder die fünf Artikel." *Theologische Studien und Kritiken* 89.
d "Von indischer Frömmigkeit." *Die Christliche Welt* 30.

1917

a *Vischnu-Nārāyana: Texte zur indischen Gottesmystik.* Jena: E. Diederich.
b *Siddhānta des Rāmānuja: Ein Text zur indischen Gottesmystik.* Jena: E. Diederich.
c "Bhakti-Hundertvers (Bhakti-Śatakam) von Rāma-Candra." *Zeitschrift für Missionskunde und Religionswissenschaft* 32.

1922

a "Aus Rabindranath Takkurs väterlicher Religion." *Die Christliche Welt* 36.
b "Zum Verhältnisse von mystischer und gläubiger Frömmigkeit." *Zeitschrift für Theologie und Kirche* 3.

1923

a *Aufsätze das Numinose betreffend.* Munich: C.H. Beck.

1924

a "Östliche und westliche Mystik." *Logos* 13.

1925

a "Meister Eckhart's Mystik im Unterschiede von östlicher Mystik." *Zeitschrift für Theologie und Kirche* 6.
b "Indischer Theismus." *Zeitschrift für Missionskunde und Religionswissenschaft* 40.

1926

a *West-östliche Mystik: Vergleich und Unterscheidung zur Wesensdeutung.* Gotha: L. Klotz.

1928

a "Zum Verständnis von Rabindranath Tagore: Ein Stück altindischer Theologie." *Die Hilfe* 34.
b "Christianity and the Indian Religion of Grace: A Comparison." *National Christian Council Review*, New Series 6 (a lecture at Olaus Petri Lectures in Uppsala, 1926).

1929

a *Christianity and the Indian Religion of Grace.* Madras: Christian Literature Society for India.
b "Ein Stück indischer Theologie, Übertragen aus Yāmunamuni's 'Dreifacher Erweis.'" *Zeitschrift für Theologie und Kirche* 10.
c "Bewusstseins-Phänomenologie des personalen Vedānta." *Logos* 18.
d "Die Methoden des Erweises der Seele im personalen Vedānta." *Zeitschrift für Religionspsychologie* 2.

1930

a *Die Gnadenreligion Indiens und das Christentum: Vergleich und Unterscheidung*, Gotha: L. Klotz.
b *India's Religion of Grace and Christianity, Compared and Contrasted.* London: Student Christian Movement Press; New York: Macmillan. (The English translation of *Die Gnadenreligion Indiens und das Christentum.*)

c "Rāmānuja." *Die Religion in Geschichte und Gegenwart* 4.
d "In Brahmas Tempel." *Münchener Neueste Nachrichten,* 1, April 7.
e "Der verlorene Sohn in Indien? Ähnlichkeit und Unterschied indischer und christlicher Religion." *Münchener Neueste Nachrichten,* 3, October 9.

1931

a *Rabindranath Tagore's Bekenntnis*. Tübingen: J.C.B. Mohr.
b *Religious Essays: A Supplement to "The Idea of the Holy."* London: Oxford University Press.
c "'Meine Religion' von Rabindranath Tagore." *Westermanns Monatshefte* 75.

1932

a *Gottheit und Gottheiten der Arier*. Giessen: Alfred Topelmann.
b *Mysticism East and West: A Comparative Analysis of the Nature of Mysticism*. New York: Macmillan. (The English translation of *West-östliche Mystik.*)
c *Das Gefühl des Überweltlichen: sensus numinis*. Munich: C.H. Beck.
d "Hymne an Varuna." *Die Christliche Welt,* 46.

1934

a *Die Urgestalt der Bhagavad-Gītā*. Tübingen: J.C.B. Mohr.
b "Nārāyana, seine Herkunft und seine Synonyme." *Zeitschrift für Missionskunde und Religionswissenschaft* 49.
c "Mystische und gläubige Frömmigkeit." *Commemoration Volume of the Science of Religion in Tokyo Imperial University,* Tokyo: Herald Press.

1935

a *Der Sang des Hehr-Erhabenen: Die Bhagavad-Gītā*. Stuttgart: W. Kohlhammer.
b *Die Lehrtraktate der Bhagavad-Gītā*. Tübingen: J.C.B. Mohr.
c "Krishna's Lied." *Zeitschrift für Missionskunde und Religionswissenschaft* 50.

1936

a *Die Katha-Upanishad.* Berlin: Alfred Topelmann.
b "Die Katha-Upanishad in ihrer Urgestalt." *Zeitschrift für Missionskunde und Religionswissenschaft* 51.
c "Vom Naturgott zur Brautmystik." *Zeitschrift für Missionskunde und Religionswissenschaft* 51.

Otto's Posthumous Works

1938

a "Briefe Rudolf Ottos von seiner Fahrt nach Indien und Ägypten." *Die Christliche Welt* 52.

1939

a *The Original Gītā: The Song of the Supreme Exalted One*, translated and edited by J.E. Turner, with Otto's "Author's Preface" (1935). London: Allen and Unwin.
[The original books in German: *Der Sang des Hehr-Erhabenen, Die Urgestalt der Bhagavad-Gītā, Die Lehrtraktate der Bhagavad-Gītā*.]

1948

a *Varuna-Hymnen des Rig-Veda*. Religionsgeschichtliche Texte, Heft 1.

1951

a *Mystique d'Orient et mystique d'Occident*. Paris: Payot. (The French translation of *West-östliche Mystik*.)

1981

a *Aufsätze zur Ethik*. Herausgegeben von Jack Stewart Boozer. Munich: C.H. Beck.

From the list, it becomes clear that Otto spent a considerable amount of time and effort studying Indian religious thought. The content of his research can be broadly classified into the following four main categories:

1. Translations of Sanskrit documents on Vaiṣṇavism (1916-a, c; 1917-a, c; 1929-b; 1935-c), *Katha Upaniṣad* (1936-a, b), and *Bhagavadgītā* (1934-a; 1935-a, b; 1939-a) etc.
2. Hermeneutical study of Indian religious thought (1916-b, d; 1917-b; 1922-b; 1925-b; 1929-c, d; 1930-c; 1931-b; 1932-a, c; 1934-b; 1936-c).
3. Research on Tagore (1922-a; 1928-a; 1931-a, c).
4. A comparative study of Christianity with Indian religious thought, especially the Vedānta philosophy (1912-a; 1913-a; 1924-a; 1925-a; 1926-a; 1928-b; 1929-a; 1930-a, b, c; 1932-b; 1934-c).

In 1917, when he published *Das Heilige*, Otto also published two books on Hinduism and a German translation of a Sanskrit text. This is important for understanding the characteristics of Otto's religious theory. At the same time, he engaged in multiple studies on Indian religious thought as well as Christian theology and the philosophy of religion. For the rest of his life, Otto continued his study of Indian religious thought as well as of Christian theology and the philosophy of religion. The year before his death, he published articles on the *Bhagavadgītā* and the *Katha Upaniṣad.* After his 1911–12 trip to the East, during which he became interested in the Indian independence movement, he became friends with the Indian poet Rabindranath Tagore (1861–1941). When Tagore visited Marburg in August, 1930, and delivered his lecture there, Otto was his interpreter.

Among Otto's works on Indian religious thought, two books deserve special attention: *West-östliche Mystik* (1926) (English translation: *Mysticism East and West*, 1932) and *Die Gnadenreligion Indiens und das Christentum* (1930) (English translation: *India's Religion of Grace and Christianity*, 1930). By comparing Śaṅkara's position that emancipation can be attained through a knowledge of non-attributed (*nirguṇa*) Brahman, with Meister Eckhart's position in medieval Christianity, he clarifies the similarities and differences between them. Later, he compares faith in the personal God of the Vaiṣṇava tradition of *bhakti* with that of Christianity. Bhakti, represented by Rāmānuja, as a "religion of grace" (*Gnadenreligion*) constitutes a parallel to Christianity. In *Die Religion in Geschichte und Gegenwart* (2nd edition), an encyclopedia of religions, Otto wrote the article, "Rāmānuja" (1930) which detailed these ideas.

Moreover, Otto translated into German the *Bhagavadgītā*, one of the most important scriptures. According to Otto, although the *Bhagavadgītā* is regarded as the "fundamental doctrinal *Text* of Hindu '*Bhakti* religion,'" the "present-day guise of *The Bhagavad-gītā*" is not "its original version." The present *Bhagavadgītā* corresponds to Chapters 23–40 of the sixth volume of the ancient Indian epic *Mahābhārata*. It can be speculated that the scripture of the Bhāgavatas, who worshiped Kṛṣṇa as the supreme God, originally incorporated this section into the *Mahābhārata*. Based on his judgment that the *Bhagavadgītā* was a text that emphasized *bhakti*, Otto attempted to clarify the "prototype" of this text with his own philological method. In regard to the *Bhagavadgītā*, Otto says:

> In India again, and also by Western commentators, the Work is regarded principally as the fundamental doctrinal *Text* of Hindu "*Bhakti* Religion." This, in the first place, is the religious attitude which in trust, faith and love turns to the Personal God Who is the Redeemer from the evil of *samsara*—of a wandering existence or migration in the Universe; but in its modern form it combines, together with the theology that originates from the spiritual attitude just referred

> to, doctrines selected from the expanding systems of *Sānkhya* and *Yoga*, from the ancient moralistic doctrine of the three *gunas* or "constituents of Nature", from the theology of the old Vedic sacrificial cult and, finally, from Vedantic speculation and soteriological teaching about the transcendent, super-personal Brahman which arise from this cult.[7]

Otto continues.

> The present-day guise of *The Bhagavadgītā*, however, is not its original version; and I trust that I have succeeded in proving, in Chapter IV, that it is actually based upon a primitive *Text*—The Original *Gītā*—which itself was in no sense whatever specifically doctrinal writ, and therefore no "Upanishad," but simply a fragment of most magnificent epic narrative. The Book is, in fact, embedded in the vast ancient Epic, *The Mahābhārata*, which has itself undergone the most diverse transformations, interpolations and perhaps even occasional abbreviations: it recounts the great and horrible fratricidal battle between the Kauravas and the Pāndavas.[8]

According to Otto, the original form of the *Bhagavadgītā* was not a text of teachings of the "Bhakti Religion" or "doctrinal writ" but simply "a fragment of most magnificent epic narrative." In the "Author's Preface" to his book *The Original Gītā*, Otto emphasizes that "*The Original Gītā*" is "no doctrinal *Text*, no doctrinal writ of *Bhakti* religion, but rather Krishna's own voice and deed, referring directly to the situation in which Arjuna finds himself."[9] Thus, Otto believes, it was derived from the words which the God Kṛṣṇa told Arjuna on the battlefield; such words constituted the original text; the rest of the verses were later inserted.

Otto's attempt to establish the original text of the *Bhagavadgītā* has not met with the approval of either Western scholars of Indian studies or of Hindu scholars, as the historian of religions Eric Sharpe and the Indologist Franklin Edgerton point out.[10] Otto's attempt to elucidate the original form of the *Bhagavadgītā*, however, was backed by the Indologist Richard Garbe (1857–1927). In 1905, Garbe, whom Otto respected as his "teacher," published a German translation of the *Bhagavadgītā* and included an interesting explanation of the historical formation of its text. According to Garbe, the *Bhagavadgītā* was originally a scripture of the Bhāgavata tradition; its monotheistic teachings, based on the Sāṃkhya philosophy of dualistic realism, were incompatible with the pantheism of Upaniṣads and Vedānta philosophy. In addition, he said that, although the 170 verses which contained pantheistic contents, were added at a later time, the original text was a monotheistic teaching centered on Sāṃkhya philosophy. According to Otto, the original text of the *Bhagavadgītā*, translated by Garbe, expresses the power, impression, beauty, and loftiness of this school. At that time, however, Garbe's theory was no longer supported, having been refuted by the Indologist Hermann G. Jacobi (1850–1937), as well as others.[11] Otto, however, regarded the *Bhagavadgītā* as containing teachings parallel to those of the Christian New Testament, especially the "Gospel of John."

4 Research on Christian Theology and Indian Religious Thought

What did it mean for Otto to study Indian religious thought? His religious studies were consistently based on his Christian theology, even when they dealt with Indian religious thought. He argued that all religions, including Christianity, are rooted in *numinous* experiences, which cannot be understood simply by concepts. The word "the numinous" (*das Numinöse*) was coined by Otto to express the primordial sense of *the holy*. Although different religions have different ideas, they share similar aspects; the various faiths of human beings have much in common.

Otto not only recognized the common aspects among religions, but claimed the superiority of Christianity to other religions. He says, *the holy*, which constitutes the essence of religious phenomena as the criterion of religion, is a complex union of the rational elements and the non-rational ones. This union is shared by Christianity and various religions in the East; whether a certain religion is higher or lower depends on how the rational and non-rational are combined. In *Das Heilige*, Otto says:

> The degree to which both rational and non-rational elements are jointly present, united in healthy and lovely harmony, affords a criterion to measure the relative rank of religions—and one, too, that is specifically religious. Applying this criterion, we find that Christianity, in this as in other respects, stands out in complete superiority over all its sister religions. The lucid edifice of its clear and pure conceptions, feelings, and experiences is built upon a foundation that goes far deeper than the rational. Yet the non-rational is only the basis, the setting, the woof in the fabric, ever preserving for Christianity its mystical depth, giving religion thereby the deep undertones and heavy shadows of mysticism, without letting it develop into a mere rank growth of mysticality. And thus Christianity, in the healthily proportioned union of its elements, assumes an absolutely classical form and dignity, which is only the more vividly attested in consciousness

> as we proceed honestly and without prejudice to set it in its place in the comparative study of religions. Then we shall recognize that in Christianity an element of man's spiritual life, which yet has its analogies in other fields, has for the first time come to maturity in a supreme and unparalleled way.[12]

In short, from the criterion of measuring the "relative rank of religions," i.e., the unity "in healthy and lovely harmony" between the rational elements and non-rational ones, Otto says, Christianity "stands out in complete superiority over all its sister religions;" the "lucid edifice of its clear and pure conceptions, feelings, and experiences" is constructed "on a foundation that goes far deeper than the rational." Otto's study of Indian religious thought was not derived from his academic interest in Indian studies or in Indian philosophy, nor from that of the comparative study of religions. Rather, it was from his reflection as a Christian theologian. From 1917, the year when he published *Das Heilige*, until 1929, as professor of Systematic Theology at Marburg, Otto made his study of Indian religious thought part of his Christian theological task. In regard to his own research orientation, Otto writes:

> Our main interest in *Das Heilige* was not in the history of religions or in the psychology of religion, but in theology, that is, Christian theology. That is, we prepared for a sharper and better understanding of the experience of God in the Bible, especially in the New Testament, by the investigation of the holy and its non-rational and rational contents, and also their connections and mutual interactions.[13]

As noted above, even though the content of his research resembled the history of religions, its purpose for Otto was "a sharper and better understanding of the experience of God in the Bible, especially in the New Testament." His main interest in religious studies was in "Christian theology." In 1917 when he published *Das Heilige*, he also published a book on Hinduism, *Vischnu-Nārāyana: Texte zur indischen Gottesmystik*. In the introduction, he says that the book was not intended to be for Indian studies or for the history of religions, but rather, "for the study of religion" (*religionskundlich*) and "for theology" (*theologisch*).[14]

5 Otto's Visit to Japan: Encounter with Zen Buddhist Thought

On his first trip to the East, Otto traveled to Japan through Burma after visiting India. During his stay in Japan, which lasted about five weeks, since he was funded by the German government, he seems to have been busy greeting members of the Japanese government and the German embassy, giving lectures, and visiting temples. First of all, in Tokyo, Otto delivered a special lecture on March 28, 1912, following the regular meeting of the Philosophical Association of Japan. His lecture was on "Evolution and Religion" (in Japanese, *Shinka-ron to shūkyō*). It was reported in the *Roku-dai shinpō* (literally in Japanese, "Six Great News") newspaper, No. 445, April 7, 1912:

> The Philosophical Association held an extraordinary meeting for Dr. Otto on the following day, on the 28th, and invited him to give a lecture. Dr. Otto talked in fluent German under the theme of the theory of evolution and religion. He said that the religion of civilization which discourses the inherent pantheistic God is never inconsistent with the theory of evolution; while the religion of the undeveloped period seeks the power of God in mysterious things, the religion of the civilized period recognizes the power of God in the various things of the world. By quoting the words of such various scholars as Goethe and Scheler, he argued, the infinite and supernatural Power works in the natural world and that the theory of evolution helps the development of religion.[15]

According to the article in the *Roku-dai shinpō*, citing the words of Johann Wolfgang von Goethe and Max Scheler, Otto discussed how "the infinite and supernatural Power" works in the natural world; "the theory of evolution may help the development of religion." This article shows that Otto presented some of his ideas regarding the world history of religions, according to which "religions begin with religion." The "infinite supernatural Power" described in this article implies Otto's "das Numinöse."

On April 11, 1912, he gave a lecture entitled "Parallelisms in the Development of Religion East and West" at the Asiatic Society of Japan. I shall discuss the content of this lecture below. During this trip, he visited Mt. Kōya, a sacred Buddhist center, on April 27, and on the next day, gave the lecture "My View of Japanese Religion" (in Japanese, *Yo no nihon-shūkyō-kan*) to the students and monks at Kōyasan University. The *Roku-dai shinpō* (No. 452, May 26, 1912) reported about this visit:

> Dr. Otto, a professor of Göttingen University in Germany, who was inspecting religions around the world under the auspices of the German government, climbed Mt. Kōya on April 27 and visited our university. On the 28th, in the number one classroom of the university, he lectured for many hours on "My View of Japanese Religion."[16]

During his stay in Japan, Otto wanted to learn about Japanese lifestyles as well as the various religions. For example, at a Zen Buddhist temple, he discussed religion with the Zen monks. While staying at a Zen Buddhist temple, one may guess that he himself practiced the Zen meditation called *zazen*. Based on his dialogue with the Zen monks, Otto wrote his essay "Numinous Experience in Zazen" ("Numinoses Erlebnis im Zazen") in *Das Gefühl des Überweltlichen* (in English, *The Feeling of the Otherworldly*, 1932):

> At a quiet Zen Buddhist temple in Kyoto,* I asked a question to a venerable old monk, "What is the fundamental idea of Zen?" Since he was asked such a question, he would have to answer with the "idea." He said, "We believe that *saṃsāra* and *nirvāṇa* are not different but are the same and that everyone should find the heart of Buddha (Buddhaherz) in one's own heart." In reality, however, this is not the key point, either. For it is still "spoken," "teaching," and "transmitted" knowledge. The gist of Zen is not a root-*idea* but a root-*experience*; this experience does not only reject the concept, but also the idea itself. Zen reveals its essence in the following moments, which Zen artists have drawn in the faces, actions, attitudes, facial and body expressions of their masters, without words incomparably, vividly in front.[17]

In relation to the same content regarding *zazen*, Otto wrote an article entitled "On *Zazen* as the Extreme of the Numinous Non-rational" (Über Zazen als Extrem des numinosen Irrationalen), which was published in his book *Aufsätze das Numinose Betreffend* (1923). As the passage above shows, he had the opportunity to deepen his understanding of the religious significance of the *zazen* practice in Zen Buddhist thought through his dialogue with a Zen master in Kyoto. Judging from his religious theory, one can guess that Otto had a deep interest in the *zazen* practice; he may be the first Western scholar of religious studies who practiced *zazen* under the guidance of an old Zen monk. Did he then understand Zen Buddhist thought?[18] As Otto argued, the gist of Zen is "not a root-*idea* but a root-*experience*;" "this experience not only rejects the concept, but also the idea itself." The Zen experience as the numinous experience is itself a "root-*experience*." Thus, the essence of this experience is expressed "without words" in the face, action, attitude, facial and body expression of a Zen monk. Otto's discussion of *zazen* exemplifies the inexpressibility of a *numinous* experience, which constitutes the core of his religious theory.

After he returned to Germany, Otto maintained his interest in Zen Buddhist thought; he regarded Zen mysticism as the ultimate of Mahāyāna Buddhist mysticism. In 1925, after more than ten years had passed since his visit to Japan, the Japanese student Shūei Ōhazama (1883–1946), who studied philosophy and theology at the University of Heidelberg for two years, from November 1921 to May 1923, published a German version of the Zen texts, i.e., Schûej Ôhasama,

Zen: Der lebendige Buddhismus in Japan, with the help of the lecturer August Faust. Ōhazama was a disciple of Sōkatsu Shaku (1871–1954), the successor of Sōen Shaku (1860–1919) who was known as the teacher of D.T. Suzuki. For Ōhazama's book, Otto wrote the "Preface" (*Geleitwort*). This book provides an introduction to the history of Zen Buddhism and a German translation of Hakuin's *Wasan*, Sōsan's *Shinjin-mei*, Yōka's *Shōdō-ka*, and thirty-one *koans*.[19] Considering how Otto's religious theory changed after his visit to Japan, one can imagine how he attempted to learn about Japanese religion by visiting sacred places and temples while he stayed in Japan. He later incorporated what he learned into his views on religion.

6 Significance of Otto's Journeys to the East

Otto's journeys to the East were a significant part of his life. First, these trips gave him the idea that a collection of various religious objects helps to understand religions in different cultures. "Words" are important for understanding religions in different cultures. At the same time, it is also important to understand the aspects of religions by means of "materials" that cannot be expressed in words. His understanding of the religious significance of "materials" led to his founding the Marburg Museum of Religions at Marburg University, i.e., "Marburger Religionskundliche Sammlung." Second, because he recognized the importance of the cooperation of religions, Otto conceived of the idea of the Religious League of Humanity, "Religiöser Menschheitsbund." On August 1, 1922, the first official meeting was held in Wilhelmshagen near Berlin, with the participation of representatives from eight religions.[20]

Third, Otto became more involved in the study of non-Christian religions. Through his journeys to the East, he learned that a deeper understanding of religions in different cultures could lead to a deeper understanding of his own religion. Just as Christianity played an important role in the lives of Christian adherents, so religions in the East were also important in peoples' lives, even though these religions differed from those of the West. Moreover, in the latter half of Otto's life, after the publication of *Das Heilige*, the weight of his comparative studies between Christianity and other religions increased. His academic interests were not limited to his previous theological studies; he gradually incorporated comparative religious studies into his Christian reflection.

Regarding the foundation of the Marburger Religionskundliche Sammlung at Marburg University, Otto became aware of its significance through his encounter with non-Christian religions in different cultures on his journey to the East. He found that religious artifacts, as well as literature, could be very helpful for understanding religions. Thus, the idea of a museum was born in Otto's mind. In regard to this idea, Martin Kraatz (former director of the Marburger Religionskundliche Sammlung, 1933–), a historian of religions, argues that while traveling in the East, Otto learned about non-Christian religions and recognized that in order to understand them, it was not enough to study only their classical and authoritative texts.[21] In this regard, Kraatz points out that in his several journeys, Otto experienced that "seeing, grasping, sniffing, and listening" were the "means of recognition which complement the intellect and which are quite equivalent to it." On the basis of his own experiences, Otto recognized that it was essential to know religions not only through texts but also through the sensual forms of religious expression. What scholars grasp through their own senses is often a direct expression of religious feeling, an expression that is not yet refracted. When the Marburger Religionskundliche Sammlung celebrated its sixtieth anniversary in 1987, in his essay "Religionskundliche Sammlung 60 Jahre alt," published in *MARBURGER Universitäts-Zeitung*, Kraatz says:

> What the scholar grasps with the help of his senses is often even an immediate, at least only slightly broken expression of religious consciousness—while the written word as preferred by many scholars of religion can only be the product of reflecting distance.[22]

As Kraatz emphasizes, Otto recognized that it was essential to know religions not only through texts, but also with the sensual forms of religious expression. In his journeys, Otto saw the various aspects of religions with his own eyes and touched them with his own hands; he noticed how the sensual forms of religious expression were important for understanding religions. As the Japanese historian of religions Tsuyoshi Maeda says, Otto's above-mentioned perception was "never obvious for the scholars of religious studies at that time, let alone for the systematic theologians of the Department of Theology."[23] Otto continued his efforts to realize his idea of the "museum of religions" which arose in his mind during his journey to the East. Finally in 1927, "Die Marburger Religionskundliche Sammlung" was founded on the 400th Anniversary of Marburg University.

It is noteworthy that while Otto continued his efforts to establish a museum of religions, he also helped start a series of translations intended as the German counterpart to the *Sacred Books of the East*. This became the *Quellen der Religionsgeschichte* (fifteen vols, 1909–1927), published by the Göttingen

Academy of Sciences. Although most of the volumes in the series were the translations of classic religious texts, the first three volumes, published in 1909–1911, were adopted into the *Quellen der Religionsgeschichte* (in English, *Sources of the History of Religions*) from an earlier series, *Religionsurkunden der Völker* (in English, *Religious Documents of the People*).[24]

According to Otto, the term "religionskundlich" used in the name of this Marburg Museum does not mean what is implied by the term "the science of religion" (*religionswissenschaftlich*), which implies the theoretical and systematic study of the essence and structure of religions; it points to "gathering of materials," that is, observing, collecting, and organizing religious objects. It is noteworthy that in his study of Christian theology, Otto combined the term "religionskundlich" with the word "theologisch." In Otto's approach, what is implied by the term "religionskundlich" is a "purely phenomenological" way of considering religion as "a phenomenon," "from the outside," i.e., "with a category that is not religious in itself." On the other hand, with the term "theologisch," Otto implies a method of considering "religion itself," "with categories derived from religion itself."[25] In other words, in his Christian theological perspectives, both "religionskundlich" and "theologisch" researches are complementary. It is significant to note that the collection of the Marburg Museum of Religions was also a resource for Protestant missionary activities.

During his first years as a professor of Systematic Theology at Marburg University, Otto was highly praised by his colleagues and students. After 1921, however, when the dialectic theology of Karl Barth (1886–1968) became popular, the students of the Department of Theology became interested in the theology of Rudolf Karl Bultmann (1884–1976) and began to attend the philosophy lectures given by Martin Heidegger (1889–1976). In 1919, two years after the publication of Otto's *Das Heilige*, Barth published his commentary *Der Römerbrief* (in English, *The Epistle to the Romans*), and the interests of the students gradually shifted away from Otto. The dialectical theology seems to have had a greater influence on the students. Bultmann who was Otto's colleague at Breslau University moved to Marburg University in 1921; he was critical of Otto's understanding of religion in *Das Heilige*. Otto's position in the Department of Theology at Marburg University was weakened, probably because of his feud with Bultmann. In the words of the historian of religions Tsuyoshi Maeda, "for theological students of that time, Otto's theology seemed to have faded in the face of Bultmann's theology, which developed hermeneutics to make decisions about faith, being based on the thorough self-criticism of liberal theology and historical theology." According to Ernst Benz (1907–78), who taught church history and doctrinal history as a professor of Marburg University, the Religionskundliche Sammlung, founded by Otto, was sometimes ridiculed as "the temple of idols" (*Götzentempel*) by the students, influenced by Bultmann theology and existential philosophy.[26]

During his trips to the East, Rudolf Otto "experienced" the importance of materials for Hindus and Buddhists in Asian religious cultures. In attempting to establish the Religionskundliche Sammlung, Otto anticipated later developments. In recent decades, the study of material expressions in religion and culture has gradually come to the fore. Historians of religions now attempt to explore the "living" religious experiences through their material expressions. As the historian of religions David Morgan argues, quoting the words of anthropologist Webb Keane, "Religions may not always demand beliefs, but they will always involve material forms." Such forms of materiality as sensations, objects, spaces, and performance constitute "a matrix in which belief happens as touching and seeing, hearing and tasting, feeling and emotion, as will and action, as imagination and intuition."[27] Thus, the emphasis of belief and faith in religious studies is being challenged by a recent focus on the physical and material objects of religions inasmuch as religious belief or faith manifests itself in a variety of material forms. As William Keenan and Elisabeth Arweck emphasize, "Without their material expressions, religions float in theological ether, and spiritualities enter the void, lifeless and deracinated."[28] It is very important for scholars of religious studies to recognize the characteristics of material forms as vital to specific religions and cultures. At the same time, it is also significant for the historians of religions to recognize the essential characteristic of materiality, i.e., the "border transgression" of time and space. Through the exhibition of material forms in museums, one is able to learn about the lives and customs of peoples in the past as well as in different geographic locations. The most valuable of these forms may be the "materiality of writing," especially scripture, which teaches doctrine through the written words. Moreover, there are other objects such as divine images or icons, pictures, ritual materials, and architectures. All of these are capable of crossing space from one place to another and of transcending the time constraints of one period to another. Thus, from the contemporary viewpoint of the History of Religions, there is no doubt that Otto had a profound understanding of the importance of the visible forms in religion and culture.[29]

In regard to his concept of the inter-religious league of humanity, "Religiöser Menschheitsbund" ("Religious League of Humanity"), Otto participated in the international conference "World Congress for the Progress of Free Christianity and Religion" (Weltkongreβ für freies Christentum und religiösen Fortschritt), held in Paris in 1913, the year following his journey to the East in 1912. In his lecture at this congress, Otto stressed the need for the cooperation of religions to overcome their diversity. His advocacy of this cooperation was expressed in the inter-religious league called "Religiöser Menschheitsbund." In collaboration with his disciple Jakob Wilhelm Hauer (1881–1962), Otto called for its establishment in 1920 to complement the League of Nations, both intellectually and ethically. From 1924, Hauer became chair of this alliance; later, as an anti-semitic Nazi ideologue, he founded the "German Faith Movement" (Deutsche Glaubensbewegung). At the international level, however, Otto's Inter-religious League was affiliated with liberal religious organizations from all over Europe and even from Japan (Daisetsu Suzuki's "The Eastern Buddhist Society").[30]

The first official meeting of the Inter-religious League was held on August 1, 1922, with 470 representatives of eight religions in attendance in Wilhelmshagen near Berlin. The conference had 470 participants, including many from non-Christian religions. At this conference, Ryōhon Kiba, a Shin Buddhist monk from Kyoto, gave a lecture entitled "Buddhismus und sittliche Weltgestaltung" (in English, "Buddhism and the Moral Formation of the World"). Otto notes that it was "impressive." Otto himself delivered a lecture on the idea of the "World Conscience" (Weltgewissen) and the path towards achieving it. The American historian of religions Gregory Alles says that the Religiöser Menschheitsbund reflected Otto's conviction as a "religious left liberal." In the light of later movements after the establishment of the "Religiöser Menschheitsbund," one may imagine that Otto intended to create a location for encounters and forms of cooperation between various religious organizations. This might bring together the powers of religions that attempted religious innovation on the periphery of their organizations, and also in the case of the liberal Protestantism to which he belonged.[31]

From October 1927 to May 1928, Otto, together with the Swedish minister Birger Forell, embarked on a journey from India to Egypt, Palestine, and Turkey. They arrived in Ceylon on November 4, 1927. The main theme of Otto's lectures in Ceylon and also South India was the Religiöser Menschheitsbund. For example, at the Buddhist Youth Association in Ceylon (YMBA) as well as in Madras (now Chennai) and Mysore in South India, Otto emphasized interreligious cooperation. Otto called for the participation of Hindus in the World Congress of Religions, scheduled for 1930. Many people whom Otto met on his travels agreed with his ideas.[32] In his essay entitled "An Inter-Religious League" (1931), he states:

> The meaning and purpose of this league, put in a nutshell, is to create an authoritative world conscience, and to unite men of principle everywhere that the law of justice and the feeling of mutual responsibility may hold sway in the relationship between nations, races, and classes, and that the great collective moral tasks facing cultured humanity may be achieved through a closely-knit cooperation.[33]

In Otto's words, at that time, the Religiöser Menschheitsbund had the "interest of all faiths in undertaking a truly cultural mission, in which all denominations, religions and idealisms of the West would willingly play their part." Recognizing the necessity of religious cooperation, this league was formed, with Otto as honorary president and Hauer and Gustav Mensching as co-presidents.[34] However, as international politics and economics were then in turmoil, the League's activities diminished, and came to an end in 1933. The League was re-established as a German branch of the "World Congress of Faiths," founded in England in 1936 by Sir Francis Edward Younghusband (1863–1942). Swedish Archbishop Nathan Söderblom (1866–1931), a historian of religions, who had close contact with Otto, received the Nobel Peace Prize in 1930 for his contribution to the international cooperation of the Christian churches. After First World War I, many scholars in religious studies were active in solving real world problems.[35] Younghusband's Association was modelled on the League of Nations, founded in 1920.

Otto's journeys to the East enabled his encounter with living non-Christian religions. Through his trip, he not only confirmed his Christian faith, but also expanded his research beyond Christianity into other world religions, thereby deepening his understanding of Christian theology. As mentioned above, among all religions in the East, Otto was primarily interested in the study of Hinduism and its philosophy. He published numerous works, including the German translations of the *Upaniṣads* and *Bhagavadgītā* and philosophical commentaries on these works. Among his works of comparative religious studies focusing on Indian religious thought were his representative books; *West-östliche Mystik: Vergleich und Unterscheidung zur Wesensdeutung* (1926) and *Die Gnadenreligion Indiens und das Christentum: Vergleich und Unterscheidung* (1930). The publication of such books on the comparative study of religions was possible not only because Otto was a Lutheran theologian, but also because he widened his study to include Indian religious thought. His Indian religious studies include his evaluation of Christianity as superior to other religions. From a contemporary perspective of religious studies, it is obvious that he would be sharply criticized for holding this view.

From the present viewpoint of Indian philosophical studies, too, Otto's study of Indian religious thought is inadequate. But what is most important from a contemporary perspective of religious studies is that for Otto as a Christian theologian, the study of Indian religious thought was not based solely on academic interest, but with an effort to demonstrate the truth of Christianity. His posture toward Hindu studies was sympathetic in that during his journeys to India, he attempted to understand Hindu thought and faith as they were. Thus, from the perspective of "comparative theology" to which the historian of religion Francis Clooney refers, both Christian theological studies and his research on Indian religious thought were "mutually enriching" for Otto. According to the comparative theologian Hugh Nicholson, Otto was in a certain sense "a precursor of today's comparative theology." In Nicholson's words, "Otto's later comparative work represents a model for the kind of philologically rigorous and theologically sensitive comparison espoused by contemporary comparative theoligians."[36]

Despite his sympathetic attitude toward Hinduism, his approach was unfortunately biased and constrained by his Western Christian views. His theological views of Hinduism did not recognize the limitation of the Western religious ideas. His research on Indian religious thought was indispensable for his religious studies, but its purpose was to deepen his understanding of Christian faith. In his encounter with non-Christian religions, Otto could build his own religious theory. In the next chapter, I will examine the core concept of *the holy* in Otto's Christian theology.

3

Comparative Religious Perspectives on *the Holy*

In the academic and philosophical context of the early twentieth century, Otto incorporated a comparative religious perspective into Christian theological studies and with the framework of religious evolution, attempted to create a pluralistic history of religions. After the 1930s, however, with the decline of the theory of evolution in the social sciences, the view of the development of religion has received little attention. Against such a background, Otto's theory of religious history became less appealing, but his theory of *the holy* has been the focus of scholarly attention over the generations. In regard to such themes as the methodology of the phenomenology of religion, the essence of religious experience, and the relationship between the sacred and the profane, Otto's religious theory has often been employed in research.

In the academic world of religious studies, the concept of *the holy*, argued in Otto's *Das Heilige* (1917), has been used repeatedly as a term to express the essence of religion. In Western culture influenced by Jewish and Christian religious traditions, the adjectives "sacred, holy, sacré, heilig" were used before modern times, while the abstract nouns "the sacred, the holy, le sacré, das Heilige" have been widely used since the latter half of the nineteenth century. This fact suggests that the concept of "holiness" reflects not only Western monotheistic traditions, but modern times.[1] One of the earliest scholars who used the concept of "holiness" in religious studies was the French sociologist Émile Durkheim (1858–1917), a contemporary of Otto. Both Otto and Durkheim built the foundation for the modern study of religions in maintaining that *the holy* is the essence of religion and that in any religion a relationship exists between "the holy" and "the secular." In both Otto's *Das Heilige* and Durkheim's *Les formes élémentaires de la vie religieuse* (1912), "holiness" constitutes an essential concept of argument.

In this chapter on the concept of "holiness" in the study of religion, I will examine Otto's methodological views of religious studies, focusing particularly on his book *Das Heilige*. These views are helpful in understanding his comparative religious perspectives, influenced by his encounter with Indian religions in his journeys to the East. An examination of Otto's theory in *Das Heilige* will clarify the theoretical background of this book, which historians of religions understand as a classic of religious studies rather than that of Christian theology.

1 Comparative Perspectives of Religion in Christian Theology

According to Friedrich Heiler, Otto's disciple and professor at Marburg University, the greatest impetus toward the publication of Otto's *Das Heilige* was his first trip to the East. Previously, at a Jewish synagogue in North Africa, he was deeply moved by the prophet Isaiah's cry of "Holy, Holy, Holy." This experience was further strengthened by his visits to Islamic mosques, Buddhist shrines, and Hindu temples. Heiler says:

> Even before undertaking his world travel he had emphasized that "in the true scientific sense" "a new affirmation of the truth of Christianity will be possible only when it is understood in its affinity and its relation to the conception of religion in general, i.e. on the background of History of Religions and Comparative History to Religions." In fact, Otto made this the focal point of his research. In *The Idea of the Holy* as well as in its supplements, *Essays Concerning the Numinous* (Title I: Gotha, 1923; 5th & 6th ed., 1932 under the title, *The Sensation of the Divine*; Title 2: Gotha, 1923, 5th & 6th ed., 1932 under the title, *Sin and Original Guilt*, published together in the English translation, *Religious Essays*, London, 1937) the examples he gave in demonstrating his new conception were mostly taken from non-Christian religions. *Eastern and Western Mysticism* (Gotha 1926, 2d ed. 1929; English tr., New York, 1932), and *India's Religion of Grace and Christianity Compared and Contrasted* (Gotha 1930; New York, 1930) are typical examples of such comparison and evaluation, in which Otto brings out not only what the several religions have in common, but also their individual characteristics.[2]

As Heiler points out, Otto incorporated the comparative religious perspective, emphasized by the Religionsgeschichtliche Schule, into his framework of Christian theology to confirm "Christian truth" from a new perspective. He pursued the truth of Christianity in the light of concrete examples from non-Christian religions. In other words, his inclusion of a comparative religious perspective in the study of Christian theology became an important factor for many scholars who regard *Das Heilige* as a classic of religious studies.

As mentioned above, one of Otto's contemporaries was the Christian systematic theologian Ernst Troeltsch (1865–1923). Troeltsch preached the truth and absoluteness of Christianity in considering the relationship between Christianity and other religions. Troeltsch suspected that with the rise of modern natural sciences, Albrecht Benjamin Ritschl (1822–89) and his school were attempting to reduce religion to the moral dimension. In order to reconstruct Christian theology, Troeltsch intended to secure religious *a priori* or religious independence as the basis for interpreting religion. To affirm the absoluteness of Christianity in world religions while recognizing other religions, Troeltsch published *Die Absolutheit des Christentums und die Religionsgeschichte* (in English, *The Absoluteness of Christianity and the History of Religions*) in 1902. In social or intellectual situations, Troeltsch tried to elucidate the absolute nature of Christianity, taking the existence of other religions into consideration. Confronted by the view of natural science, Otto recognized the need to present Christian theological perspectives and the views of non-Christian religions. Adolf von Harnack, a Lutheran theologian like Otto, argued that Otto's *Das Heilige* had the same significant impact as Schleiermacher's *Über die Religion*. One can imagine how influential Otto's religious theory was at that time.[3]

2 Characteristics of *the Holy*

Otto's book, *Das Heilige: Über das Irrationale in der Idee des Göttlichen und sein Verhältnis zum Rationalen* (1917), the English translation: *The Idea of the Holy: An Inquiry into the non-rational factor in the idea of the divine and its relation to the rational*, 1923) was published during World War I (1914–18). The book *Das Heilige* was Otto's main work written at Breslau University, where he was appointed to a full professorship in 1915. In December 1916, he already sent his colleagues the first copies of this book although it was officially published in 1917 when he was appointed to the chair of professor at Marburg University. In his academic life, Otto never left the framework of his religious theory which he argued in *Das Heilige*, but modulated it in his short essays again and again, by changing or supplementing phrases in its new editions. Not only has this book been repeatedly re-published in Germany, but it was also translated into English (1923), Swedish (1924), Spanish (1925), Italian (1926), Japanese (1927), Dutch (1928), and French (1929). Many editions of *Das Heilige* appeared during Otto's lifetime; apparently he continued to work on it until he died. He was reportedly very surprised by the success of his book.[4] It is noteworthy that, as Otto himself said, the main thrust of this book was Christian theological studies. At that time when the obviousness of Christianity came into doubt, or when it was argued that the religious worldviews were no longer adequate, Otto published *Das Heilige*. This book was Otto's response as a Christian theologian to a changing world environment.

Today, this book is widely known as one of the classics of the History of Religions among scholars around the world. It is often considered as the beginning of the phenomenology of religion. However, Otto never called himself a "phenomenologist of religion." When he referred to the term "phenomenological" (*fänomenologisch*), it suggests, rather, a "negative view of the study of religion."[5] For Otto, the orientation of *Das Heilige* was directed toward Christian theological studies. The reason why Otto's "theological" research was widely interpreted as a phenomenological study of religion was probably due to the influence of Edmund Husserl's disciple, phenomenologist Max Scheler.[6] In the summer of 1918, Husserl, who is regarded as the founder of phenomenology, read *Das Heilige*, recommended by Martin Heidegger and Heinrich Ochsner (1891–1970). After reading this work, Husserl sent a letter to Otto, in which he called *Das Heilige* "a first beginning for a phenomenology of the religious" (*ein erster Anfang für eine Phänomenologie des Religiösen*). At the same time, however, since Husserl found in Otto's book the existence of a "metaphysician (theologian)" (*Metaphysiker (Theologe)*), he criticized Otto's academic attitude.[7] Moreover, Max Scheler, who was one of Husserl's disciples, also praised *Das Heilige* as a book of the phenomenology of religion. Scheler certainly evaluated Otto's description of *the holy* as "phenomenological," but he was still critical of Otto's argument presented in the conclusion of *Das Heilige*. According to Scheler, Otto returned to the view based on Kant and Fries; he did not regard *the holy* as the "definiteness of an object" (*Gegenstandsbestimmtheit*), but as a "subjective category of reason, 'imprinted' on the given sensory material" (*einer subjektiven Vernunftkategorie, die dem gegebenen Sinnesmaterial <aufgeprägt> werde*). Thus, Scheler interpreted the book as saying that from the epistemological viewpoint of Kant and Fries, Otto regarded *the holy* as an *a priori* capacity of emotion. Although he was critical of Otto's views, it may be noteworthy that in Otto's *Das Heilige*, Scheler found "a different kind of phenomenological approach" (*andersartiger phänomenologischer Ansätze*) in his "determination of the essence of the holy" (*Wesensbestimmung des Heiligen*).[8]

Another evaluation by Scheler of Otto's religious theory is based on Scheler's phenomenological method of religion. In order to express the non-rational and transcendent aspect of *the holy*, Otto coined the term *the numinous* (*das Numinöse*). *The numinous* is totally "unique" (*sui generis*). It cannot be defined in the strict sense, even though one can discuss it. Even though it can be discussed, it cannot be grasped conceptually. Otto says:

> Then we must add: "This *X* of ours is not precisely *this* experience, but akin to this one and the opposite of that other. Cannot you now realize for yourself what it is?" In other words our *X* cannot, strictly speaking, be taught, it can only be evoked, awakened in the mind; as everything that comes "of the spirit" must be awakened.[9]

In other words, Otto says, each person has to wake up *the numinous* "out of the spirit" (aus dem Geiste). Scheler considered Otto's methodological perspective on *the holy* as a method that may lead to the "phenomenological intuition of the essence" (*phänomenologischer Wesensschau*). Scheler's phenomenological approach is a negative method in which the phenomena to be manifested are successively stripped in comparing them with similar or contrasting phenomena. It means "revealing" the phenomena "in front of the eyes of the spirit" (*vor den geistigen Blick Hinsetzen*).[10]

Otto attempted to return to the level of religious experience that supports religion from its depth, intuitively grasping its essence and further clarifying its uniqueness. At that time, Husserl and Scheler, who were leaders in the academic world of phenomenology, highly praised his approach as phenomenological. This suggests that for these phenomenologists, Otto's religious theory attracted attention as a phenomenology of religion in the early stage of its development. Subsequently, such phenomenologists of religion as Gerardus van der Leeuw (1890–1950) and Claas Jouco Bleeker (1898–1983) developed the methods and concepts of the phenomenology of religion. As Douglas Allen points out, Otto's emphasis on the uniqueness of religious experience was an important contribution to the phenomenology of religion.[11]

From Husserl's perspective of phenomenology, it may be obvious why he criticized Otto's religious theory. But from Otto's position in constructing a certain Christian theological framework, Husserl's criticism was inadequate and misleading, for it misunderstood Otto's Christian theological view. Otto's main concern was not to construct a phenomenological view of religion, but to construct a Christian theological view. Even though Otto's methodological view of religion seemed to be phenomenological, it was essentially based on his Christian theological perspectives. As suggested before, one can say that Otto had three "faces:" that of a Christian theologian, a philosopher of religion, and a scholar of religious studies. Evaluation of Otto's religious theory depends on which aspect of his three "faces" was emphasized.

Kurt Rudolph (1929–2020), a professor for Religionsgeschichte of Marburg University, also criticized Otto's religious theory as "crypto-theology" (*Kryptotheologie*) from the standpoint of the History of Religions in a narrow sense, and regarded Otto's religious theory as leading to a biased development of the German study of religion. Rudolph felt this approach deviated from the primordial direction of Religionswissenschaft.[12] However, Rudolph's criticism was based on a superficial understanding of Otto's religious theory. For from Otto's theological perspectives, it would be more appropriate to interpret his religious theory as his own Christian theological view, rather than as his "disguised theology." Otto attempted to clarify the essence and structure of religious experiences shared by religions, including Christianity; his intention was to clarify the truth and absoluteness of Christianity by comparing it with other religions.

3 Location of *the Holy* in Otto's View of Religion

Otto had a deep knowledge of Hinduism as well as Christianity. When he visited Japan, he was introduced to Zen Buddhist thought and later became interested in it as a type of mysticism. By publishing *Das Heilige*, he intended to clarify the essence of religion that permeates the religious faith of human beings, regardless of the differences in religion or culture. This book, which has received wide attention not only in Germany but also throughout the world, is Otto's representative work. It has been widely accepted as well as criticized; among his books, there is a tendency to regard only this one as special.

In order to understand Otto's religious theory, it is necessary to remember that his description of religion in *Das Heilige* was rooted in his Christian theology. His true academic interest was in Christian theology. As Robert F. Davidson (1891–1960) also states, Christian theology was "Otto's principal and enduring interest;" "history, psychology, and philosophy were for him simply 'handmaidens of theology.'" According to Davidson, however, the term "theology" to which Otto refers does not mean "a dogmatic or systematic exposition of Christian faith," but "primarily an historico-psychological 'science of religion,' designed to provide understanding of concrete religious experience."[13] Otto emphasized that his academic interests were in his Christian theological studies. But it is true that his approach had large similarities with the approaches adopted by the contemporary phenomenologists in Germany. *Das Heilige* was written during the mid-life of his religious studies research, when he was about forty years old. The Japanese historian of religions Noriyoshi Tamaru (1931–2014) points out that this book was not only written in the middle of his research years, but it was also in the "intermediate position" from the viewpoint of Otto's religious studies development. Tamaru continues:

> While it [*Das Heilige*] incorporates the insights and perceptions gained in his early works that preceded it as an important premise, it included some of the subjects, developed in later years, in advance at least in a nascent form. Such as his religious arguments of the *sui generis* of religion and religious *a priori*, which cannot be reduced to other kinds of activities, belong to the former, while his comparative study of religions in the East and the West (especially, Indian religion and Christianity) and ethical studies can be said to be the latter example.[14]

As Tamaru points out, the insights and perceptions gained in his early works depend on Otto's study of the philosophies of Friedrich Schleiermacher (1768–1834) and Jakob Friedrich Fries (1773–1843). By combining Schleiermacher's religious theory and the Kant-Friesian philosophy of religion, Otto opposed a naturalist view while supporting a religious one and insisted on the uniqueness of religion that cannot be reduced to anything else. Not only are these points of view incorporated into *Das Heilige*, but comparative religious or ethical issues are also introduced. They are developed in such later works as *West-östliche Mystik* (1926) and *Die Gnadenreligion Indiens und das Christentum* (1930). As Davidson pointed out, the Christian theology to which Otto referred was "an historico-psychological 'science of religion,' designed to provide understanding of concrete religious experience." Incorporating the perspective of comparative religion within the framework of Christian theology, Otto developed Christian theological studies, relating them, for example, to Indian religion. His Christian theology was no longer the traditional review of Christian doctrines. As Davidson says, "as a result there is large similarity between his approach and that adopted by the contemporary phenomenological school in Germany. Indeed his own enduring contribution to modern theology may perhaps best be seen as a penetrating and highly suggestive 'phenomenology of religion.'"[15] As Davidson argues, *Das Heilige* contains content which can be called the beginning of the phenomenology of religion.

Das Heilige had Christian theological intentions, but its content is roughly divided into two parts. The first half, Chapter 1 to 15, is a phenomenological analysis of the experiences of *the holy*, while the second half, Chapter 16 to 23, is a religious philosophical analysis of the *a priori*-ness of the experiences of *the holy*. The first part describes the experience of *the holy* and its general characteristics; the second part discusses the experiences of concrete *holy* objects and events.[16]

In the study of Christian theology, Otto attempted a deeper understanding of the philosophical features and originality of Christianity by studying the ideas of other religions from a comparative study of religions, while considering such various religions as Indian religion. For this reason, although *Das Heilige* was a book on Christian theology for Otto, it was accepted as a book on religious studies, especially the phenomenology of religion, unlike his own Christian theological intention. For this main reason, Otto's work *Das Heilige* was undoubtedly recognized as a classic of religious studies.

4 The Rational and the Non-rational Aspects of *the Holy*

For Otto, the purpose of *Das Heilige* was, as its subtitle suggests, first to inquire into "the non-rational factor in the idea of the divine" and then to investigate "the relation of the non-rational to the rational." Focusing on the *a priori* relationship between the non-rational aspect and the rational one in religion, Otto attempted to clarify the relationship between the two. In the Foreword to the English translation of *Das Heilige*, that is, *The Idea of the Holy*, Otto states:

> In this book [i.e., *Das Heilige*] I have ventured to write of that which may be called "non-rational" or "supra-rational" in the depths of the divine nature. I do not thereby want to promote in any way the tendency of our time towards an extravagant and fantastic "irrationalism", but rather to join issue with it in its morbid form. The "irrational" is to-day a favourite theme of all who are too lazy to think or too ready to evade the arduous duty of clarifying their ideas and grounding their convictions on a basis of coherent thought. This book, recognizing the profound import of the non-rational for metaphysics, makes a serious attempt to analyze all the more exactly the *feeling* which remains where the *concept* fails, and to introduce a terminology which is not any the more loose or indeterminate for having necessarily to make use of *symbols*.
>
> Before I ventured upon this field of inquiry I spent many years of study upon the *rational* aspect of that supreme Reality we call "God", and the results of my work are contained in my books, *Naturalistische und religiöse Weltansicht* (English translation "Naturalism and Religion", London, 1907), and *Die Kant-Friesische Religions-Philosophie*. And I feel that no one ought to concern himself with the "Numen ineffabile" who has not already devoted assiduous and serious study to the "Ratio aeterna".[17]

According to Otto, before exploring and understanding the non-rational *numinous* aspect of *the holy*, it is important to explore the rational one. Thus, he emphasizes that the exploration of the non-rational side of *the holy* is premised on the exploration of its rational side.

At the beginning of the publication of *Das Heilige und das Profane: Vom Wesen des Religiösen* (1957), Mircea Eliade (1907–86), who was influential in the History of Religions in the latter half of the twentieth century, noted that when Otto's *Das Heilige* was first published in 1917, it evoked a worldwide reaction. Commenting on the "relationship between the non-rational and rational aspects" in religion, proposed by Otto, Eliade interpreted the relationship between them as "the sacred in its entirety." He further argued that "the first possible definition of the *sacred* is that it is *the opposite of the profane*."[18] Thus, Eliade says, the sacred and the profane *simultaneously exist* in their paradoxical relationships. Otto's concept of *the holy* was interpreted in Eliade's "dialectic of the sacred." Otto's conceptual framework of religion, inherited by such historians of religions as Eliade, has been widely used in contemporary religious studies. Although it has not been used, or not much used, in Germany since the 1970s, there is no doubt that, seen from this perspective, Otto's view of *the holy* indeed constitutes the foundation of the History of Religions.

According to Eliade, although the sacred and the profane are in conflict with each other, they are in a complementary relationship. In this way, he emphasized the importance of understanding the whole picture of the sacred as complementary parts, and called the relationship between them a religious "hierophany." In other words, Eliade grasped the relationship between the non-rational and the rational aspects of *the holy*, presented by Otto, as the complementary reality of the sacred and the profane, two parallel yet paradoxical components. Eliade's way of understanding the dialectical relationship between "the sacred" and "the profane" was severely criticized after his death as having the characteristics of a "hidden theology." However, in a sense, the criticism of Eliade's religious theory may be justified, for his conceptual framework was developed on the basis of Otto's theological viewpoint.

5 *The Numinous* as the Non-rational Overplus

First, let us focus on Otto's use of *the holy*, to express "the idea of the divine." He refers to "the divine" as *the holy* experienced in the so-called "feelings of the numinous." In describing *the numinous*, it is obvious that Otto is basing it on the Lutheran framework. For Luther, the "feelings of the numinous" in faith involves an independent apprehension of God and provides an access to the depth of reality, inaccessible to rational speculation. Schleiermacher also regards *the holy* as the central concept of religion in *Über die Religion*. Otto says that the word *holy* is usually understood in an ethical or rational sense; it is a purely ethical term meaning "completely good." He then explores the fundamental and deeply felt meaning of this word.

The Numinous and Its Associated Feelings

First, according to Otto, the ethical meaning of *the holy* is what was added in the historical development of religion; such a usage of this word is not accurate. Otto states:

> It is true that all this moral significance is contained in the word "holy", but it includes in addition—as even we cannot but feel—a clear overplus [*Überschuß*] of meaning, and this it is now our task to isolate. Nor is this merely a later or acquired meaning; rather, "holy", or at least the equivalent words in Latin and Greek, in Semitic and other ancient languages, denoted first and foremost *only* this overplus: if the ethical element was present at all, at any rate it was not original and never constituted the whole meaning of the word.[19]

In his search for the meaning of the word *holy*, Otto coined the term *the numinous* (*das Numinöse*) to express the non-rational "surplus" (*Überschuß*) or "'the holy' minus its moral factor or 'moment'" and "minus its 'rational' aspect altogether."[20] By subtracting all other elements that accompany the concept of *the holy*, that is, all rational elements other than non-rational elements, Otto says, one can reveal the true nature or essence of *the holy*.

According to Otto, in Semitic religions, such ancient words for *holy* as the Hebrew *qādosch*, the Greek *hagios*, and the Latin *sanctus* (or more precisely the *sacer*), were originally the words which expressed only the non-rational "surplus" in its early stages of development. The term, *the numinous* (*das Numinöse*), was coined from the Latin *numen* which means "divinity," and represents the non-rational part of *the holy*. Otto says that one can make *numinös* from Latin *numen*, just as one can make *ominös* from the Latin word *omen* that means "aura." The category of *the numinous* is totally "unique" (*sui generis*) and, cannot be precisely defined; it can only be discussed. Otto writes that "while it admits of being discussed, it cannot be strictly defined. There is only one way to help another to an understanding of it."[21] Thus, he says, "the nature of the numinous can only be suggested by means of the special way in which it is reflected in the mind in terms of feeling." In other words, it can be suggested only through the special "feeling-reaction" (*Gefühls-reaktion*) that it evokes in the feelings of the person that experience it, as it cannot be understood as a concept.[22] The fact that it evokes a "special feeling reaction" suggests that *the numinous* presupposes an objective reality. Otto states that what is experienced as *the numinous* is the "object outside me" (*ein Objekt außer mir*).[23] He suggests that it is the non-rational "surplus." In other words, by pointing out the characteristics of feeling that are "associated with the object" (*Objekt-bezogen*), it indicates that the feelings of *the numinous* are related to the object of *the numinous.*

Otto says that *the numinous* can be merely grasped by feelings. In a supplementary note on "feelings" in *Das Gefühl des Überweltlichen: sensus numinis* (in English, *The Feelings of the Otherworldly: sensus numinis,* 1932), in regard to the "feelings" in the "otherworldly," while following the "linguistic usage of old and traditional words," Otto does not consider the "feeling" as a "subjective state" (*subjektive Zuständlichkeit*), but as "an act of reason itself, a way of cognition" (*ein Akt der Vernunft selber, eine Weise des Erkennens*). This way of cognition is not based on concepts or definitions, logical analysis or theorization, but begins mostly with a grasp "according to the feelings" (*gefühlsmäßig*). Even if one cannot make a successful transition to a thing "according to the understanding" (*verstandesmäßig*), many "feelings" can be very sure convictions or confirmations. Thus, in regard to the key term *numinous*, in each new edition of *Das Heilige,* Otto emphasizes the objective reality of *the numinous* and states that his description is based on Luther's framework. As Davidson rightly points out, for Luther, on whom Otto depends for his theological stance, the nature of faith is derived from "its objective reference to a transcendent reality;" the emotional aspects of experience are simply the "means by which religious reality is immediately apprehended."[24] In short, in Otto's religious theory, the "feeling of the numinous," which is an intuitive function of "cognition" (*Erkennen*), is the emotional response in human awareness of an objective transcendent reality.

The Numinous and Its Analogies

Otto argues that *the holy* consists of an *a priori* relationship of the rational aspects with the non-rational ones. If one does not understand this fact properly, he says, one would be led to a completely false irrationalism. In the "Foreword by the Author" to the English translation of *Das Heilige*, i.e., *The Idea of the Holy*, he challenges this kind of false irrationalism. In the first chapter of *Das Heilige*, he emphasizes the significance of rational elements in *the holy*.[25] In order to understand the non-rational elements of *the holy*, Otto explains, it is important first to understand the characteristics of the rational elements. Eliade's argument on the relationship between the sacred and the profane is a development of Otto's view of the relationship between the rational element and the non-rational one. One can say that Eliade's theory of the sacred and the profane fundamentally has a structure in common with Otto's religious perspective.

Now, as Otto emphasizes, the essential feature of Christian theism is that "divinity" (*Gottheit*) is understood by accurately defining the idea of God. It may be considered by an "analogy" (*Entsprechung*) to the personal and the rational that humans sense within themselves in an inadequate and limited way. At the same time, all terms related to the divine are considered "absolute" or "perfect." Otto says, "All these attributes constitute clear and definite *concepts*: they can be grasped by the intellect; they can be analyzed by thought; they even admit of definition."[26] Moreover, if one regards such objects that can be clearly understood as "rational," the essence of divinity described in these rational terms can be expressed as "rational;" religion which recognizes God in such a way is, to that extent, "a rational religion" (*eine rationale Religion*).[27] However, the non-rational part of *the holy*, that is, the aspect of *the numinous*, is shown only by analogy or similar expressions.

Here, Otto considers the position of Christian theology that a religion "conceptually" expresses a perception of the extrasensory (i.e., the recognition of faith) as showing the high degree of that religion. Moreover, from the perspective of Christian theology, Otto says, the fact that Christianity has a concept, outstanding clarity, obviousness, and richness, as opposed to religions which take other stages and forms, shows the superiority of Christianity over other religions.[28] He also notes that one must be careful about the misunderstanding that comes with the phrase, "the essence of divinity is exhausted" (*das Wesen der Gottheit erschöpften*).[29] All languages attempt to convey concepts above all, because they consist of words. The more clear and unambiguous a discourse is, the easier it is to understand, but when a rational predicate appears in the foreground, it does not exhaust divinity and has meaning only for the non-rational.

Elements of *the Numinous* and Their Associated Feelings

According to Otto's analysis of the elements of *the numinous* in *Das Heilige*, the essence of religion is the experience of *the holy*; the content of its experience is the "feeling" (*Gefühl*) of the non-rational *numinous*. Therefore, the word "feeling" is a key to understanding Otto's religious philosophy. *The numinous*, which cannot be grasped or expressed by language, is reflected in a "feeling-reaction," or is inherently understood as such. According to Otto, "feeling" is not a "mere subjective mood" but contains "some vague symbolic content." In other words, as Jörg Lauster, who is a Christian systematic theologian familiar with Otto's Christian theological studies, points out, Otto shared Schleiermacher's views in that he considered the basic definition of religion to be "feeling." Unlike Schleiermacher, however, Otto emphasizes that religion is more than such a feeling. Based on Otto's discussion, Lauster says:

> On the one hand, religion is a subjective act, the feeling is an accompanying interpretation of an inner experience. On the other hand, this experience is caused by something outside the individual. The subjective interpretation has a referent, it is something like a reaction, an answer, a reflex—of course, always under the conditions of individual subjectivity.[30]

According to Lauster, in the "accompanying interpretation of an inner experience" of "feeling," its object always exists under the condition of individual subjectivity. In other words, feelings are "like a reaction, an answer, a reflex" that subjectively interpret what *the numinous* vaguely suggests. Otto calls this first element of *the numinous* the "creature-feeling" (*Kreaturgefühl*). It is "a reflection of feelings caused by a numinous object in self-feeling." In regard to this experience, while Schleiermacher named it the "feeling of 'dependence'" (*das Gefühl der "Abhängigkeit"*), Otto called it the "creature-feeling." According to Otto, this feeling is "the emotion of a creature, submerged and overwhelmed by its own nothingness in contrast to that creature which is supreme above all creatures."[31] In other words, the feeling of "absolute dependence" presupposes that of "absolute superiority" (and even inaccessibility).[32]

Otto's explanation of "feelings" relies on Fries' epistemological position, which represents a unique development in the interpretation of Kant's philosophy. Otto received severe criticisms for this view. In his Christian theological studies, on the basis of Schleiermacher's religious theory, Otto attempted to incorporate "feeling" (*Gefühl*) and "intuition" (*Anschauung*) into his methodological perspectives. In this process, he became interested in Fries's philosophy. Fries's philosophy divides human perception into three parts: "knowledge" (*Wissen*), "faith" (*Glauben*), and "feeling" (*Ahndung, Ahnung*), and discusses their relationships. Fries's division is based on Kant's division of understanding, reason and judgment, but Fries reconsidered it a multilayered structure of cognition.

For Fries, knowledge of the eternal in the finite is possible only through pure feeling. Religious and aesthetic feeling, i.e., "feeling" (*Ahndung*), is characterized by "truth-feeling" (*Wahrheitsgefühl*). The world of "faith" appears in the world of "knowledge" by "feeling." Religion arises through "feeling." Fries says that, although "feeling" is felt positively, it cannot be analyzed or expressed conceptually.[33] Fries's cognitive structure constitutes the basic framework of Otto's religious theory.

For Fries, when considering the rational aspects of *the holy*, the knowledge of God is a general *a priori* aspect. Moreover, when considering the non-rational aspect of *the holy*, the *numinous* experience, like "feeling," is a unique experience as well as the ultimate source of all religions. The "feeling" and the *numinous* emotions are formally the same, but specifically, both of them are different. According to Fries, "feeling" has no autonomous meaning or value. It only links the domains of faith and knowledge. On the other hand, for Otto, religion includes not only unique experiences (or those identified as aesthetic experiences) but also completely autonomous meanings and values. The meanings and values of *the numinous* are determined by an analysis of the contents of religious consciousness.[34]

Regarding elements of *the numinous*, Otto introduces the concepts of "mysterium tremendum" and "mysterium fascinans." *The numinous* cannot be conceptually clarified; it can only be felt. It is inaccessible in conceptual thinking and is only suggested in the mind that experiences it, through the special "feeling-reaction" (*Gefühls-reaktion*) which it evokes. It is experienced as the "daunting" as well as the "fascinating." "Mystery" (*mysterium*) means something hidden that cannot be conceptually expressed. Although it does not say anything more positive in itself, it is intended to be quite positive. Something positive can be experienced as a "feeling." Not only is it the terrifying element of the "daunting," but it is also a distinctly unique attraction and fascination (*das Fascinans*). Both elements combine in a strange "contrast-harmony" (*Kontrast-harmonie*).[35] The positive aspect implied in this feeling is the adjective *tremendum*. The word *tremor* itself means "fear" (*Furcht*), a common "natural" feeling. *The numinous* causes such feelings as the unlimited "awe" and "wonder" in those who experience it. Yet, it is also *the fascinans*; that is distinctly attractive, captivating, and fascinating. Otto quotes Luther's words: "It is just as we honor a sanctuary with fear and yet do not flee from it but penetrate it more."[36] According to Otto, it is characteristic of *the numinous* that both elements are in harmony, though they are opposite. This can be seen in religions throughout the world.

In the *tremendum* element of *the numinous*, Otto says, there are three dimensions. They are "awe," "majesty" (*majestas*), and the "energetic" (*Energisch*). In regard to "awe," Otto argues that the antecedent stage of the "religious awe" (*religiöse Scheu*) in the *numinous* feeling was the "daemonic dread" (*dämonische' Scheu (=panischer Schrecken)*) that constituted the most "primitive" (*roh*) stage. Moreover, Otto says, "daemonic dread" first begins to stir in the feeling of "something uncanny," "eerie," or "weird." "This feeling which, emerging into the mind of primeval man, forms the starting-point for the entire religious development in history." In Otto's view, both "daemons" and "gods" spring from this root; "All the products of 'mythological apperception' or 'fantasy' are nothing but different modes in which it has been objectified."[37] Otto emphasizes that the emergence of these *numinous* feelings has begun a new era of "humanity" (*Menschentum*). He regarded this first *numinous* feeling as unique to humans and tried to show its originality and universality. In the latter part of *Das Heilige*, especially in Chapters 16 and 19 entitled "The Holy as an *a priori* Category" ("Das Heilige als Kategorie *a priori*"), he provides a theoretical basis, introducing the concept of *a priori*.

For Otto, the feeling of "awe" is everywhere present throughout the history of religion. In religion's early stage of development, "awe" gives consistency to the history of religion as a "warp;" in each religion, the specific nature of *the holy* that appears through the "schematization" (*Schematisierung*) of the object of "awe" forms the weft. In his later collection of papers, i.e., *Das Gefühl des Überweltlichen: sensus numinis*, Otto says, "It is self-evident that the numinous feeling, at first found only in vocalization, in a sound without words."[38] In other words, the "first" (*erst*) and "primitive" (*roh*) stage of the numinous feeling was historically not verbal, but expressed in pre-verbal vocalizations. In any case, the "awe" feeling always exists in religious tradition as the original sensation of the "numinous feeling," that is, *sensus numinis*, "the source of the heterogeneity of religious feelings."[39]

Another element of *the numinous* is what Otto calls "das Mysterium," that is, *the wholly other* (*das ganz Andere*). Otto describes "mystery" minus the *tremendum* element more accurately as "surprising" (*Mirum*) or "wonderful" (*Mirabile*).[40] In the religious sense, the term *mirum* meaning the mysterious and the "amazing" is said to be "wholly other." It means "other" and "totally other," represented by such words as *thāteron* (Greek), *anyad* (Sanskrit), *alienum* (Latin) and *aliud valde* (Latin). According to Otto, *the wholly other* is also seen in the first stage of the "numinous feeling" in very early religion.[41] Later, I will elaborate on the concept of the "wholly other" in Chapter 6 of this book, especially in relation to Indian religious thought.

Otto's religious theory was based on Lutheran theological thought. Although Otto had begun his Christian theological studies by the time he published his first book, *Die Anschauung vom heiligen Geiste bei Luther* (1898), it is not surprising that he developed his perspective with the help of Luther's theological terminology. For example, in *Das Heilige*, Otto says:

> It is the absolute numen, felt here partially in its aspect of *maiestas* and *tremendum*. And the reason I introduced these terms above to denote the one side of the numinous experience was in fact just because I recalled Luther's own expressions, and borrowed them from his *divina maiestas* and *metuenda voluntas*, which have rung in my ears from the time of my earliest study of Luther. Indeed, I grew to understand the numinous and its difference from the rational in Luther's *De Servo Arbitrio* long before I identified it in the *qādôsh* of the Old Testament and in the elements of 'religious awe' in the history of religion in general.[42]

As one can see from the sentences quoted here, the main theological terms that Otto uses are derived from Lutheran theology. For example, the elements of *tremendum* and *majestas* that compose *the numinous* are derived from "divine majesty" (*divina majestas*) and "terrifying will" (*metuenda voluntas*) that Luther quotes. Regarding the differences between the non-rational (*numinous*) and the rational of *the holy*, Otto had already found a clue in Luther's works long before the writing of *Das Heilige*.

6 *A priori* Category of *the Holy* and Its Schematization

As Otto says, *the holy* is a complex category composed of the rational and the non-rational elements, as a "purely *a priori* category" (*eine Kategorie rein a priori*) of meaning and value. It conditions the religious interpretation of human experience and provides the knowledge of an objective and transcendent reality. In the development of religion, its non-rational core is gradually filled with a rational and ethical sense. With the concept of "*a priori*" derived from Kant's epistemology, Otto attempted to clarify the structure of *the holy* as a complex category.

The non-rational *numinous* feeling is qualitatively different from natural or everyday feelings. It is "a qualitatively specific and unique feeling" (*ein qualitative eigenartiges originales Gefühl*), the "original feeling" (*Urgefühl*). The word "original" (*Ur-*) is not in the sense of time but in a fundamental *a priori* sense, as found in Kant.[43] The feeling of *the numinous* as the "original feeling" is prior to all *a priori* experiences and exists in the structure of human cognition, whether one experiences it or not. Otto says that it is similar to high-level cognitive ability. He states:

> It [the numinous] issues from the deepest foundation of cognitive apprehension that the soul possesses, and, though it of course comes into being in and amid the sensory data and empirical material of the natural world and cannot anticipate or dispense with those, yet it does not arise *out of* them, but only *by their means*. They are the incitement, the stimulus, and the "occasion" for the numinous experience to become astir, and, in so doing, to begin—at first with a naive immediacy of reaction—to be interfused and interwoven with the present world of sensuous experience, until, becoming gradually purer, it disengages itself from this and takes its stand in absolute contrast to it.[44]

The feeling of *the numinous* breaks out from the "foundation of the soul" (*Seelengrund*), that is, from "the deepest foundation of cognitive apprehension that the soul possesses." Events and things in the everyday world are "the incitement, the stimulus, and the 'occasion' for the numinous experience to become astir." As Otto understands, the concept of *a priori* is related to Kant's concept insofar as it means to precede all experiences, but is separated from Kant as long as it is accompanied by some kind of "ability," that is, "feeling" or "higher reason."[45] Since Otto uses the term "*a priori*" in a very broad sense, there is also an argument that there are few mental phenomena that are not *a priori*. For Otto, however, the feeling of *the numinous* as the "original feeling" is qualitatively unique and therefore *a priori*. Unlike any other spiritual phenomenon, it is involved in the understanding of a unique object or *numen*. Therefore, as Almond pointed out, "both the rational and non-rational elements of the category of the Holy are *a priori*; the incipient Kantian tradition is reflected through a Friesian prism."[46] It is obvious that Otto's emphasis on "feelings" in his arguments of the experience of *the holy* was partly due to his reliance on Friesian philosophy, which inherited and developed Kantian philosophy. The non-rational element of religious *a priori* is the foundation of religion. It represents the fundamental characteristic of Otto's religious theory. Religion exists only when the rational and non-rational elements are inextricably linked. Here, Otto introduces the concept of "schematization" (*Schematisierung*) in order to explain the relationship between the two elements. In *the holy*, he says, the rational element "schematizes" the non-rational element of *the numinous*. Otto's vague explanation of the term "schematization" makes it very difficult to understand his intent. As pointed out by Bernhard Häring (1912–98) and Almond, Otto's "schematization" of *the numinous* with the rational and ethical was criticized because of his vague explanation of the term.[47]

According to Otto, "schematization" represents "the relation of the rational to the non-rational in the complex idea of the holy" (*das Verhältnis des Rationalen zum Irrationalen in der Komplex-Idee des Heiligen*). The non-rational *numinous* is "schematized by the rational concepts and becomes the complete and comprehensive category of the "holy" in the complete sense."[48] The genuine schematization is not simply a coincidence in that the religious feelings of truth (*Wahrheitsgefühl*) grow and develop, and in that they are not disassembled or separated, and more clearly recognized.[49] Therefore, with Otto's so-called "schematization," the non-rational *numinous* can be expressed for the first time, and it is understood as a doctrine of religion.

The specific elements of *sensus numinis* are schematized by their corresponding rational concepts. The *tremendum* element of *the numinous* is schematized by the rational concept of justice and moral will, and is understood as the holy "wrath of God." The *fascinans* element of *the numinous* is schematized by the concept of goodness and love, and is disclosed as the infinite "grace of God." The concrete moment of *sensus numinis* is schematized by a corresponding moral or rational concept. In this regard, Davidson says:

> The *tremendum* (the daunting or repelling moment of the numinous), schematized by the rational ideas of justice and moral will become known as the holy "Wrath of God." The *fascinans* (the attracting or alluring moment of the numinous), schematized by the ideas of goodness, mercy and love, is revealed as the infinite "Grace of God." The essential mysteriosum of the numinous, schematized by the idea of absoluteness, fundamentally transforms all rational attributes when applied to the deity.[50]

This statement makes it clear that Otto attempted to construct his own position in Kant-Friesian philosophy. Otto's theory of "schematization," however, received a lot of criticism. According to Joachim Wach, for example, the greatest weakness in Otto's analysis of religious experience is the concept of "schematization." In his article published in 1951, "Rudolf Otto and the Idea of the Holy," Wach says:

> The word he took from Kant, but he changed its meaning. Religious experience becomes schematized in entering into relationships with other modes of experience or of judgment. The central religious notions of sin and of redemption,

> even that of the Holy, have moral associations. A phenomenological demonstration of the foundation of moral values was the aim of the last endeavours of Rudolf Otto.[51]

By incorporating Kant-Friesian philosophy, Otto explained that in religion the rational elements "schematize" the non-rational elements of *the numinous*. It is an important point of Otto's argument that the non-rational and rational elements of religion exist in harmony through the so-called "schematization" which in turn represents the supremacy of religion. In Otto's argument of the *a priori* involvement of the rational and non-rational elements in *the holy*, what is of particular importance is the relationship with the *numinous* feelings. Furthermore, at the basis of the a *priori* involvement, lies the underlying "feeling of truth" (*Wahrheitsgefühl*), which Fries points out.

Before ending my discussion in this chapter, I would like to briefly mention the continuity and discontinuity between Otto's religious theory and Kant-Friesian philosophy. In *Das Heilige*, Otto incorporated the framework of Kant-Friesian philosophy. Before the publication of *Das Heilige*, in his book *Naturalism and Religion* (1904), Otto had already defended religious faith against scientific naturalism in Friesian terms; in his *Kantisch-Fries'sche Religionsphilosophie und Ihre Anwendung auf die Theologie* (1909), he more explicitly adopted Friesian "transcendental idealism." As Davidson points out, Otto was influenced by Friesian emphasis upon the essential mystery in religion and his theory of *Ahndung* as a certain apprehension in religious feeling.[52] In this respect, there is continuity between Otto and Kant-Fries. At the same time, however, there is a discontinuity between the two. According to Almond, the discontinuity between the two does not mean that Otto changed his Kant-Friesian basic philosophical approach, but rather that he modified his own approach in order to understand data that he gained through his encounter with other religions. Moreover, as Davidson also points out, as a result of the historical and psychological analysis of religious experience, which Otto undertook in his later studies, he modified the position adopted in his early *Kantisch-Fries'sche Religionsphilosophie und Ihre Anwendung auf die Theologie*. In examining the issues of religious pluralism in the modern world, Otto's religious theory is an important attempt as a pioneer of the Kantian manner.[53] The arguments provided by Almond and Davidson are based on the results of their detailed research on Otto. It is my view that they are the proper interpretations of Otto's religious theory.

4

Influences of the History-of-Religions School on Otto's Religious Theory

The Religionsgeschichtliche Schule (the History-of-Religions School) consisted of a group of Protestant theologians, who developed a school of thought in Germany from the end of the nineteenth century to the beginning of the twentieth century; it supported the liberal theology centered at the University of Göttingen. German Protestant theologians belonging to this school, including Ernst Troeltsch, applied the methods of the history of religions to the interpretation of the Bible. Otto was a good friend of Troeltsch. After he became a lecturer at the University of Göttingen in 1899, Otto was influenced by the Religionsgeschichtliche Schule whose influence was gradually increasing at that time. Although this school began as a movement within Christian theology, it did not fit within the traditional framework.[1]

The History-of-Religions School was characterized in two ways.[2] First, "history" was meant to clarify "historical facts" which underlie the literature. In order to clarify historical facts, scholars emphasized "comparison" in historical studies and its related disciplines, while taking into account traditional philological studies. The other characteristic is that scholars of the History-of-Religions School emphasized the differences between religion and theology. They thought that religion did not mean theology, but the totality of religiousness and rituals as sociological facts. They attempted to understand religions as psychological phenomena. After Otto became a lecturer at the University of Göttingen, he attempted to incorporate the methodology of a "comparative" study of religions, used by the History-of-Religions School; he pursued his Christian theological studies, going beyond their traditional content.

1 Uniqueness of the Historical Approach to Religions

Otto has been often introduced as a pioneer in the phenomenology of religion. However, he regarded his work as Christian theological study and never considered himself a phenomenologist of religion. Rather, the method of those religious studies which Otto called "phenomenological" (*phänomenologisch*) or "religionskundlich" was to study religion as a "phenomenon" from the outside, i.e., "considering religion in a category which is not religious in itself." His "theological" (*theologisch*) study was "a method of considering religion itself according to itself," and that of applying "a category, derived from religion itself, to religion in regard to religion itself." For Otto, a Lutheran theologian, the "theological" method of study was to elucidate the unique meaning of religion (especially Christianity). Irrespective of his own desires, however, Otto's "theological" writings have been often regarded as the phenomenological study of religion.[3] Otto's Christian theological studies were designed on the premise of the uniqueness of religion and incorporated comparative religious methods. His method was similar to the phenomenological methods used by Edmund Husserl and Max Scheler. While going beyond the framework of traditional Christian theology, Otto's research contained the characteristics of the wide range of religious studies that explores the meaning of religion by comparing such various religions as Hinduism within the scope of religious research.

Otto, always aware of being a Lutheran theologian, was particularly interested in Indian religions and in other non-Christian religions. From a modern perspective of the History of Religions, he was a historian of religion as well as a Christian theologian. In his comparative study of religion, he proposed the "law of parallel lines of development" in order to understand similar phenomena found in Western and Eastern religions. He interpreted religions in the world as containing parallel phenomena. Through his two journeys to non-Western cultures, Otto gradually constructed his own framework of religious history, especially touching on concrete aspects of Indian religion and its faith.

In his religious studies, Otto regarded such Eastern religions as Hinduism and Buddhism as parallel to Christianity. In describing the history of world religion, Otto interprets the historical development of Eastern religion and Christianity by the "law of parallel lines of development." However, since he attempted to understand Indian religion and thought on the basis of the framework of Christian concepts, he failed to observe the diverse and multilayered structure of Indian religion, especially the polytheistic characteristics of Hinduism.[4]

From a methodological viewpoint, Otto's study builds on two views: "the uniqueness of religion" (*sui generis*) and "the comparative study of religions." These two were basic to the whole History-of-Religions School. From early on, Otto had a deep sympathy with Schleiermacher's religious theory and attempted to clarify the essence of religion on the premise of its uniqueness. The theoretical foundation consisted of Schleiermacher's "intuition" (*Intuition*) and "feeling" (*Gefühl*). In 1899, Otto republished Schleiermacher's *Über die Religion* (in English, *On Religion*) with a preface and a postscript to commemorate just 100 years since the publication of the first edition of Schleiermacher's book, published in 1799. The subtitle of this book was "Speeches to the Cultured among the Despisers" (*Reden an die Gebildeten unter ihren Verächtern*). In this book, opposing the enlightenment rationalism of his time, Schleiermacher emphasized that religion has its own domain that cannot be captured by rational thought. He found the essence of religion in "intuition" and "feeling" rather than thought or action.

Such Christian theologians as Wrede and Troeltsch, who belonged to the History-of-Religions School, also argued that the essence of religion was a non-rational experience, while they searched for this essence in history. In the post-Schleiermacher era, this perspective that the essence of religion is non-rational became a normative view for liberal Christian theology and the philosophy of religion. In his book, *Naturalistische und religiöse Weltansicht* (Naturalistic and Religious Worldviews, 1904), Otto argued that according to Schleiermacher's religious theory, the core of "piety" (*Frömmigkeit*) is the "feeling of absolute dependence" (*Gefühl der Abhängigkeit schlechthin*) and that faith is an "experience of mystery" (*Erleben des Mysteriums*).[5] While confronting the naturalistic worldview of that time, Otto sought in the *sensus numinis* the uniqueness of religion that cannot be found in other areas of society and culture. His *Naturalistische und religiöse Weltansicht* was based on Schleiermacher's thought as well as on Fries's Kantian philosophy. His purpose was to defend the "independence and freedom of spirit" (*Selbständigkeit und Freiheit des Geistes*) against naturalism from the standpoint of Kant's transcendental idealism.[6] In his book published in 1909, *Kantisch-Fries'sche Religionsphilosophie und ihre Anwendung auf die Theologie* (*The Philosophy of Religion Based on Kant and Fries*, 1931), Otto emphasized that "the important means and starting point for the study of religion (*Religionswissenschaft*), especially for the study of Christianity, is the religious experience (*religiöse Erlebnis*) itself."[7]

Another facet in Otto's approach is "the comparative study of religions." He developed a theory of religious history pertaining to world religions through his comparative study of Christianity with other religions. In *Kantisch-Fries'sche Religionsphilosophie und ihre Anwendung auf die Theologie,* he argues that Christianity must be understood in its intrinsic affinities and associations with religion in general, and therefore in the context of the history of religions and in the comparison of religions."[8] Like other theologians in the History-of-Religions School, as the knowledge of world religions increased in the Western world, Otto had to confront the question of the relationship between Christianity and other religions. Otto shared this outlook with other theologians of the History-of-Religions School. They attempted to describe the development of Christianity as a history of religious people, rather than as a history of doctrines. Otto's comparative study continued to be normative, presupposing the superiority of Christianity.

In his comparative study of religions, Otto mainly paid attention to the following three points. First, similar phenomena in different religions suggest a fundamental similarity in the experience of humankind.[9] His "law of parallel lines of development" shows how Eastern religions are related to Western Christianity. For Otto, religion is essentially similar in different societies and cultures, as long as it is a human experience. Before Otto was actively engaged in research, various evolutionary views of religion were under discussion in the European academic world. Non-Christian religions were assessed in relation to the absolute criterion of Christianity. By modifying the previous views of religious progress, Otto presented his own "narrative" concerning world religious history.

Otto's second point is that in the comparative study of religions, focusing only on the similarities of religions, one risks overlooking their individual characteristics. Otto thought that religions historically manifest similarly, but they still have their own distinct differences. As he says:

> [I]n the comparison of religions we are prompted to use an even finer discrimination in ascertaining the manner in which the common basic force, despite all apparent parallelism, takes on perfectly distinct forms in its individual manifestations.[10]

Here, Otto distinguishes religion itself from its various manifestations. This understanding of religion reflects the structure of the *numinous* "schematization." An even more important point for Otto was "to compare the contents and values of religions in order to see where one could find the values of higher and more fulfilling religions." From the perspective of his comparative research, Christian religion is thought to parallel Eastern religions, especially such Hindu ideas as *īśvara* (Lord; God), *bhakti* (devotion), and *prapatti* (self-surrender). In this regard, Otto says:

> [D]espite all their similarity these most similar manifestations are subtly but decisively distinguished in the spirit which informs them. The spirit of India is not, even in these instances, the spirit of Palestine. There are fundamental spiritual values that separate these two worlds of the spirit, in spite of astonishing similarities and convergences of type.[11]

The results of Otto's comparative study are presented in *West-östliche Mystik* (1926) and *Die Gnadenreligion Indiens und das Christentum* (1930). Acknowledging the similarities between Christianity and other religions, Otto's comparative study of religions tried to demonstrate the superiority of Christianity.

2 Characteristics of the Historical Study of Religions

Next, I consider Otto's "narratives" in his study of religious history. He modified the single-line evolutionary theory of religion, that had influence until the beginning of the twentieth century, to the "pluralistic evolutionary theory". According to the Japanese historian of religions Noriyoshi Tamaru, the interpretation of religious history can be broadly classified into the following four types: (1) the denial of the view of development and evolution, (2) its modification, (3) the abandonment of history, and (4) the view of circular religious history, based on different principles.[12] Position (1) is best represented by the primitive monotheistic doctrine (*Urmonotheismus*), presented by Wilhelm Schmidt (1868–1954); position (2) is found in the work of Otto and Nathan Söderblom. It was the phenomenologists of religion who strongly asserted the position (3). For example, Gerardus van der Leeuw emphasized that the phenomenology of religion had nothing to do with the historical development of religion. Position (4) passed from Schleiermacher to Joachim Wach through Otto in modification expressed in (2); it is represented by Otto's disciple, Gustav Mensching. At its foundation, there is a rejection of such concepts as"religion in general"and"religion itself." These have theological and enlightenment characteristics and the treating of concrete "religions" as the object of their historical research.

Otto, who exemplifies position (2), interpreted similar religious phenomena in the world as the "parallel" (*Parallele*) or "convergence" (*Konvergenz*) in the development of religions. He viewed the history of religions as the "development" (*Entwicklung*) in a double sense. First, he considered the development of the *numinous* itself, for example, as feelings such as spiritual awe develop into the fear of gods (or God). At the same time, he interpreted the development of religion as the process of ethical interpretation of *the numinous*. That means that Otto's "schematization" of *the numinous* proceeds.[13] In his argument on the development of religion in the first sense, as the source of various religions, Otto set a foundation that can hardly be called "religion," but rather, "pre-religion" (*Vorreligion*) from which "religion" develops.

As elements that form the foundation of this "pre-religion," Otto cites daemonic awe, shamanistic possession, primitive mysticism with daemonic hustle and ecstatic dance, and magical rites. These elements cannot yet be called "religion." Although his criteria for distinguishing "pre-religion" from "religion" are not very clear, Otto holds that "religion" developed on the basis of "pre-religion." Moreover, he says, the "pre-religious" element that precedes "religion" is deeply involved in "religion" and continues to function in it like the front yard of a house. While emphasizing that "this transition to the higher plane proceeds in varied fields of culture, the manifestations being unrelated to one another, independent, and of diverse individuality," Otto argued for parallelism of religions in the history of religions.[14] According to Otto, Greek thought, a decisive factor in Western culture, developed in the period 800–500 BCE; *logos* was separated from *mythos*, and *theologia* (the knowledge of divinity) was separated from *mythologia* (the knowledge of myth). On the other hand, in the Eastern cultures at about the same time, Confucius and Lao-tzŭ appeared in China, and Gautama Buddha in northern India and Nepal. There were religious phenomena similar to Western religions. As the mythological foundations were overcome and religion was ethically and spiritually sought, the absolute began to be explored.

By paying particular attention to the history of Indian religion in the history of Eastern religions, Otto emphasizes that Indian religious history is parallel to Western development.[15] For example, in the religion of the Vedas, Varuṇa, the governing and judicial deity of the universe, parallels the ancient Israelite Jahweh. Classical Upaniṣad thought contains the idea that all reality is one. When Brahmanism was established (900–800 BCE), it was based on primitive sacrificial mysticism and meditation on the gods. Its Indian development parallels Eleatic philosophy in Greece, an early Pre-Socratic philosophy, founded by Parmenides in the fifth century BC. According to Otto, what later became a philosophy was conceptually mysterious and religious. Moreover, in the Brahmanic world, the practical "religious life" (*vita religiosa*) involved philosophical reflection, and at the same time, developed as the experience and practice of salvation (enlightenment). Otto says that, although such development was not as prominent in the West as in India, both were obviously parallel.

In China, Lao-tzŭ preached withdrawal from the world to realize the *Tao*. This closely corresponds to the *logos* of the Greek philosopher Heraclitus, who argued that fire forms the basic material principle of an orderly universe. In India, the term *brahman* was originally the "holy word" of magical hymns, but it became the ultimate principle of the world. The term *ātman* (soul) was originally "breath of life." According to Otto, however, "the *ātman* line of thought and the *brahman* line of thought converged." This *ātman* corresponds to the Western "*pneuma*" and, as Heraclitus says, "*logos* is *pneuma*, *pneuma* is *logos*." Otto points out that *logos* and *pneuma* correspond to *brahman* and *ātman*.[16]

What most interested Otto was Vedānta religious philosophy, represented by Śaṅkara and Rāmānuja in Hindu tradition. In the Preface to his work, *Siddhānta des Rāmānuja*, he states:

> Here, the two wholly great (*ganz Große*) confront each other in Śaṅkara and Rāmānuja, which only play their respective roles; almost uncanny great, world-surpassing, ultimately non-rational, incomprehensible, undefinable, All-One theopantistic mysticism (*All-Eins theopantistischer Mystik*) wrestles with the Lord, the feeling, willing, personal, rational, loving and beloved God of heart and conscience. Nowhere in world literature are these two opponents (are they opponents? Or are they poles?), so sharply, clearly, and definitely clashed as here, in this first section of the [*Śrī-*]*Bhāṣya* of Rāmānuja.[17]

As Otto states in this passage, there are "All-One theopantistic mysticism" and faith in "the Lord" (the "God of heart and conscience"), i.e., "Savior-mysticism" as the "two opponents" or "poles." Rāmānuja, who emphasizes the latter, is in a sharp and decisive conflict with Śaṅkara, who has an affinity for the former. Otto calls these thoughts "Vedānta-Mystik." He argues that Indian mysticism parallels Western mysticism found in Christianity and Islam. This point is presented in detail in his comparative study of Śaṅkara and Eckhart, i.e., in his book *West-östliche Mystik*. Otto also finds in Bhakti a remarkable parallel between Eastern and Western religions.

In *Die Gnadenreligion Indiens und das Christentum*, Otto analyzes the similarities and differences between Hindu and Christian religious traditions, focusing on the Vaiṣṇava tradition of Hinduism as parallel to Christianity. In his analysis, he tries to understand the concepts of "god," "grace," and "salvation" in the Indian "religion of grace" by comparing them with concepts in Christianity. He pays particular attention to Rāmānuja's emphasis on salvation through bhakti and the Vaiṣṇava tradition in general. He considers as "Savior-mysticism" (*Heilandsmystik*), faith in Kṛṣṇa and Rāma and also faith in the Savior as preached by Caitanya, a contemporary of Luther. Otto regards the Vaiṣṇava tradition that he calls "Bhakti-religion" as "a rival to Christianity" (*ein Konkurrent des Christentums*). Otto compares the Christian doctrine of *gratia sola* with Vaiṣṇav's *bhakti*. In *Die Gnadenreligion Indiens und das Christentum*, Otto argues that the legitimate "rival" to Christianity developed in Indian culture.[18] For Otto, study of the history of religions provided a path to understanding the essence and spirit of Christianity. This approach was also essential to his Christian theology.[19] From a comparative perspective, he noticed a "very curious coincidence" between these religions. Otto attempted to show parallel developments of religions all over the world, despite differences between East and West. A clear line of development is suggested: "pre-religion" (*Vorreligion*) → faith in spiritual beings → polytheism → monotheism.[20] On the basis of this interpretation, Otto maintained his Christian theological position. In defining the essence of religions that underpins the "mysterious coincidence" of religious phenomena as *sensus numinis*, Otto pointed to similarities in Eastern and Western religions that supported his view of religious parallels. In short, Otto's study of religion is based on his interpretation of the history of religions that the essence of religion shared by all human beings, regardless of East or West, penetrates the differences among religions in the world.

3 Historical Study of Religions and India

As discussed above, Otto's perspective on the history of religions was a view, seen through the viewfinder of modern Western religious culture. His framework of religion was constructed of trends in Western Protestant theological study from the end of the nineteenth century to the first half of the twentieth century. This may be obvious from tracing his "narrative" on the history of religions. What characterized Otto's study of religious history was his hypothesis that the Indian history of religions paralleled the Western one. A comparative study of the Vaiṣṇava tradition with Christianity reveals that these two religions are both religions of "salvation." According to his interpretation, the Vaiṣṇava concept of *bhakti* corresponds to the Christian concept of "faith" (*Glaube*); the Vaiṣṇava concept of *prasāda* corresponds to the Christian concept of "grace" (*Gnade*). Therefore, Otto called the Vaiṣṇava tradition the "religion of grace" (*Gnaden-religion*) in India.

From Otto's perspective, the Vaiṣṇava tradition is a concrete example of universal religiousness. Although Christianity and Hinduism historically have different origins, they contain very similar religious forms. In the similarity of these religious phenomena, Otto hypothesized parallels in world religious history. What made him strongly aware and convinced of this were his own experiences when he first traveled to the East and encountered Hindu and Buddhist religious traditions. Otto's framework of religious history was still vague when he was influenced by the Religionsgeschichtliche Schule (the History-of-Religions School). His theory of parallelism in the development of religious history had not yet been constructed. From this period onward, his religious studies presented an impression of him as a "historian of religions" (*Religionswissenschaftler*) as well as a Lutheran theologian and a philosopher of religion.

Returning from his journey to the East, Otto began to study Hindu and Buddhist religious traditions, in particular. From 1912 until 1915, records showing the books that he borrowed from the university library underscore his interest in Hindu and Buddhist religious traditions. His close friendship and academic exchange with Heinrich Friedrich Hackmann (1864–1935), a German Protestant theologian, religious historian and sinologist, also played a role. Hackmann belonged to the Religionsgeschichtliche Schule. By voraciously reading books by Hackman, he deepened his understanding of the Eastern religions.[21]

Before his journey to the East, Otto thought that humans had *a priori* "numinous feeling" as a human ability and that the history of religions was its "development." He specifically discussed his concept of "parallelism" in the development of religious history for the first time when, during his stay in Japan, he delivered a lecture on April 11, 1912, at the Asiatic Society of Japan, entitled "Parallelisms in the Development of Religion East and West."[22] The main point of his lecture was a comparative consideration of the Jewish-Christian traditions with the Buddhist traditions. This lecture still makes no mention of Hinduism in India, which attracted his later academic interests. The comparisons in this lecture were still rough; this may be understandable, since his lecture was based on what Otto had just noticed or encountered on his journey to the East. In his lecture at the Asiatic Society of Japan, Otto focused on eight similarities of religions in the East and the West: the contemporaneity of Jewish-Christian and Buddhist traditions; the similarities of their contents; the development of these traditions from the historical to the speculative; the similarities of the "church" system; syncretism; adaptation; cultural by-products; and religious reformations. All of these items derived from Otto's Christian traditions. Using his understanding of the Jewish-Christian traditions, Otto examined the ideas and phenomena of Buddhist traditions that corresponded to the Jewish-Christian. The points that he included in his lecture in Japan became the basis for his view of parallelism in the development of world religions.

Moreover, his second trip to India was from mid-October 1927 to mid-May 1928. At that time Otto was with his disciple, the Swedish minister Birger Forell (1893–1993). He stayed in India longest on his whirlwind journeys to Ceylon,

India, Egypt, Palestine, Asia Minor, and the Balkans. In India he traveled to South India, including Mysore, and Ceylon, which he was unable to visit on his first trip to the country. When Otto returned to Germany after his second trip to India, he published the book, *Die Gnadenreligion Indiens und das Christentum: Vergleich und Unterscheidung* (1930), as a result of the research he conducted on the trip. Before he left for India, he gave a lecture at the Parish General Assembly in Kassel in 1924, and at the University of Uppsala, from which he received an honorary doctorate, and the University of Oslo in 1926, entitled "Bhakti Religion in Comparison to Christianity" (Die Bhakti-Religion im Vergleich mit dem Christentum). Thus, the main content of this book was already completed before Otto left for India. After his return from India, he revised his lecture manuscript and published this book. In this regard, in May 1926, in his letter (dated May 15, 1926) addressed to the historian of religions Nathan Söderblom, Otto wrote to him that in his lectures which he delivered before his trip to India, he attempted to provide the unique and sufficiently prominent features of the Christian faith of salvation, not only by just treating the history of religions but also by comparing the similarities and differences with Hinduism.[23]

A major purpose of Otto's second journey to India was to collect material for the Marburger Religionskundliche Sammlung. At the various places he visited, however, he met a wide range of Buddhists and Hindus. With them, he discussed the "Religiöser Menschheitsbund" (Religious League of Humanity), and, more specifically the outline of the "Universal Religious Peace Conference," scheduled to be held in 1930. This trip was subsequently significant to Otto for two reasons: first, during three days on the Elephanta Island in the Gulf of Mumbai, he was impressed by the mural carvings in the cave temples and later reported that he had experienced *the holy*. He explained that one of these, the three-sided image of Śiva, had led to an experience of *the holy*. Friedrich Heiler described Otto's holy experience as one of the most important religious experiences, together with his experiences in the synagogue of Morocco's coastal city of Mogador where he was deeply impressed by the chanting of the "three holies" (*Kadosch*).[24] During his trip, Otto wrote a letter (dated January 4, 1928) to his niece, Margarete Ottmer, in Germany, detailing this experience of *the holy*. He wrote:

> The stillness and the majesty of the image is complete. It portrays Śiva as the creator, the preserver, and the destroyer of the world, and at the same time as the savior and bestower of blessings. Nowhere have I seen the mystery of the transcendent expressed with more grandeur or fullness than in these three heads.

He further wrote:

> To see this place would truly be worth a trip to India in itself, and from the spirit of the religion (*von dem Geiste der Religion*) that lived here one can learn more in an hour of viewing than all the books ever written.[25]

By looking at the Hindu image of Śiva, which had such beauty and majesty, he experienced *the holy*. Through this Śiva statue, Otto recalls the image of Christ in the old Byzantine Church of early Christianity. Through the image of Śiva who brings the grace of salvation, he had the feelings of *fascinans* and *tremendum* occurring in the experience of *the numinous*. His religious experience at that time was the "feeling of *the numinous*" that Otto claims to be shared by all humanity, even though various religions are different. Through this experience in India, Otto confirmed the parallelism of religious development between Christianity and Hinduism. In this sense, his journey to India was important to him in that he understood the depth of Indian religion through his own experience as the "feelings of *the numinous*" just like in Christianity.

In an additional sense, Otto's trip to India was also very significant. As he encountered scholars, students, and government officials, he explained the "World Religious Peace Conference" to be held in 1930. For example, in Mysore, Otto met Parakāla Svāmī, the patriarch of the Parakāla Maṭha of the Rāmānuja School (Vadagarai School), while being treated as a guest of the Mysore king (Mahārāja). According to Birger Forrell, who accompanied Otto, although Parakāla Svāmī, the patriarch of the Parakāla Maṭha, was a professor of Sanskrit at Rāmāṇuja College in Mysore, he was devoted to his work as the patriarch of the monastery. Otto says that the encounter with Parakāla Svāmī was most memorable for him. Through such meetings, he notes that he experienced "a unique brotherhood with the faithful in other religions."[26] Moreover, he was also able to confirm the relationships between the two lines of thought existing in Hindu religious tradition, namely, "theism" and "mystic non-dualism." Here, Otto's "theism" refers to Rāmānuja's qualified non-dual Vedānta philosophy and that of bhakti in the Vaiṣṇava tradition. On the other hand, Otto's "mystic non-dualism" refers to Śaṅkara's non-dual Vedānta philosophy and that of Śaṅkaran religious tradition.

During his stay in Mysore, Otto also visited the Śṛṅgeri Maṭha, the main shrine of the Śaṅkaran religious tradition, founded by Śaṅkara. He hoped to meet the Jagadguru, the "world teacher." For many years, the patriarch of Śaṅkaran Maṭha has been called the Jagadguru Śaṅkarācārya, a figure who has been widely respected by Hindu adherents. Unfortunately, during Otto's stay in Mysore, the Jagadguru happened to be away. In his *Report*, the accompanying Forrel did not write that

Otto had met the Jagadguru of Śṛṅgeri Maṭha. Today, however, the Marburg Museum, i.e., Marburger Religionskundliche Sammlung, includes a portrait of the thirty-third Jagadguru, i.e., Saccidānandaśivābhinavanṛsiṃhabhāratī (world-renunciation in 1866 and videha-mukti [death] in 1912), presented from Śṛṅgeri Maṭha and a statue of Śaṅkara obtained by Otto in India. These bestowed artifacts testify that Otto had some interaction with the Jagadguru of Śṛṅgeri Maṭha.

On Otto's journey to India, he became convinced that the difference between Christianity and Hinduism was not in their non-rational components, but, rather, differences in their doctrines and ethics. This view is related to his emphasis on ethics in his later years. In *Die Gnadenreligion Indiens und das Christentum* (1930), he argues that in the theistic flow of Hinduism, there is a consciousness that *the holy* is present in the same way as in Christianity. Even in the non-dual Vedānta philosophy of Śaṅkara, Otto clearly recognized theistic elements of faith, which were based on his own experiences in India. He thought that bhakti in Hindu tradition especially corresponds to faith in Christianity. According to him, Christian faith and Hindu bhakti are essentially the same; both of them teach the doctrine of salvation. Otto argues that in bhakti, the God of salvation (*Heilsgott*) has been conceived, believed, pursued and even unquestionably experienced. Thus, bhakti might be respected as a "rival" (*Konkurrent*), though they turn on a different axis.[27]

Hindu theistic thoughts are strikingly similar to Christian thoughts about God and *the holy*. Otto, however, argues that Hinduism lacks values that are derived from God, such as the value of the created world. Otto's understanding of Indian religion based on his Christian criteria is said to have disappointed some Indian people.[28] Indian religion, which Otto described throughout his journey to India, was Hindu tradition and its philosophy—but only as far as he could see it from his own perspectives of religion. His account of Hinduism was constructed from his Christian perspectives. It was not the "living religion" of the Hindus, but rather a Hindu tradition, interpreted by the filter of Otto's Christian religion or theological interests, i.e., a "reconstructed religion" based on the Western religious paradigm. In short, Otto's experiences in India were of great significance in his construction of a religious theory, rooted in the experience of *the numinous*.

4 Tasks of the Historical Perspectives of Religions

From his Christian theological perspective and philosophy of religion, Otto reflected on the essence of religion that humans inherently possess. At the same time, from his comparative religious perspective, he constructed his own methodology in exploring the phenomena in the history of Eastern religions, especially that of India. Otto overlaid his comparative religious views with Christian theology and philosophy of religion, always conscious of himself as a Lutheran theologian and professor of Christian systematic theology. He expressed his theory of religion in comparative religious perspectives, reframed from his Christian theological position.

Concrete aspects of interpretations from his theological perspectives of religion can be found in his particular attention to the Vaiṣṇava tradition; one can find his interpretations in that he perceives the Vaiṣṇava tradition as a "religion of grace" in India. In seeing the Vaiṣṇava tradition as a Christian theologian, he interpreted that religious tradition in non-Western cultures as parallel to Christianity in the West. It is noteworthy that he viewed the Christian God and the Hindu God Viṣṇu in parallel as the "wholly other" (*das ganz Andere*). What his religious hermeneutical perspective could essentially treat within its framework was the theology of Rāmānuja or that of bhakti, represented by the Vaiṣṇava tradition. It was possible for him to interpret that the conceptual framework of Hinduism, described as bhakti, as corresponding to that of Christianity. From a monotheistic perspective, Otto could appreciate the parallelism of religious development in East and West. When he attempted to understand Hindu tradition, including its polytheistic aspects, he focused on its "monotheistic" aspects alone. Otto's study of Indian religion shows us that he could not fully understand it in its own context, because he relied too much on Christian conceptual frameworks.

Otto's theory of religion was derived from the religious context of the modern West. As the American historian of religion William A. Graham, who is known in Islamic and Scriptural studies, emphasizes, all concepts in a religion are constrained by particular religious and cultural context in the modern West. Therefore, these concepts necessarily have a provisional character. We have to say that the concepts of religion and the conceptual framework composed of them inevitably have historical and cultural prejudices.[29] Thus, the concepts and theories of religion that have seemed self-evident in traditional religious studies must be reexamined by returning them to specific religious contexts. In this sense, Otto's journey to the East had the potential to be an important opportunity of reconsidering Western concepts of religion in Eastern religious context. Otto, however, tried to argue the resemblance or the parallelism of religions in the East and West, while relying on the modern Western concepts of religion from the standpoint of Christian theology. In short, we must conclude that Otto's theory failed to recognize polytheistic aspects of Hindu religious tradition. As is often seen in the study of religion by such Western religious scholars as Eliade, in the core of Otto's study of religion, one can find the deep-rooted influences of the modern Western Christian worldview. The correction and revision of the description of religious history may be one of the more important tasks in the contemporary study of religion.

As the historian of religion Wilfred C. Smith points out, scholars of religion begin from the premise that they can understand religions other than their own. Western scholars of religion have had the tendency to regard non-Western religious traditions impersonally as "them." By clarifying doctrines and symbols, they thought it was possible to understand religion. However, such a scholarly attitude may lead to misunderstanding the practices carried out by those involved in a particular religion, or a lack of respect for the religious contexts. Given a particular religious tradition, one can understand the doctrines and symbols only in relation to adherents and communities. Bearing in mind Wilfred Smith's "personalization of the faiths observed," one needs a hermeneutical perspective that relies on empathetic understanding.[30] In short, it could be called a religious contextualization.

In Otto's theory of religion, the historical or comparative study of Christianity with other religions was important for understanding Christian truth. Methodologically, he relied on his Christian theological studies. His theistic perspective, however, suggests a conceptual limitation in understanding Indian religious thought. From his Christian theological perspective, he accepted Hindu religious tradition as one of "salvation," but argued that it lacks the values of the world created by God. Hindu religious tradition, discussed from his Christian theological perspective, was not a "living religion," practiced by the Hindus, but rather a "reconstructed religion."[31] Thus, it may be argued that Otto failed to fully present Indian religious thought as it exists in reality. His perspective had limitations in understanding Hindu tradition, since it lacked contextualization within its Indian religio-cultural setting.

5

Parallelism of Mysticism in Religions East and West

In this book, I have explored Otto's view of comparative religion. In works, such as *West-östliche Mystik,* Otto developed his own understanding of religion. Now, I will clarify how Otto understood Eastern and Western religious thoughts from his comparative religious perspective, with a focus on his theory of mysticism. Among worldwide religious phenomena, he stressed the importance of "mysticism." The concept of "mysticism" in the contemporary study of religion is derived from Western religious traditions. It is important to clarify the extent to which this concept is valid for the understanding of Eastern religions. The issue of whether "mysticism" is a universal concept is not always self-evident, as the American historian of religion John B. Carman points out.[1] To clarify the perspectives from which Otto regarded Śaṅkara's thought as "mysticism," I will focus on his understanding of Indian religious thought. Thus, I wish to examine Otto's theory of mysticism and its characteristics, while taking up the discussion of "mysticism" in recent religious studies.

Otto's most methodological significance is that he first of all asserted the uniqueness of religion, an issue that is debated among historians of religions. To clarify that religion cannot be understood from other phenomena, Otto introduced the concept of "holiness" (*Heiligkeit*) into his study of religion. The other methodological significance in Otto's theory of religion is that he attempted to explore the essence of religion at the level of religious experience. To capture the essence of religion, he emphasized the feeling of *the numinous*. These two points have influenced the study of religion, especially the phenomenology of religion. They constitute the foundation of Otto's Christian theological perspective.

1 Religious Concept of "Mysticism" and Its Research

I would like to briefly discuss research on "mysticism" (Mystik) as a religious concept. The term is said to have been established in the mid-eighteenth century. According to the American historian of religions Leigh Eric Schmidt (1961–), by the turn of the twentieth century, mysticism was known as the universal quintessence of religious experience. In the first half of the eighteenth century, the English category of "mysticism" did not exist. An alternative general classification was "mystical theology," indicating a special division in Christian theology.[2] It was at least by, or shortly after, the nineteenth century that the term "mysticism" became a concept that implies a non-rational divinity and the mysterious immediate experiences.

After the word "mysticism" was recognized as a religious concept, it was applied not only to phenomena in Western traditions, but also to those in the East. It was gradually accepted as one of the universal categories in modern religious studies. As Schmidt points out, the spread of the term "mysticism" as a category became a means of interreligious involvement; it was a sympathetic meeting point of increasing global encounters. The word "mysticism" became a conceptual bridge that enabled countless religious contacts in the nineteenth century.[3] In Europe, research on non-Christian religions progressed with Indology as its starting point. Through these studies, mystical elements were gradually recognized, not only in Christianity but also in various religions. From the latter half of the nineteenth century to the twentieth century, as the Japanese historian of religions Hidetaka Fukazawa points out, "the mystical as the 'common essence' of religions was praised." On the other hand, since the period of Kant, for other scholars of rationalism and science, the term "mysticism" has been synonymous with "obscurantism," which referred to all the non-rational elements of religion. This corresponds to the fact that in the mystical discourse, the word "mysticism" was extended to the non-rational phenomena outside religion. Moreover, "while talking about the universality and super-historicity of mystical experiences, which can be said to be the non-rationalization of natural religion, the historical genealogy of the phenomenal forms of religious mysticism was attempted."[4]

The word *mysticism/Mystik* is originally derived from the Greek word *myo*. It means, to "close," especially to "close the eyes," but in conceptual meaning, it is derived from the adjective *mystikos*.[5] This word shows "a spiritual tendency which is universal," that is, the "tendency of the human soul which is eternal." In short, mysticism should not be seen as religion itself, but rather as the most vital element in all true religions.[6] According to L.E. Schmidt, it was especially Robert Alfred Vaughan (1823–57) who popularized the term "mysticism" as "the highest form of spirituality."[7] In any case, not only Rudolf Otto, but also such scholars of religion as R.C. Zaehner (1913–74), W.T. Stace (1886–1967), Ninian Smart (1927–2001), and S. Radhakrishnan (1888–1975) agreed that mystical experience was a main element in religion.[8]

Mysticism means the "union" of the soul with the ultimate reality. The goal of mysticism is for the mystics to "find the object of personal love and establish a conscious relationship with the absolute" in a mysterious union. Religion is generally perceived as separating divinity and humanity, while mysticism explores the close "union" with the divine, the penetration of the divine in the soul, and the disappearance of the personality in the divine, i.e., the personality with all modes of action, thought, and emotion. In other words, mystics "go through all the phenomenal and all the lower forms of reality, and attempt to be the existence itself."[9]

Mysticism in religious studies should be approached in a particular context (historical, cultural, linguistic). This approach has become increasingly popular for the last twenty-five years. For example, according to the American philosopher Steven T. Katz (1944–), "There is no pure (i.e., non-mediated) experience;" mystic experience is constrained by previous experiences and complicated beliefs, patterns of attitude and expectations. According to the American historian of religions Wayne Proudfoot (1939–), the development of mysticism after Schleiermacher was a larger "protective" plan to secure the "protected area" of religious experience. It is said to be part of a "protective strategy." As Proudfoot points out, mysticism is an area that is protected from both the reductionist explanations and the influx of science. Therefore, Proudfoot says, researchers of religion point out that it is necessary to stop securing mysticism as an autonomous and universal territory that cannot be attributed to other phenomena.[10]

Moreover, the American historian of religions Hans H. Penner (1938–2016) severely criticizes the universality and transcendence of "mysticism." In his article, "The Mystical Illusion" (1983), Penner, who agreed with Katz in regarding mysticism as a "false category" and an "illusion," criticizes the validity of this concept. According to Penner, "'Mysticism' is an illusion, unreal, and a false category which has distorted an important aspect of religion." This does not imply that "the assertions made by yogis, Śaṁkara, St John of the Cross, or Eckhart are unreal or illusory." Penner says, "It is precisely such puzzling data that have led scholars to construct so-called mystical systems and in turn, to see 'mysticism' as the essence of religion."[11]

In regard to the study of mysticism, there are classical studies by such scholars as Rudolf Otto, Evelyn Underhill (1875–1941), W.T. Stace, and R.C. Zaehner. There are many differences in their works, but they all attempted to describe mysticism by exploring its essence. In other words, mysticism is treated as the ultimate experience that transcends the self and the world and is qualitatively different from an everyday experience. It is what Otto calls the *numinous* experience. In response to this view, Penner emphasizes:

> I suggest that we must reverse such approaches to the study of mysticism. We must remember that all we have for understanding mysticism is language, not experience. It is not mystical experience which explains mystical traditions or languages, rather it is mystical language which explains mystical experience. In fact it is useless to appeal to mystical experience as the basis of our explanation because it is precisely this experience that needs to be explained.[12]

As an alternative approach for studying mysticism, Penner proposes the perspective of studying diverse examples in context. The central point of his argument is that "mystical languages cannot be thought of as referring to the same Reality, because Reality is relative to a language system."[13] What Penner emphasizes is that different mystical languages express different mystical worlds.

There is also a deconstructive study of mysticism. For example, the Canadian theologian Grace M. Jantzen (1948–2006) attempts to overcome traditional mystical interpretations from a feministic perspective. According to Jantzen, in Christian history, there is nothing that can be defined as the "essence" of mysticism; the thought of mysticism is a "social and historical construction." Jantzen says:

> When current philosophers and theologians opt for a particular understanding of mysticism this is also, intentionally or not, to opt for a particular social construction of mysticism which inevitably contains and conceals issues of power and authority.[14]

In short, according to Jantzen, mysticism is "a constantly shifting social and historical construction." Moreover, in order to explain mysticism, the American scholar of Judaism, Steven Wasserstrom, coins the term "mystocentrism." With this word, Wasserstrom expresses strong doubts about the long-standing dominance of mysticism in religious studies. According to Wasserstrom, "religious reality," of course, usually creates a mystical meaning, although scholars only study its texts and contexts. As the American historian of religions Jonathan Z. Smith points out, there are never "religious phenomena" available in the classroom; only the "epiphenomena" exist.[15]

2 Background of Otto's Study of Mysticism

How did Otto perceive "mysticism"? His encounter with the "mystic" world of the East, especially in India and Japan, was a major turning point for his religious studies. He later described his impressions at that time: "For the first time, the view of the strange parallelism between the feeling and experience of the East and West became more concrete to me. At the same time, the recognition of intimate peculiarities and heterogeneities became more concrete to me."[16] Otto's view of Eastern religions was based on his own experiences through his journey to the East. In his lecture at the Asiatic Society of Japan on April 11, 1912, Otto says:

> They [the religions of the East and West] are truly parallel, their similarities being now recognized as due to the working of an underlying power called in religious language, revelation, and in scientific language, common religious feeling. If there is a general consciousness throughout the human race then similar phenomena are to be expected. This principle is one of the most significant deductions of modern critical study.[17]

Moreover, he concluded his lecture at the Asiatic Society of Japan with the following words:

> In both the East and the West there is a crisis in all religions to-day. We in the West now realize that we have no monopoly on religious truth. We must in honesty change our attitude toward other faiths, for our watchword must be "Loyalty to Truth." This changed attitude, however, does not weaken, but rather, instead, reinforces one's faith in God, for He is seen to be not a small or partial being but the Great God who is working throughout all times and places and faiths. The historico-critical school of the study of religion is now in full swing in the East as well as the West. We may feel confident that its results hereafter, as in the past, will be to demonstrate that religion is a universal fact, and that it is not primarily dependent upon history but rather lives by its own divine strength and power.[18]

According to Otto, "religion is a universal fact" and "lives by its own divine strength and power." For Christians in the West, he says, their attitude toward other faiths on the basis of the watchword "Loyalty to Truth" "re-inforces one's faith in God" who works "throughout all times and places and faiths." This perspective provides the basis for Otto's subsequent religious research. In his article on "Parallel and Convergences in the History of Religion," Otto proposed the "law of parallel lines of development" to summarize the history of world religions. From this stance, he regarded the Vedānta philosophy in India as "mysticism."[19]

Otto conceived of mysticism as "the essence of a mysterious spiritual phenomenon" (*das Wesen der seltsamen geistigen Erscheinung*). His major books on mysticism include *Das Heilige*, *West-östliche Mystik*, and *Die Gnadenreligion Indiens und das Christentum*. Regarding the word "mysticism," Otto refers to the etymological analysis of the Sanskrit word:

> Mysterium, Mystēs, and Mystik are probably derived from the stems that still remain in the Sanskrit √muṣ. √muṣ means "hidden, lurking, sneaking" (hence, the meaning of deceiving or stealing). In general understanding, "mysterium" is a secret in the sense of something strange, incomprehensible, unexplainable in general, and in that respect, even "mystery" which represents what we try to say is just a similar concept from the realm of the natural. In other words, it is brought up as a display just for some kind of analogy, and it does not really say anything.[20]

Otto regarded Vedānta philosophy as containing "mystery" that could not be reasonably understood or explained in words. Even though one attempts clarification, "mystery" is still impossible to discuss. For Otto, Vedānta philosophy represented "the essence of mysterious spiritual phenomena." The term *unio mystica* suggests that it is based on the experience of the union of oneself with the absolute or transcendental reality. Otto regards mysticism as "the experience of the immanence of the divine, the essential union or the essential unity with the divine" (*Erfahrung der Immanenz des Göttlichen, Wesenseinigung oder Wesenseinheit mit dem Göttlichem*). The mystical experience is the "experience of the divine as the transcendent" (*Erfahrung des Göttlichen als des Transzendenten*), which is different from the commonly understood religious experience.[21] Mysticism emphasizes a "mysterious union" or the union of the self with the transcendent, while in general religious experience, transcendence implies a gap between the transcendent and human existence. For it is based on the understanding of human beings that there is an infinite gap between the two. Otto acknowledged "the inherent experience of the divine, the essential union or the essential unity with the divine" as one of the characteristics of mysticism. However, Otto's theory of mysticism is subtly different from the general understanding of it. Although Otto's book, *West-östliche Mystik*, has often been quoted in discussions about mysticism, it can be said that the discussions were based on an interpretation that deviated slightly from the essence of Otto's "mysticism."[22]

Otto focuses on the difference of the relationship between the self and the "divine" in mysticism and general religious experience, particularly the meaning of the word "divine" (*göttlich*). In mysticism, "divinity" means "divinity as an immanent principle" (*'Gottheit' als immanentes Prinzip*), or "intrinsic God." On the other hand, the "divine" in general religious experience means the "transcendent God" (*der transzendente Gott*), the object of worship for devout adherents. This difference of meaning suggests that religious experience in mysticism and general religious experience have a fundamentally different structure. The word "divine" really points to a difference in the nature of religious experience. In Otto's view of mysticism, the "divine" means "God without modes" (*Deus sine modis*), a non-rational and impersonal God. Thus, "mysticism" is recognized as a religious phenomenon by the concept of "God without modes." He says, "Unity is not mysticism for the first time, but living under the wonders of God as the "wholly other" is already predominantly mysticism." Otto continues:

> As soon as a person embraces such a concept of God, one is already a "mystic," and as is often the case with mystics, even though the momentum of "union" recedes or is not emphasized, it is still the case. Such a notion of God, which has a completely non-rational characteristic and which is different from the trusted personality and transformed God of the rustic form of theism, makes one a "mystic."[23]

In Otto's "mysticism," the experience of mystical union is actually a moment of living under the "wonder" (*Wunder*) of God as the "wholly other." For Otto, "mysticism" emerges when the object of religious feelings becomes predominantly "non-rational," or *numinous*, as they define one's emotions. This is the core of Otto's mysticism. When "mysticism" is understood according to the above interpretation, the boundaries between the mystical experiences and commonly understood religious experiences become ambiguous. His point represents the essential characteristic of Otto's theory of religion, which puts mystical experience at the core of religion.

3 Mysticism East and West: Śaṅkara and Eckhart

From "mystical intuition" (*intuitus mysticus*), Otto says, ontology and philosophy were born in the East and West. Thus, in his book *West-östliche Mystik*, he chooses as representative thinkers Śaṅkara in India and Meister Eckhart in the West. According to Otto, both of them are "teachers of salvation," "theologians" as well as "philosophers." Otto places Śaṅkara as active around 800 CE (according to the Japanese philosopher Hajime Nakamura, his dates are about 700–750), while Eckhart lived from 1250 to 1327 CE According to Otto, for both of them, the way to salvation is "knowledge." These mystics resemble each other in their method of reaching salvation. Otto found their mystic similarity was unaffected by climate, geographic location or ethnic differences. Both of them show an "inner affinity" (*innerliche Verwandtschaft*) of spirit and experience.[24]

According to Otto, both men were "mystics" and "scholastics" in personality, and attempted to "reproduce the content of their mysticism with the means of their trained scholasticism."[25] Otto recognizes the existence of "mystical intuition" (*intuitus mysticus*) at the foundation of their ideas.[26] Since there is also an "internal affinity" between the two, Otto says, it is possible to show a similar ontological structure by comparing words and phrases. According to Otto's insight, behind the similar ontological structures of the two thoughts lies the metaphysical intuition that underpins their ontologies. By extracting the corresponding forms of expression from their ideas, Otto attempted to show almost the same "metaphysics."[27] According to Otto, for Eckhart, God is "Being" (*esse*) itself. Eckhart goes one step further and says, "Being is God" (*Esse est Deus*). Likewise, commenting on the *Chāndogyopaniṣad* (6.2.1), Śaṅkara says that at the beginning of the world, there was only "Being" (*sat*) or Brahman, which was "one without a second" (*ekam evādvitīyam*). Eckhart's "Being" (*esse*) and Śaṅkara's "Being" (*sat*) are "Being itself" (*das Seiende selbst*). Thus, Otto emphasizes the similarity or identity of these two ontologies in the East and the West.

The word *esse* expresses the primordial essence of "God" in scholasticism. Thus, God does not have Being, but God is Being itself. Just as *sat* is Brahman (=Ātman), *esse* is God. Moreover, *sat* is expressed as "non-attribute" (*nirguṇa*) or "not this, not that" (*neti neti*), while *esse* is the "absolute, simple, and non-additional Being" (*Esse absolutum, simpliciter nullo addito*) and "pure and simple Being" (*esse purum et simpkex*). As Śaṅkara's "Being" (*sat*) is the identification of the subject and the function of being, Eckhart's "Being" (*esse*) includes both existence and the existing subject. Thus, arguing the similarity or identity of these philosophies, Otto emphasizes that the pure Being itself cannot be captured by concept or expressed in words. As Davidson rightly points out, in mystic intuition as described by Eckhart, Otto finds an explicit defense of the immediate and non-conceptual apprehension of God; Eckhart emphasizes the inadequacy and limitation of ordinary and conceptual knowledge, condemning it as "a means of hiding the true knowledge of God from us."[28]

A further notable similarity between the two is "the relationship of this wholly superpersonal divinity with the personal God" (*das Verhältnis dieses ganz überpersönlichen Göttlichen zum persönlichen Gott*). Śaṅkara formulates this as the relationship between higher Brahman and lower Brahman, and identifies the lower Brahman as the Lord (*īśvara*). On the other hand, Eckhart unites Deitas and Deus, that is, "divinity" (*Gottheit*) and God (*Gott*). For Eckhart, there is a pure "divinity" at a height which exceeds "God." This divinity is the "foundation of God's potentiality," and, like Śaṅkara's higher or attributeless Brahman, is the higher and wholly "one" (*Eine*).[29] From the perspective of comparative religions, Otto argues that in comparing the two ontologies in the East and the West, these two thoughts are strikingly similar. Above all, Otto emphasizes, both of them resemble each other in the fact that they are not "metaphysical;" they both are guided by their interest in something which lies outside metaphysical reflection, that is, the salvation of the soul. In the writings of both Śaṅkara and Eckhart, the idea of pure Being is merely the "utmost which concept or 'ratio' can offer in the approach to the highest of all things;" it "reveals itself as only a rational 'schema' (model) of something which is fundamentally transcendent—something numinous."[30]

Recognizing the similarity of these two religious thoughts, Otto treats Śaṅkara's thought as "the main type of Oriental mysticism." Since Otto was a Lutheran theologian, his argument relied on Luther's theology. According to Otto's classification, there are two types of mysticism: "soul-mysticism" (*Seelenmystik*) and "God-mysticism" (*Gottesmystik*). "God-mysticism" is found where God becomes the "mystical" reality. On the other hand, "soul-mysticism" is not accompanied by the concept of God, which is not important to the ultimate experience itself. In this mysticism, the *numinous* essence of the soul becomes alive.

As the concrete expressions of "soul-mysticism," Otto suggests Yoga and Buddhism. These two are religious phenomena as "excessive rise of the numinous meaning of soul." Yoga is divided into theistic and atheistic Yoga; theistic Yoga teaches mystical union with God, while atheistic Yoga seeks to free Ātman from all false unions by the use of Yogic methods. Emancipation (*nirvāṇa*) in Buddhism, which denies God, is grasped as the "mystical state" which is completely non-rational and which cannot be described. Furthermore, Otto perceived that in Buddhism, the idea of "no soul" (an-ātman) further strengthened the mystical characteristics.

Otto also categorizes these types as the "mysticism of introspection (*Innenschau*)" and the "mysticism of unifying vision (*Einheitsschau*),"[31] which aims to return to the depth of one's soul. It starts with a "soul-mysticism" and almost remains there as "soul-mysticism" itself. On the other hand, the "mysticism of unifying vision" seeks unity under diversity. When mystical intuition is based on the existent theism, the experienced One has the name "God." The orientation of "soul-mysticism" seems to be quite different from that of "God-mysticism." Since the "mysticism of introspection" and the "mysticism of unifying vision" are different, these two are difficult to combine. However, the Upaniṣad thought, which Śaṅkara's thought presupposes, contains the ontological structure that makes that possible; it is the identity of the highest reality Brahman in the world with the essence of human existence Ātman, i.e., *tat tvam asi* (That thou art). In this structure of thought, Otto points out the possibility of the co-existence of "soul-mysticism" and "God-mysticism," or, alternately, the "mysticism of introspection" and the "mysticism of unifying vision."

In his view of mysticism, Otto argues that "mysticism of introspection" and "mysticism of unifying vision," also called the "way of introspection" (*Weg der inneren Schau*) and the "way of unifying vision" (*Weg der Einheitsschau*), may complement each other. Otto finds the fundamental identity in these two, saying:

> But in Eckhart as well as in Śaṅkara (or more exactly in the mystical direction which Śaṅkara and his school summarize and complete) the two ways have *come together*. In Śaṅkara, it is on the ground that they had long converged in the Indian tradition. In Eckhart, it is on the similar ground.[32]

As Otto says, both in Śaṅkara's philosophy and in the Śaṅkaran religious tradition, the founder of which is believed to be Śaṅkara, the "way of introspection" and the "way of unifying vision" are well combined. In other words, the "way of knowledge" by which world renouncers aim to attain "emancipation" (*mokṣa*) by acquiring the "knowledge" (*jñāna*) of Brahman (=Ātman), and the "way of devotion" by which the ordinary devotees seek salvation from God (the attributed Brahman) by "devotion" (*bhakti*)—both of them "come together."[33] Otto emphasizes that "Eckhart is more than just a representative of tradition," arguing that Eckhart's case is based on similar reasoning to that of Śaṅkara. In other words, in Eckhart, Otto says, the "way of introspection" and the "way of unifying vision" join together. These two ways, however, are uniquely reborn and flow out of his heart.[34]

In the context of Indian philosophy, the theoretical motif of "soul-mysticism" can be described as "Ātman-mysticism" as Otto puts it. But even though it may be called "Ātman-mysticism," Śaṅkara's mysticism is in sharp conflict with the pure "Ātman-mysticism" of Yoga. The confrontation means that Śaṅkara is not a "mystic," as generally expressed, but rather represents a unique combination of "soul-mysticism" and "God-mysticism." By regarding Śaṅkara's thought as "specially limited mysticism" (*eine bestimmt qualifizierte Mystik*), Otto interprets it from his theistic perspectives. There is no doubt that Otto accurately grasps the essential structure of Śaṅkara's thought, which is characterized by the identity of the supreme Brahman and the essence of individual Ātman. But one can say that the characteristic of Otto's discourse is that Indian thought has been reinterpreted through the filter of his monotheistic conceptual framework, found in Christian religious tradition. In other words, Otto's explanation of Śaṅkara's thought represents an interpretation of Vedānta philosophy from a theistic perspective. In his attempt to understand Otto's interpretation of Śaṅkara's thought from a Hindu perspective, the Indian religious scholar S.P. Dubey points out that the interpenetration of theism and mysticism in Śaṅkara may provide a unique characteristic to Śaṅkara's mysticism.[35]

According to Dubey, Otto in fact understands Śaṅkara's Advaita Vedānta philosophy from his theistic point of view; however, neither the successors of Śaṅkara nor the opponents of Śaṅkara's thought claimed that his philosophy was theologically oriented. As Dubey says, Otto's attempt as a "theologian" to understand Śaṅkara seems to be unreasonable. It is noteworthy that in modern times, the adherents of Śaṅkaran religious tradition, collectively called *smārtas*, regard him as "an incarnation of Śiva" (*śivāvatāra*), who emphasized the significance of "devotion" (*bhakti*) to gods for the attainment of salvation. In Śaṅkara's Advaita Vedānta philosophy, *bhakti*, which leads indirectly to "emancipation" (*mokṣa*), is concerned with the personal God or the "Brahman with attributes" (*saguṇa-brahman*). But with the *Bhakti-stotras* or devotional hymns to the deities, traditionally ascribed to Śaṅkara, the modern Śaṅkaran religious tradition, represented by Śṛṅgeri Maṭha, often called *Śrī Śāradā pīṭha* ("the throne of Śrī Śāradā) by its adherents, advocates Śaṅkara's philosophy as what may be called Vedānta theology being "theologically oriented," assuming that he recognized bhakti as a means of attaining salvation especially for lay adherents, by acquiring the grace of a deity. In fact, in his journey to South India in 1927, during his stay in Mysore, Otto had a chance to visit Śṛṅgeri Maṭha. Although he was unable to meet the Jagadguru there, he undoubtedly observed many pilgrims visiting Śṛṅgeri in order to worship Śrī Śāradā, well-known in South India as the mother goddess or goddess of education, whose image is believed to have been installed by Śaṅkara.[36] What he observed there with his own eyes may have influenced Otto's interpretation of Śaṅkara as a theologian.

4 The Bhakti Type of Indian Mysticism and Christianity

Otto has detailed two types of mysticism in Indian religious tradition: the "knowledge" (*jñāna*) type of mysticism that is non-theistic and the "devotion" (*bhakti*) type that is theistic. The former corresponds to the "soul-mysticism" to which Otto refers, a perspective shared with the "non-dual" (*advaita*) interpretation of the Upaniṣads, represented by Śaṅkara. The latter corresponds to the "God-mysticism" to which Otto refers, a perspective shared with the theistic interpretation of the Upaniṣads, represented by Rāmānuja. In his book *West-östliche Mystik*, Otto says:

> In Śaṅkara's time and environment, the exact correspondent [to the emotional element in Western mysticism] was the emotional bhakti, the *bhakti-mārga* (the way of love; Weg der Liebe) in place of the *jñāna-mārga* (the way of knowledge; Weg der Erkenntnis). Bhakti and *bhakti-mārga* could also be truly a name for the "way" of simple love of God and of personal relationship to God. For instance, it is so with Rāmānuja, who here resembles Luther.[37]

The "way of knowledge" (*jñāna-mārga*), characterized by Śaṅkara's Advaita Vedānta philosophy, corresponds to the "soul-mysticism" to which Otto refers; it also resembles Eckhart's philosophy in the West. On the other hand, the "way of devotion" (*bhakti-mārga*), characterized by Rāmānuja, corresponds to the "God-mysticism" or "bhakti-mysticism" (*bhakti-Mystik*) to which he refers; it attempts to attain "the 'unity' with the Highest" (*die 'Einung' mit dem Höchsten*) through coalescence by emotional exaggeration and glow of feeling. According to Otto, this type of mysticism resembles Luther's theology in the West.

In relation to Otto's categorization of the two types of mysticism, I would like to explain how Otto interprets his worldview of religions in relation to the East and West. From the viewpoint of comparative religion, it is often claimed that the faith of India is "world-denying" (*weltverneinend*), while that of Christianity is "world-affirming" (*weltbejahend*). According to Otto, in Indian thought, the world is regarded as "unreal" because it is "a product of mere *māyā* and the cosmic 'illusion' of *avidyā*," while in Christian thought, the world is regarded as "real." However, Otto states that this distinction is inaccurate and does not touch the most essential point. For, he says, throughout all Christian literature, there is a vein of "world-denial." In the West, too, the world is regarded as "a handful of sand, trouble of soul, fleeting, transitory, unstable, vain, yes, even a dream, and vain phenomenon of the sense."[38] Thus, a radical renunciation of the world is found in Christianity; also in India, there is a theory of the world as a "mere phenomenon," represented by Śaṅkara's Vedānta thought. Otto argues, however, that this is not the case in Rāmānuja's Vedānta thought. In his understanding of Indian mysticism, Otto interprets Rāmānuja's theology as characterized by "bhakti-mysticism." He emphasizes the significance of *bhakti* (devotion) to the personal God for the attainment of salvation or "the 'unity' with the Highest." He affirms the reality of the world and ascribes a certain validity to the *māyā* i.e., the creative miraculous power of the Lord (*īśvara*).[39] Thus, Otto understands that, while Rāmānuja affirms the reality of the world, he lacks the "positive *evaluation* of the world," which "belongs inseparably to the essence of Christianity." In Otto's words, "India gives no genuine *worth* to the world because it knows nothing of the *goal* of the world"; the world is "a *real* creation of God," but "this creating, sustaining, dissolving, and re-creating is the *līlā* of *Īśvara*, his eternal 'play.'"[40]

In comparison with the Hindu worldview, Otto attempts to clarify the characteristics of God in Christianity. He says that the "conception of creation must become a true *necessity* to the religion, and has an origin quite different from that of India." He says further that, although in India, religion arises "from what Schleiermacher calls the feeling of absolute dependence," it does not arise exactly from the concept of salvation; it would be enough for eternal salvation with *Īśvara* that he has the power to save.[41] In fact, Otto argues that some theistic traditions, except for the Vaiṣṇava, are satisfied with this designation. In Christianity, however, he emphasizes that God is "*necessarily* the creator of the world in consequence of the idea of salvation." Thus, Otto concludes:

> In Christianity the creation by God is not derived from the mere idea of absolute dependence, but from the purpose of the creation, that it should become the place and scene of the honour of God in "his kingdom."[42]

As discussed above, by comparing Hindu and Christian doctrines, Otto explains that in Christianity, characterized by the idea of salvation, God is "*necessarily* the creator of the world in consequence of the idea of salvation." Thus, in his comparative study of Christian doctrine with Indian religious thought, especially Vaiṣṇava, Otto obtained a deeper understanding of Christian doctrine.

Otto also notes that, in the "doctrine of grace," there are many striking similarities and differences between Hindu and Christian doctrines. In regard to the similarities, he says, they emphasize "rescue of the wholly lost, as of those without claim or worth, not by their own power or merit, but by free, unfathomable grace alone." By the term "rescue of the lost," according to Otto, a Christian adherent may think of "rescue from the lost condition in sin and guilt, from the terrors of the conscience smitten by God and his holiness," while a Hindu adherent may think of "rescue and release from the 'bonds,' viz., the bonds that bind him to *saṃsāra*, and their cords, from the misery of this world of wandering, and from the torturing 'wheel of birth and rebirth,' the wandering of the soul from existence to existence."[43] In Indian religious tradition, Otto says, this idea is stated in both the "'classical' theology of the extreme Vedānta mysticism" and the "Bhakti-religion."

To clarify the relationship between God and the world, Otto uses the figure of an "ellipse," suggested by the German Protestant theologian Ritschl (1822–89). The religious relationship between God and the soul, Otto says, is not to be compared to "a circle with only one focus," but to "an ellipse with two foci, God and the world." This metaphor is also quite supported by Indian theologians, whether they are of the "mystic-monistic school," i.e., Śaṅkara in Advaita Vedānta philosophy, or "bhaktas," i.e., Rāmānuja and adherents of the Vaiṣṇava religious tradition. The pressure of a world that is to be overcome and deliverance from it are "hinges upon this and other mystic religions in turn." According to Otto, the theory of salvation held by the Advaita Vedānta philosopher is quite "elliptical;" "the evil in the world in *saṃsāra*, and liberation from it by the *ekatā*, the identification with that which is entirely super-mundane, is the great theme of this religion." He continues that this is also the same case with Bhakti-religion. In Bhakti-religion, too, the world is "only an 'enchainment' from which to be delivered." For a Christian, however, the world has the "immeasurable value of being the sphere of service to the divine will."[44]

As one of the main differences between Hindu and Christian doctrines, Otto discusses "sin": he quotes a statement in Luther's *Small Catechism*: "Where forgiveness of sin is, there is *also* life and blessedness." Otto is not concerned with "the *lack* of the idea of sin in India, or with the lack of the idea of *ātma-siddhi* [the realization of the "self"] in Christianity," but rather with "an essential *transfer of the axis*." In ancient India, Otto says, the axis of the search for salvation is given in the *Bṛhadāraṇyakopaniṣad* (I. iii. 28):

> Lead me from *non-being* to *being*,
> Lead me from darkness to the light,
> Lead me from death to the super-death.
> *Asato mā sad gamaya*
> *Tamaso mā jyotir gamaya*
> *Mṛtyor mā 'mṛtaṃ gamaya*

But the fundamental theme of the religion of Palestine is given in the ancient words of the Bible:

> Ye shall be *holy*, for I am *holy*.[45]

This passage supports Otto's view that the axis of Christianity is the idea of *the holy*. Otto considers this to show a difference between the two religions: the fundamental principle of Bhakti-religion is *karma* and *mokṣa*, while that of Christianity is the idea of *the holy*. Otto does recognize that Bhakti-religion has "profound ideas of forgiveness and intimate renewal," while Christianity has "profound ideas of soul and the life of the soul, of transitoriness, and of 'that which endures forever.'" In comparing these two religions, Otto argues that although the idea of "sin" is not lacking in India, it "never has the depth and weight which it has in the West."[46] In his comparison of Christianity with Bhakti-religion, Otto emphasizes that both of them share some common points in doctrine: in Bhakti-religion, the grace (*prasāda*) of Īśvara liberates the soul from *saṃsāra*, while in Christianity, the grace of God redeems the soul from sin. In his analysis, Otto points out that both religions come close to each other in the concepts of grace and salvation.

Because of their similarities in several concepts, according to Otto, Bhakti-religion can be seen as a "competitor" to Christianity. By emphasizing the idea of *the holy*, he sees Christianity as superior to other religions. Otto's research, derived from his Christian theological perspective, was ahead of its time although the contents of his research were still insufficient. While Otto's theological viewpoint was open to such other religions as Bhakti-religion, his understanding of them was biased toward Christianity. From a comparative viewpoint, it is intriguing that Otto's encounter with other religions became an important stimulus for him to gain a deeper understanding of Christian thought.

5 "East is West, and West is East"

The term "mysticism," originally derived from classical Greek, became widely used to represent various religious phenomena in the world from the eighteenth century to the nineteenth century. The spiritual aspect of religious traditions came to be called "mysticism," which is even now widely used as an important concept for understanding religious thought. It is necessary to reconsider the conceptual meanings of mysticism in the context of specific religious phenomena.

From a more recent comparative viewpoint of religions, it is important to reconsider the Indian religious traditions that Otto treats, especially Vedānta, and his interpretation of them.

In the Introduction to his book *West-östliche Mystik*, Otto cites the poem "The Ballad of East and West" by the English poet Rudyard Kipling (1865–1936): "East is east, and west is west, never the twain shall meet." The full stanza is:

> Oh, East is East, and West is West, and never the twain shall meet,
> Till Earth and Sky stand presently at God's great Judgment Seat;
> But there is neither East nor West, Border, nor Breed, nor Birth,
> When two strong men stand face to face, though they come from the ends of the earth!

Otto asks, "Are the thought worlds of East and West so different and incomparable that they can never meet and therefore, at the deepest level, never understand each other?" In reply, he says, "There is no more fitting sphere in the spiritual life of man than that of mysticism and mystical speculation, for they rise from the very depths of the human spirit."[47] In addition, he gives a bird's-eye view of mysticism:

> It is often claimed that mysticism is *the same* in all ages and in all places, that timeless and independent of history it has always been identical. East and West and other differences vanish here. Whether the flower of mysticism blooms in India or in China, in Persia or on the Rhine and in Erfurt its fruit is one. Whether it clothes itself in the delicate Persian verse of a Jelaleddin Rumi or in the beautiful middle German of a Meister Eckhart; in the scholarly Sanskrit of the Indian Śaṅkara, or in the laconic riddles of the Sino-Japanese Zen School, these forms could always be exchanged one for the other. For one and the same experience speaks here, only by chance in varying dialects. "East is west, and west is east."[48]

This passage explains why, for many years, Otto was interested in mysticism in the world history of religions. In his words, "Mysticism is *the same* in all ages and in all places," and "One and the same experience speaks here, only by chance in varying dialects." Even though the languages are different, the forms of mysticism "could always be exchanged one for the other." Thus, the words, "East is west, west is east," symbolically express Otto's views, especially of mysticism.

In his book *West-östliche Mystik*, Otto attempted to understand Śaṅkara's Advaita Vedānta thought as parallel to Eckhart's Christian doctrine, and Rāmānuja's Vedānta thought as parallel to Luther's Christian doctrine. According to Otto, in the relationship between the personal God and human beings, "salvation" is implicitly based on the "grace" of God as the "wholly other." He presented a hermeneutical perspective on Vedānta through his understanding of Vedānta philosophy as "mysticism" through a theistic conceptual framework. Śaṅkara's thought is based on the identity of Brahman as the highest reality of the world and Ātman as the essence of individual beings. In other words, this provides a theory that asserts the reality of the world as the development of Brahman; at the same time, its epistemological view centers on the human individual essence Ātman. Otto was well aware of the fundamentals of Śaṅkara's thought. However, since he attempted to place his understanding of it in the theistic conceptual framework of Christianity, his interpretation of the Advaita Vedānta came closer to a realistic theory of world development. It must be said, however, that he could not properly grasp the epistemological structure rooted in Ātman. Śaṅkara puts the concept of "nescience" (*avidyā*) at the core of his theory. Thus, one can say that Śaṅkara's thought, which emphasizes the theory of illusion, is deconstructed from the basis of that thought.[49] Otto's theory of mysticism has not fully grasped Śaṅkara's thought. It suggests the conceptual limitation of Otto's interpretation of Śaṅkara, and also implies that his hermeneutical framework contained conceptual limitations in understanding the structure of Vedānta philosophy. I shall discuss this in detail in Chapter 7 of this book.

Whether "mysticism" is a real religious experience has been actively questioned, especially since the 1980s. This is an important issue under discussion in the study of religion. Must a scholar choose between an essentialist or reductionist view of mystical experience? This question will be discussed in more detail later, but in brief, "mysticism" is perceived as "reality" or a "real" religious experience by one who has this religious experience. Thus, it could be considered as a phenomenon of "meaning" for such people. Here, the semantic interpretation of Otto's "holiness" suggests the possibility of a semantic understanding of religion.

6

The Concept of the "Wholly Other" and the Experience of the Depth

The History of Religions, which was established in the West in the latter half of the nineteenth century, has been given various names. Max Müller, the founder of the History of Religions, called it the "science of religion." Other names include Religionswissenschaft, "comparative religion," the "history of religions," the "history of religion," "religious studies," and the "study of religion." Most studies have been based on Christianity and modern Western cultures; concepts such as "religion" and "mysticism" have been consciously or unconsciously used in the contemporary research. Inevitably, these concepts had Western Christian implications. They were never "transparent tools," but were produced in the modern West as the "concepts with intentional loads"[1] Although the comparative study of religions tried to treat all religions from the same vantage point and to comprehend them in a value-free manner, their viewpoints had Western Christian implications. This was perhaps inevitable.

In recent years, however, this cultural bias has been recognized; these concepts have been re-examined by positioning them in their specific religious context. For example, Judaism, Christianity, and Islam are "monotheistic," while Hinduism and Shinto are "polytheistic." At first glance, these understandings seem accurate, but they do not necessarily reflect the reality of a practiced religion. This is becoming increasingly apparent. Such words as "monotheism" and "polytheism" were constructed and conceptualized within the framework of modern Western religious traditions when religious studies were established in the nineteenth and early twentieth centuries. The concept of the "wholly other" (*das ganz Andere*) was one of these concepts constructed within such a religious and cultural context.

In his description of the elements of *numinous*, the "wholly other" is a term that Otto considered particularly important. As he says, however, this concept is the most difficult to explain of all the elements of the numinous.[2] Here, I first consider the concept of the "wholly other" in the context of Otto's theory of religion. Then, while clarifying the Western implications attached to this concept, I would like to treat the meaning of the "wholly other" as a religious concept and examine its validity in Otto's study of Indian religious thought. Otto found a religious idea corresponding to the concept of the "wholly other" in the Upaniṣads in India. But to what extent could Otto understand and present this concept of the "wholly other" within Hindu thought? How well could he capture the reality of Hindu religious tradition with a Western concept of religion? In this chapter, I will discuss these issues in Otto's religious theory and revisit his theory of comparative religion.

1 "Parallelism" in the Development of Religions

In order to understand the religious and cultural contexts in which Otto's concept of the "wholly other" was born, I would like to briefly mention his view of comparative religion. By traveling abroad, Otto had the opportunity to come into direct contact with the religions and cultures of the world and deepen his understanding of them. During his journey to the East from 1911 to 1912, Otto visited Japan in 1912. Throughout his trip to the East, he became particularly interested in the mystical qualities of Japanese religious traditions. In his journey to the East, Otto noticed that in such key elements as doctrine and ritual, there was a "parallelism" of development between the religious traditions of the West and those of the East. He was convinced that there were common religious feelings in these religions, and that there was a parallelism in the development of religions, which he called the "law of parallel lines of development."[3] Otto passed on this idea to his disciple Friedrich Heiler. Above all, Otto's experiences in India were significant for the construction of his comparative religious views. His encounter with Eastern religions was important for the development of his religious perspectives.[4]

When we examine the meaning of the "wholly other" (*das ganz Andere*) as Otto's understanding of religion, focusing on his view of "parallelism" between Eastern and Western religions, his objective gradually emerges. Otto was only able to claim a superiority of Christianity over Eastern religions because of his Western conceptual framework. This suggests that the conceptual framework of religion is closely related to the category of Western culture and that the framework of the History of Religions is provisional and does not have universal validity. The concept of *the holy* which Otto put at the core of religion is generally recognized by other scholars of religion as a complex combination of rational and non-rational elements. Otto thought that various combinations of these two elements could make religion higher or lower. He maintained that the degree of harmony in these elements provides the measure of superiority and inferiority in religions. According to Otto, by this scale, Christianity is superior to other religions: given its deep and non-rational foundation, pure and vivid concepts, feelings, and experiences shine in Christianity. The non-rational is simply the foundation, outer edge, and coloring, which always maintains mystical depth and gives religion the majestic tone and dark shadow of mysticism. Thus, according to Otto's argument, Christianity has classic dignity in the sound harmony of its elements.[5] In regard to religions in the East, however, he argues that the harmony between the two is still incomplete. Therefore, he concludes that Christianity is the superior religion in the world.

2 Concept of the "Wholly Other" and Indian Religious Thoughts

Among Eastern religions, especially in Indian religions, Otto sought the "wholly other" corresponding to Christian tradition. In Indian religion, he first thought that what corresponded to the "wholly other" was the highest Brahman in the Upaniṣad teachings. Although Upaniṣad thought still retained remnants of Vedic ritualism, it anticipated the emergence of various ideas developed in later periods. In the Upaniṣads, the discourse was still intuitive or mythical, but the emphasis was on philosophically exploring the essence of the universe and human existence. That was the idea of the "identity of Brahman with Ātman" (*tat tvam asi*), which is the core of Upaniṣad thought. Although Hinduism has generally been regarded as "polytheistic," the idea of the "identity of Brahman with Ātman" has some characteristics of "monotheism." In the Upaniṣads, Otto found the idea of the "wholly other" in parallel with Western religious thought.

In Otto's theory of *the numinous*, the "wholly other" (*das ganz Andere*) is a term which implies depth of *the numinous* beyond the perception of intelligence. It is the *mysterium* itself inherent in *the numinous* that goes beyond intellectual understanding. Therefore, it cannot be conceptualized. When Otto analytically considered the element of "mystery" in *Das Heilige*, he quoted the words of the German Reformed mystic and poet Gerhard Tersteegen (1697–1769): "The God who is comprehended is not God" (*Ein begriffener Gott ist kein Gott.*). This sentence suggests that the "wholly other" is "not a concept" because it is "beyond our categories." It is "the completely different which does not belong to our real world." According to Otto, it corresponds to *thāteron* in Greek, *anyad* in Sanskrit, *alienum* or *aliud valde* in Latin.[6] Otto sees the "wholly other" as "the qualitatively other of the supernatural," compared with human existence as "creatures." In the world history of religions, according to Otto, the "wholly other" can be seen in the "extremely advanced and abstract forms of theological thinking" as well as in the "elementary expressions of religious feeling."[7]

In regard to the word "wholly other," Otto says, "I did not discover this word [*das ganz Andere*]." Even though languages are different, he believed, the term has been universally used since ancient times in the religions of the world. In ancient India, more than 2,500 years ago, in the older Upaniṣads, the wholly other was called *anyad eva*. More than 1,600 years ago in the West, Augustine called the wholly other *aliud valde* or *dissimile*. Although Christianity and Indian religion are different, Otto says, "*aliud valde* is equivalent to *anyad eva*."[8] In another article, however, while Otto acknowledges the corresponding similarities between *aliud valde* and *anyad eva*, he also admits that "despite all the similarities, they are not qualitatively the same."[9] In any case, at first glance, these two words seem to share some similar meaning.

The semantic structures that these two words imply in their respective religious contexts are quite different. In Augustine's concept of the "wholly other" (*aliud valde*), the *numinous* component implies the relationship between the transcendental God as the "Creator" and human beings as the "creatures." On the other hand, the ontological structure in the ancient Upaniṣads consists of the identity of the highest Brahman with the Ātman of individual beings. At least in the ancient Upaniṣads, on which Otto relies, there is no transcendental relationship between God and human beings, such as found in Christianity. However, Otto attempted to read the Christian idea of "God's unity" into the Indian concept of the "wholly other" (*anyad eva*), i.e., the Supreme Brahman. Although Otto says that they are not exactly the same, he attempted to interpret the Old Upaniṣad thought in the framework of Christian monotheistic structure.[10] What is important for scholars of the History of Religions is that this interpretation allowed Otto to perceive Indian religious thought in the semantic world of *the holy* on the same level as modern Western Christian thought.

3 Religious Concepts in the Modern West and the Reality of Hinduism

To what extent could Otto express the reality of Hindu religious tradition, specifically Indian religious thought, with such religious concepts as the "wholly other"? We must first recognize the fact that Hindu thought contains both monotheistic and polytheistic themes. Hindus may worship any god or gods in a polytheistic spiritual climate. Throughout India, the gods are inseparable from various rituals and customs. Yet people believe in the reality of the absolute One behind all the gods. This is faith in an absolute God. In terms of religious commitment, when Hindu faith is reconsidered in relation to an absolute God, this faith may be considered monotheistic. Hinduism has not only polytheistic but also monotheistic qualities.[11] Hinduism may be understood monotheistically or polytheistically, depending on the viewpoint of the religious scholar. Alternatively, Hinduism can be understood as "henotheism," as Max Müller called it.

Initially, research into Indian religious thought began with the study of Indology by William Jones (1746–94) and others. When it was discovered that both Christianity and Indian religious thought contained mystical elements, scholars became interested in studying Upaniṣad thought and Vedānta philosophy. For example, among the scholars active during Otto's life were Max Müller (1823–1900), Paul Deussen (1845–1919), Hermann Oldenberg (1854–1920), etc. They placed the Upaniṣads at the center of Hindu thought and Vedānta philosophy. One of the reasons for their interest is that Śaṅkara's Advaita Vedānta philosophy was easy to understand from the conceptual framework of Western philosophy of religion. For Christian missionaries, the Upaniṣads were used as evidence of early monotheism within the Hindu religious tradition. For liberal Christians, this fact also provided a basis for interreligious dialogues between Christianity and Hinduism and for recognizing certain commonalities between religions.[12]

As a result of his study of Indian religious thought, Otto published such books as *West-östliche Mystik* and *Die Gnadenreligion Indiens und das Christentum* (1930). First, in *West-östliche Mystik*, Otto compares the representative Hindu philosopher Śaṅkara and the mystic thinker Meister Eckhart in medieval Christianity and the characteristics of Eastern and Western mysticisms. By doing so, he attempted to clarify the parallels and differences in Eastern and Western religious thoughts. In *Die Gnadenreligion Indiens und das Christentum*, he compared the Vaiṣṇava religious tradition to Christian doctrine and faith. In this book, he elucidated similarities and differences between Hinduism and Christianity. It was quite natural in the Western religious and cultural context at that time that the Lutheran theologian Otto focused on religious ideas and phenomena in India that he regarded as parallel to the concepts of Christianity.

Otto not only understood Indian religions as partially consistent with Christianity, but, based on his "law of parallel development" of religions, interpreted the development of Indian religions and Christianity as parallel religious phenomena. After returning home from his second trip to India, Otto published *Die Gnadenreligion Indiens und das Christentum* in Marburg. The main contents of this book consisted of his lectures delivered at the Parish General Meeting in Kassel in 1924, his lectures at Uppsala University and Oslo University in 1926, and also based on the contents of his Kassel lectures in 1924. Therefore, the book gives the readers the impression that it is biased toward Christian interpretation. At that time, ordinary Christians in Western culture knew very little about Indian religions. Most were unaware of the fact that like Christianity, Hinduism was a "religion of grace" (*Gnaden-religion*) that emphasized faith in God and salvation by God's grace. In such a context, Otto wrote his book based on the content of the lectures, conscious of its Western Christian readership. In fact, the book was at first accepted by many Hindu readers, partly because up to that time, Western scholars of Indian religious thought did not pay attention to the Hindu traditions that emphasized devotion to God.

However, as John Carman who is very familiar with the Hindu bhakti traditions points out, a number of Hindu readers from the devotional movement were disappointed by what seemed to them a number of negative conclusions. In her "book review" of Otto's *India's Religion of Grace and Christianity*, the British scholar of Buddhism C.A.F. Rhys Davids (1857–1942), who was a scholar of Buddhist texts in the Pāli language, points out that for Otto who is "too broad-minded to approach so great a subject as the religious history of India in the attitude of a sectarian," "to entitle a first chapter 'A Competitor of Christianity?' was an unfortunate start, and needed the toning down that is duly given." Davids argues that Otto's description of Hinduism looks like a Christian-biased analysis.[13]

4 India's Bhakti-Religion and Salvation by Grace in Christianity

Now, focusing on *Die Gnadenreligion Indiens und das Christentum,* I would like to clarify the characteristics of Otto's understanding of India's Bhakti-religion in comparison with Christian doctrine and faith. According to Otto, Indian thought is not characterized by speculation for the sake of mere metaphysics or theoretical views of the world, but by the doctrine of salvation. It is not properly a "philosophy," but a "doctrine founded upon 'faith.'" In his study of Hindu religious tradition, Otto argues that India's Bhakti-religion, as a "religion of grace"

(*Gnadenreligion*), is astonishingly similar to Christianity. According to Otto, the "good conferred in salvation by Christianity" is the "communion with the living, personal God;" the "means of salvation" in Christianity is God's "grace" (*gratia*), which "lays hold of the lost, rescuing and redeeming him." He argues that "these are the very slogans and distinctive terms of those forms of the Bhakti-religion" and that "there seems to have arisen in India a competitor of almost astonishing similarity—a competitor which seems to dispute the sole possession by Christianity of that which is its very heart."

In Bhakti-religion, Otto says, "salvation" has three characteristics; (1) "the salvation which comes not from profound speculation and for the wise, but is offered to all, and to the 'poor in spirit' in particular;" (2) "the salvation which comes not by mystic experiences, by the loss of personality in the impersonal primal cause of all being, but by *bhakti*, that is by surrender in simple, trusting appropriation of the 'grace' of the 'Lord,' and in love to him;" (3) "the salvation which comes not through the toil of good 'works,' but is the free gift of grace, and by the saving might of 'the Lord.'"[14] In Otto's view, salvation is bestowed on "all" or on the "poor in spirit," by *bhakti* or "surrender in simple, trusting appropriation of the 'grace' of the 'Lord,' and in love to him," and as the "free gift of grace" or the "saving might of the Lord." Thus, in regard to "salvation," he says, India's Bhakti-religion and Christianity are really similar.

Otto regards the concepts of "God," "grace," and "salvation" in India's "religion of grace" as common concepts in Christianity. The Indian "religion of grace" he referred to was Vaiṣṇavism. Although he equates Vaiṣṇava thought with Rāmānuja's thought, it must be said that his arguments, such as on the "religion of grace" and the "religion of Bhakti" are inadequate from an Indological perspective. In regard to Vaiṣṇava religious ideas, in addition to Rāmānuja's religious thought, there are such major religious thinkers as Madhva (1197–1276) who advocated the Dvaita (dual) Vedānta philosophy and Vallabha (1475–1531), a Vaiṣṇava Vedāntin, who advocated the Śuddhādvaita (pure non-dual) Vedānta philosophy that salvation arises only by the grace of God. It is essential to refer to those other positions as well. In any case, he interprets the Vaiṣṇava tradition as a religious parallel to Christianity. According to Otto, the Vaiṣṇava tradition is a "competitor of Christianity" (*ein Konkurrent des Christentums*) in the Indian religious context. He claims that the doctrines of "grace" (*gratia*) and "grace only" (*gratia sola*) in Christianity are central teachings in the Vaiṣṇava tradition as well, which emphasizes salvation by devotion to Viṣṇu. Thus, Otto describes the existence of Bhakti-religion as a "rival" that seems to vie for the exclusivity of salvation.[15]

The important point for the History of Religions is that the religious concepts of the modern West allowed Otto to shed light on Bhakti-religion, represented by Rāmānuja's thought. It was the "monotheistic" aspect of Indian religions that corresponded to the Western Christian conceptual framework. Otto regarded India's Bhakti-religion as a form of religion closest to Christianity. The fact that Otto's concept of the "wholly other" was able to clarify the characteristics of Indian religion by focusing on its "monotheistic" aspects illuminates a certain effectiveness of this religious concept.

At the same time, however, it must be admitted that as a result, the "polytheistic" characteristics of Indian religion or religious thought were overlooked. One cannot say that Otto clarifies all of Hindu religious tradition. It can be said that the concept of the "wholly other," derived from Western monotheistic tradition, lacks a comparative religious perspective sufficient to set it apart from Christian thought. In other words, Otto's study failed to grasp Indian religions or religious thoughts as a whole, because he relied too much on Christian concepts in explaining them. In short, he lacked the perspectives to properly position Bhakti-religion in its actual Indian religious context.

5 Experience of the "Depth" and Its Interpretation

How did Otto interpret the experience of the "depth" (*Tiefe*) in religion? As yet, no detailed research on his study of Indian religious thought has been conducted. I would like to examine Otto's interpretation of the experience of the "depth" and its main characteristics. According to Otto, *the numinous* is a non-rational element of religion that is conceptually difficult to grasp, but "experienceable" (*erfahrbar*) in its dimension of feeling.[16] Spirit (*Geist*) and soul (*Seele*) are the "numinous miraculous beings" (*numinoses Wunderwesen*), and the experience of the "depth" or "feeling of the numinous" (*sensus numinis*) is at their foundation. Otto thought that characteristics applied to the non-rational "God" may also be applied to spirit and soul as the copies of "God" in creatures. Otto argues that there is an experience of "depth" in the spirit and soul with the "feeling of the numinous," to quote the words of Gregory of Nyssa (*c.* 330–394), "Since one of the characteristics of divine essence is its incomprehensibility, its image (the soul) must also resemble the archetype (divine essence) here."[17] In mysticism, the basis of human existence itself is perceived as *numinous*, and the soul is considered to be "secret" (*Geheimnis*) and full of "wonder" (*Wunder*). Accordingly, spirit and soul contain the non-rational support to experience the depth of existence.

In regard to the experience of "depth" in religion, however, when it is expressed in concepts and scholastic terms, its non-rationality is hidden. According to Otto, the "feeling of the numinous" cannot be "transmitted" (*übertragen*) in the true sense.[18] For example, rational speculation conceals the non-rational and mysterious "God" with the concept of God and theological terms. According to Otto, however, "before God is *ratio*, absolute reason, and personal spirit, and moral will, God is the wholly non-rational (*das ganz Irrationale*), the "wholly other" (*das "Ganz Andere"*), totally mysterious (*das völlige Wunderding*)."[19] The experience of "depth" in religion is not conveyed by mere words, but through empathy and re-experience etc.; it is "only stimulated, shaken, and awakened."

Otto thus acknowledges the essential differences between the deep experience of the "feeling of the numinous" and its rational concepts or doctrines. At the same time, he also recognizes that the "feeling of the numinous" is alive in the paradoxes and mysteries of the rituals and doctrines in various Western religious traditions. Otto says:

> In Catholicism the feeling of the numinous is to be found as a living factor of singular power. It is seen in Catholic forms of worship and sacramental symbolism, in the less authentic forms assumed by legend and miracle, in the paradoxes and mysteries of Catholic dogma, in the Platonic and neo-Platonic strands woven into the fabric of its religious conceptions, in the solemnity of churches and ceremonies, and especially in the intimate *rapport* of Catholic piety with mysticism. For reasons already suggested, the mysterious is much less in evidence in the official systems of doctrine, whether Catholic or Protestant.[20]

From his view of the parallels in religious development, Otto focused not only on Christianity but also on Eastern religions, and attempted to explore the essence of religion in various religious traditions. According to Otto, the word "Ātman" (soul) in Hinduism is the "wholly undefinable wonder" (*das ganz indefinible Wunderding*), that is, the "wholly other" (*das "Ganz andere"*), which is essentially beyond all concepts. In his article, "The Depth of the Numinous Sense" ("Tiefen des *sensus numinis*," 1932), he cites verse 2:29 of *Bhagavadgītā* when he explains "Ātman." In this quoted sentence, "him" means "Ātman."

> One looks at him mysteriously (*āścaryavat*). Another talks about him mysteriously.
> Moreover, another hears about him mysteriously. No one knows him, even if one hears him.[21]

āścaryavat paśyati kaścid enam āścaryavad vadati tathaiva cānyaḥ /
āścaryavac cainam anyaḥ śṛṇoti śrutvā 'py enaṃ veda na caiva kaścit //

Based on this sentence, in order to clarify the "emotional tone" (*Gefühlston*) of this verse more clearly, Otto expresses its meaning as follows.[22]

> One looks at him as the "wholly other." One who talks about Ātman talks about the "wholly other." One who learns about Ātman learns the "wholly other." No one knows him (Ātman), even if one learns about him (Ātman).

Otto emphasizes that the feelings of *the numinous* are "alive" at the deepest dimension of these words. Using the word "mysterious" (*acintya*) in verse 2:25 of the *Bhagavadgītā*, he argues that "Ātman" cannot be grasped by reflection.[23] Ātman is intuited in the depth of the spirit. Ātman is said to be equivalent to the "ground of the soul" (*Seelengrund*) and the "inner abyss" (*innere Abgrund*), as called by Western mystics. He says that here, one can see the fundamental feelings of *the numinous*, i.e., the "fundamental horror" (*Urschauer*) and "self-abandonment" (*Sich-verjagen*) toward "wonder" (*āścarya*) and "marvel" (*adbhuta*).

The inner "wonder" of the soul, according to Otto, manifests itself through a "breakthrough" (*Durchbruch*) or "sudden inspiration" (*plötzliches Aperçu*) for those who experience it. Then, he says, it contains two moments: The first moment is "the moment of inspirational entry or penetration" (*das Moment des inspirativen Eintretens oder Eindringens*). It is accompanied by the characteristics of suddenness, directness, and once-occurring, at which time the depth of the *numinous* feeling is intuited. The other moment is "that of anamnesis, of remembering something" (*das der Anamnesis, des Sicherinnerns an etwas*). It is already "obsessed with and familiar with vague feelings" before recognizing the wonder of the soul. Otto says that verse 4:30 of the *Kena Upaniṣad*, referring to Brahman, i.e., Ātman, is based on these two moments.[24]

> Now, in regard to Ātman:
> When something penetrates into consciousness, as it were,
> And suddenly remembers this –: Such a state of mind
> (illustrates the awakening of ātman knowledge).

6 The "Wholly Other" and Its Religious Context

Since Otto's theory of religion is based on Christian concepts of religion particular to the modern West, it has various problems. At the same time, such problems clearly present issues to be treated when considering the future of the History of Religions. As Robert F. Davidson points out in his studies of Indian religion, Otto consistently emphasized the "greater maturity and profoundness of the Christian concepts of holiness, sin and salvation, in which the moral implication of religious experience has become explicit."[25] All religious concepts, however, inevitably have "provisional characteristics," as pointed out by the historian of religion William A. Graham. Moreover, these concepts include historical and cultural prejudices.[26] Scholars must be aware that, like Otto's concept of the "wholly other," the application of Western religious concepts to other religions always contains limitations. The concepts and theories of religion that have been understood as self-evident in previous religious studies must be open to constant revision by positioning them in particular religious contexts.

Otto's full-scale study of Indian religions began with his trip to the East. When attempting to grasp the reality of religion, the way of understanding differs, depending on the level of religion or the aspect of religion on which one focuses. Otto's concepts, such as the "wholly other," have a monotheistic background in Christianity; his attempts to understand Hinduism through these concepts give too much attention to similarities between Eastern and Western religions. Only the monotheistic aspects of Hindu tradition may be highlighted. It is necessary, however, to treat both the polytheistic and the monotheistic aspects. In Hindu religious tradition, monotheistic and polytheistic components are organically connected. One must examine such concepts of religion with constant awareness of those derived from Western culture. The conceptual framework of "religion" built on the basis of modern Western religious traditions is not always valid in understanding non-Western religious traditions. Historians of religions must advance their understanding of religious thought or phenomena according to particular religious contexts. Nowadays, historians of religions are more than ever required to pursue their studies with the hermeneutical perspectives of religion. Historians of religions can deepen their understanding of other religions by critically examining concepts derived from the Christian religious tradition.

7

Vedānta Philosophy as the Discourse of Mystic Experience

The significance of Otto's theory of religion lies in the fact that he attempted to explain the essence of religion from religious experience or a sense of *the holy*, and its non-rationality. Although his theory of religion is still widely known among religious scholars, his study of Indian religious thought is generally less well known. Research on his views of Indian religious thought has not yet been seriously conducted. His interest in Indian religion was based on his own comparative insight that there was a "parallel development" of religions between the East and the West. His visit to India in the fall of 1911 was his first encounter with the Indian religious world. This led him to introduce a comparative religious perspective within the framework of Christian theology. Otto's works on Indian religious thought include his books, *West-östliche Mystik* and *Die Gnadenreligion Indiens und das Christentum*, as well as numerous articles.[1]

This chapter attempts to clarify Otto's understanding of the Vedānta philosophy, which he treats as an Indian type of mysticism. The discussion here focuses on the way Otto approached Indian religious thought.

1 World Religious History Framework: Development of Religions in the East and West

During Otto's lifetime in the nineteenth and twentieth centuries, the European world already had a great deal of information on the religions of the East. Otto himself had some knowledge of Eastern religious culture, undertaking by himself the translation of the *Bhagavadgītā* into German. As a Lutheran theologian, he enlarged his academic interest to include Eastern religions. Unlike traditional Christian theologians, he spent his life studying the philosophy of religion and comparative religion as well as Christian theology. His study of religion was intended to explore the truth of Christianity more deeply. A turning point in his interest in comparative religious research was his encounter with different religions during his journey to the East, especially with Hindu religious tradition.

Throughout Otto's 1911–12 journey, his research specifically included comparative studies of various religions. His visit to India and Japan and his exposure to the world of Eastern mysticism greatly influenced his reflection. Specifically, his view of the parallelism of Eastern and Western thoughts became more concrete.[2] In short, Otto became more specifically aware of the "parallelism of development" in Eastern and Western religions. He also acquired a new perspective on the truth of Christianity. By learning about different cultures through encounters with people who deeply believed in their own religions, he deepened his understanding of Christian teachings.

At the Asiatic Society of Japan on April 11, 1912, Otto delivered a lecture on a comparative consideration of Eastern and Western religions. The title of his lecture was "Parallelisms in the Development of Religion East and West." In his lecture, Otto emphasized the parallelism between Eastern religions (Buddhist tradition) and Western religions (Jewish and Christian tradition), although they developed almost completely independently. He argued that humankind had a universal consciousness of "common religious feelings" and that world religions had similarities.[3] These views became a basic premise in his subsequent religious studies. Instead of considering only one religious phenomenon or borrowing from only one religion, he sought to capture those religious phenomena that developed independently in parallel. In his books such as *Vischnu-Nārāyana* and *Siddhānta des Rāmānuja*, he attempted to construct his own theoretical framework. In publishing "Parallel and Convergence in Religious History," he specified parallel development in Eastern and Western religions as the "law of parallelism of development."[4] This view is basic to Otto's theoretical framework of world religious history and his understanding of Vedānta philosophy.

In seeing world religions in the light of this perspective, Otto argues that they are similar in regard to such aspects of religion as the respect and harmony of the scriptures and traditions, the interpretation of the scriptures and formation of doctrine, and the explanations of the relationship between revelation and reason. Moreover, according to Otto, in comparing religions to the biological theory of "organic evolution," similar religious phenomena can be seen in places where the geographical or social contexts are different. However, he acknowledges that each religion has its own unique characteristics. In his own words, "Historically, 'religion' is manifested as religions and these religions have no less than their characteristic differences." "In the comparison of religions we are prompted to use an even finer discrimination in ascertaining the manner in which the common basic force, despite all apparent parallelism, takes on perfectly distinct forms in its individual manifestations." Moreover, Otto says, "There are fundamental spiritual values which separate these two worlds of the spirit [the spirit of India and the spirit of Palestine], in spite of astonishing similarities and convergences of type."[5]

The History of Religions has two main research objects: to identify and clarify the structure of religion attributes common to religious phenomena and to clarify the concrete history of each respective religion. In regarding the essence of religious phenomena as the feeling of *the numinous*, Otto observed a "parallelism of development" common to all human beings in all religious phenomena, and envisioned a framework of religious history. However, by overemphasizing the universal general laws in this history, Otto's perspective became static, although he recognized the importance of a concrete history of religions. For this reason, his framework could not capture specific historical developments of religions. He did uncover the remarkable coincidence of religious experiences shared by human beings. He published a number of comparative religion works, including *Das Heilige*, *West-östliche Mystik*, and *Die Gnadenreligion Indiens und das Christentum*. In short, his research perspective was rooted in his liberal Christian theology, from which he sought a deeper understanding of Christian truth through his comparative studies.

2 Mystic Experience in Vedānta Philosophy

In the History of Religions, "mysticism" is understood to be based on one's experience of unification with the absolute or transcendental reality, as generally suggested by the term *unio mystica*. According to Otto, mysticism is "the inner experience of the divine, the essential union or unity with the divine." Moreover, mystical experiences differ from the "experience of the divine as transcendental" (*Erfahrung des Göttlichen als des Transzendenten*), which is the commonly understood religious experiences.[6] Mysticism emphasizes a "mystical union" of the transcendental and the self, while general religious experience emphasizes an infinite gap between the transcendental and human beings. Mysticism and general religious experience thus have different relationships to the "divine."

The "mysticism" to which Otto refers, however, is different from the general understanding of mysticism. He first observes the difference in the relationship with the "divine" or "God" found in mysticism and that of general religious experience. Here, what is noteworthy is the meaning of the "divine" (*das Gottliche*) or "God." In mysticism, even though the same word "divinity" or "God" is used, it means "the 'divinity' as an intrinsic principle" (*"Gottheit" als immanentes Prinzip*), that is, "immanent God." In contrast, the "divine" in general religious experience means the "transcendental God" (*der transzendente Gott*), who is the object of worship for devout adherents. Thus, the same word implies the different meanings of religious experience. Each has a fundamentally different essence and structure. In short, the word "divine" or "God," has a different meaning in mysticism and general religious experience.

Moreover, Otto argues that it is not only the "relationship with God," i.e., the structure of religious experience, that differs between these two contrasting religious experiences. I quote his words:

> The point of departure and the essential distinction is not that the mystic has another and a new relationship to God, but that he has a different God. This difference of object results in a difference of relationship, but it is the difference of the object itself which is the determining factor.[7]

In this argument, the "divine" or "God" in mysticism means "God without modes" (*Deus sine modis*), that is, the non-rational and impersonal God. When one experiences "God without modes," one is said to be a "mystic." Thus, Otto argues:

> Mysticism is not first of all an act of union, but predominantly the life lived in the "knowledge" of this "wholly other" God.[8]

In this regard, let us read his argument in more detail:

> It is characteristic of types of mysticism to seek the *Deus sine modis* (the God without modes) and to cherish Him in the soul. "God" is then experienced in an act of union. But man is a mystic as soon as he has this conception of God, even when the element of union recedes or remains unemphasized, which can easily happen in mysticism. It is the wholly non-rational character of this conception of God with its divergence from the intimate, personal, modified God of simple theism, which makes the mystic. Mysticism is not first of all an act of union, but predominantly the life lived in the "knowledge" of this "wholly other" God. God himself is mystical, for a relationship of union is only possible with an object which is itself mystical in the first instance.[9]

Thus, in Otto's understanding of mysticism, an experience of mystical union is not necessary for mysticism, but living under the "wonder" of God, which is "wholly other," is the essential factor. In other words, for Otto, "mysticism" emerges as a "non-rational" religious feeling. It is the predominant manifestation of the "non-rational" or the "numinous" of religious feeling. This is the essence of mysticism to which Otto refers. This essence manifests itself in each religion, as the "diversity of individualization."

When we understand "mysticism," as Otto says, this blurs the line between mystical experience and religious experience or faiths that are commonly understood. The essential structure of general religious experience consists of involvement in such a "non-rational" transcendental reality as God, whereas the essential structure of mystical experience is "living under the wonders of God," the "wholly other." According to Otto, this does not necessarily mean that the experience of a mysterious union is essential. The ambiguity of the boundaries between the mystical experience and the commonly understood religious experience elucidates Otto's view of the significance of the mystical experience at the heart of religion.

3 Perspectives for Śaṅkara's Philosophy

When Otto attempts to understand Śaṅkara's Advaita (non-dual) Vedānta philosophy as an Indian "mysticism," he relies on a theistic conceptual framework, partly because he was a Lutheran theologian. This point fundamentally characterizes his theory of religion.

According to Otto's classification, there are two main forms of mysticism: "soul-mysticism" and "God-mysticism." "God-mysticism" is established when God is the "mysterious" reality. In contrast, the concept of "soul-mysticism" does not involve the notion of God: "The numinous element of the essence of the soul comes alive." As examples of "soul-mysticism," Otto discusses Yoga and Buddhism, religious phenomena with an "excessive rise of the numinous meaning of the soul." On the other hand, Otto distinguishes between theistic and atheistic Yoga. Whereas theistic Yoga proposes a mystical union with God, in atheistic Yoga, there can be no "mystical union" with God (*unio mystica*), because it seeks to free Ātman from all false connections. Buddhism also denies God, but Otto says, since it "lives in the numinous," he interprets Buddhism as a religion; emancipation (*nirvāṇa*) in Buddhism provides a "mysterious state" which is "wholly non-rational" and which could be "only spoken by silence." Moreover, he says, the Buddhist view of selflessness in denying "Ātman" further strengthens its mystical characteristics.[10]

Otto also categorizes the two types of mysticism as the "mysticism of introspection (*Innenschau*)" and the "mysticism of unifying vision

(*Einheitsschau*)."[11] The "mysticism of introspection" aims to return to the depth of one's soul, turning away from everything outside. It begins with "soul-mysticism," and remains almost soul-mysticism itself. On the other hand, the "mysticism of unifying vision" does not need soul-mysticism. Involved the world of things and events, it seeks a unity under diversity. When mystical intuition is connected with traditional theism, the non-rationally underlying One comes to have the name of "God."

According to Otto, in both Śaṅkara's and Eckhart's religious thoughts, "soul-mysticism" and "God-mysticism" or "mysticism of introspection" and "mysticism of unifying vision" are deeply combined. Otto found such a combination in Śaṅkara's thought. Moreover, he says, the combination forms a unique type of mysticism in different spiritual climates. At first glance, the orientation of "soul-mysticism" seems to be quite different from that of "God-mysticism;" it seems extremely difficult for them to combine. Nevertheless, in Upaniṣad thought, which Śaṅkara's philosophy presupposes, there is an ontological structure of thought that makes its combination possible. This is the identity between the highest Brahman and Ātman, the essence of human beings. For example, a part of Otto's understanding of Śaṅkara is obvious in the following passage:

> Śaṅkara, judged by his introduction to his Commentary to the *Brahma-sūtras*, must also be placed first among the "mystics of the soul," since the quest for the Ātman and for the right knowledge of Ātman is here so predominantly in the foreground. In that very important introductory chapter of his great work the Brahman is not mentioned at all.[12]

As Otto says, the "soul-mysticism" referred to here can be expressed as "Ātman-mysticism" in the context of Indian philosophy. Even though it is called "Ātman-mysticism," Śaṅkara's mysticism is in sharp conflict with the pure "Ātman-mysticism" of Yoga; it is a unique combination of "soul-mysticism" and "God-mysticism." According to Otto, Śaṅkara's thought is a "certainly qualified mysticism" (*eine bestimmt qualifizierte Mystik*). It is interesting that Otto discusses Śaṅkara's thought by assuming the following possibilities if we think that Śaṅkara chooses a path of Yogic mysticism and Rāmānuja's "purely personal theism," then Otto presumes that, although Rāmānuja is a "great rival" to Śaṅkara, Śaṅkara dares to choose Rāmānuja's personal theism. In this way, Otto interprets Śaṅkara's thought in a theistic perspective. It is the ideal state of Yoga's mystical thought, that is, the state of the so-called "independence" (*kaivalya*), which is the wholly "godless state" (*Gottlosigkeit*). That state is incompatible with the motif of the "God-mysticism" that Śaṅkara's ontological framework contains.

Otto accurately grasped the essential structure of Śaṅkara's thought, that is, the identity of Brahman and Ātman. For example, he says:

> For Śaṅkara likewise "Brahman" appears to be the ātman (soul) come to itself, in the glory which belongs to its own eternal nature, which has only been obscured by avidyā. Brahman and Ātman appear to be simply interchangeable terms (*Wechsel-namen*) for the same thing. Where Ātman has been found there Brahman is reached. It is not easy to see what the Ātman would gain by being given now the name of Brahman also.[13]

What Otto attempts to express is not the Western metaphysical framework, but the Vedānta philosophy of the identity of Brahman with Ātman. As mentioned above, Otto was familiar with the ontological structure of Śaṅkara's thought, but his discourse was filtered through the monotheistic conceptual framework found in the Christian religious tradition. This is clear in the following passage:

> Brahman as the higher or supreme Ātman, which is identical with every ātman (soul) cannot strictly speaking be gracious. But the fact that a man can achieve the highest state not in mere isolation like the Yogin, but only in and through the attainment of Brahman, has indeed an analogy to the bhakta's "salvation by grace," so that for Śaṅkara there is here a possibility of accepting the doctrine of the Gītā. He adopts this teaching not only in the sense of the personal God who helps man along the path of knowledge by His illumination, but occasionally in the sense of the supreme Ātman Himself "bestowing grace."[14]

Moreover, Otto says that "there is salvation only within Brahman." The passage quoted here clearly shows us that Otto understands Śaṅkara's philosophy as parallel to the monotheistic thought. In other words, Otto's understanding of "salvation" is implicitly premised on the responsive relationship between the personal God as the "wholly other" and human beings; the "grace" of God is bestowed on human beings who have faith in God.

4 Vedānta Philosophy as a View of Salvation

Whether it is Christian doctrine or Indian religious thought, Otto does not understand doctrine or religious thought as merely rational or philosophical, but as the rationalization or ethicalization of the non-rational element of religious experience, namely, the feeling of *the numinous*, with theological or philosophical reflections. Otto called such a process the "schematization" (*Schematisierung*) of religion.[15] This process of "schematization," which shifts the non-rational essence of religious experience to a rational conceptual level in scriptures and doctrines, produces such doctrines and religious ideas as God being absolute. From the standpoint of religious experience, however, the doctrine and religious ideas are only secondary and derivative.

The holy is expressed at the doctrinal level through the concept of God as personal reality, or as impersonal reality. On the basis of his detailed consideration of the religious experience in such his works as *Das Heilige* (1917), *West-östliche Mystik* (1926), *Die Gnadenreligion Indiens und das Christentum* (1930), and other articles on Indian philosophy, Otto compared Christian and Indian religious thoughts, with special attention to the Vedānta thought. It was the sense and significance of *the numinous* that Otto incorporated as an indispensable component in his comparative study of religious thought. Otto considered Śaṅkara's philosophy to be, like Christian thought, not just metaphysics based on philosophical thought, but "soteriology" (*Heilslehre*) or "theology" (*Glaubenslehre*) rooted in the experience of *the holy*. Otto understood that they all represent ways (*Weg*) to salvation.

Otto was interested not only in Śaṅkara's philosophy, but also in Rāmānuja's thought, which emphasized *bhakti* (devotion) to Viṣṇu as the supreme God. Of particular note is Otto's interpretation of the commentaries on the *Bhagavadgītā*. As mentioned above, Garbe translated the text of *Bhagavadgītā* into German and claimed that it was devotional scripture. Otto agreed with Garbe that Śaṅkara interpreted Brahman in the *Bhagavadgītā* as reality without attributes, i.e., "super-personal Brahman." Otto argues that Śaṅkara's interpretation of Brahman distorted the teaching in this scripture.[16] In contrast, Otto argues that Rāmānuja challenged Śaṅkara's Advaita Vedānta philosophy by regarding the "Supreme God" in *Bhagavadgītā* as the personal God, the creator of the world.

Otto was strongly attracted to Rāmānuja's thought, which he felt had some parallels with Christian teaching. He found it similar to Luther's teaching in that it emphasized sincere faith in God. Rāmānuja's thought emphasized emotional *bhakti* or the "way of devotion" (*bhakti-mārga*) leading to salvation by God. What is peculiar to "Bhakti-mysticism" is that "it seeks to attain unity with the Highest through coalescence by an emotional exaggeration and glow of feeling." In this case, "even the Highest is thought of as responding to amorous longings."[17] According to Rāmānuja, the personal God (*Īśvara*) is the eternal Brahman; this God is the "cause of the world" (*Ursache der Welt*), forming diverse real worlds, living forever as God who transcends the world and time and who saves one chosen by his grace to move from the earthly world to Heaven, i.e., *Vaikuṇṭha*, the land of bliss.[18]

In 1927, on his second trip to India, Otto visited the Rāmānujan monastery in Melkote near Mysore. This monastery is said to have been either founded, or rebuilt, by Rāmānuja. When he visited the monastery, Otto wrote a short note in its guest book. Thirty years later, the American historian of religion John B. Carman, well known for his study of Rāmānuja's thought, visited this monastery. There, Carman found Otto's note with his signature: "When I return to Germany, I will write a book about Rāmānuja."[19] We can guess that Otto's "book" in his short note was *Die Gnadenreligion Indiens und das Christentum*, published in 1930. It was written for Christians who were unaware of India's "religion of grace." In this work, Otto writes that his stay in Mysore, where he met representatives of Bhakti-religion, was a very good opportunity for him to deepen his understanding of the Indian religion of grace.

In the study of Indian philosophy, Rāmānuja is well known as a Vedānta philosopher. When Otto introduced his philosophy to the European academic world, he gradually recognized that Rāmānuja should more appropriately be named as a "theologian" (Theolog) rather than as a "philosopher." Otto writes as follows: "The problem for him [Rāmānuja] is not the "philosophy" (*Filosofie*), but the "apologetics for a religious possession [i.e., religious experience]" (*Apologetik für einen religiosen Besitz*).[20] From Otto's viewpoint, the essence of Rāmānuja's philosophy was not in rational ontology, metaphysical logic, or philosophical reflection, but in the non-rational religious experience or *the numinous*. Similarly, in regard to the Advaita Vedanta philosopher Śaṅkara, Otto argues that he is not essentially a "philosopher" but rather a "theologian" or a "teacher of salvation" (*Heilslehrer*). Otto's interpretation of Śaṅkara as a theologian is based on his Christian viewpoint that Śaṅkara's interest was not in the metaphysical, but rather in the salvation of the soul.

According to Otto, *the holy* is a complex category of *a priori* combining non-rational and rational elements. *The holy*, which combines these two elements, is found in all religions. For behind the differences between religions, there lies a "uniform and constant function of human spirit." Otto further states:

> The degree in which both rational and non-rational elements are jointly present, united in healthy and lovely harmony, affords a criterion to measure the relative rank of religions – and one, too, that is specifically religious. Applying this criterion, we find that Christianity, in this as in other respects, stands out in complete superiority over all its sister religions. The lucid edifice of its clear and pure conceptions, feelings, and experiences is built upon a foundation that goes far deeper than the rational. Yet the non-rational is only the basis, the setting, the woof in the fabric, ever preserving for Christianity its mystical depth, giving

> religion thereby the deep undertones and heavy shadows of mysticism, without letting it develop into a mere rank growth of mysticality.[21]

The above passage clearly states Otto's position as a Christian theologian. In particular, he wants to compare the religions of the East, especially those of India, with Christianity and to demonstrate the superiority of Christianity over other religions. Otto considered Vedānta philosophy as "mystic," rooted in the experience of *the holy* and even as the "doctrine of salvation." From Otto's viewpoint, the concept of "God" (*Īśvara*) appears or disappears in Śaṅkara's "Brahman without attributes" (*nirguṇa-brahman*), that is, the higher Brahman. Śaṅkara's argument contains special features, for example, in his use of the term "Supreme God" (*parameśvara*), Otto points out that it is unclear whether by this term, Śaṅkara means the higher Brahman or the lower Brahman. Otto considered that "this ambiguity was just intentional;" Śaṅkara's focus was not on the rigor of philosophical thought, but on the salvation of the soul.[22] Furthermore, according to Otto, Brahman "is not purely opposite to God (*Deus*), but is itself the sublimated, mystical, exceeded God (*Deus*);" Brahman is not in opposition to "God" as generally understood, and is also the "mystical God."[23] Thus, from a theistic perspective, considering the higher Brahman without attributes as the excessive rise of the lower Brahman (God) with attributes, Otto understood the reality of the world and human existence.

Otto clarifies that Śaṅkara's philosophy has a theistic foundation, and then argues for the similarities between Śaṅkara and Eckhart. In both cases, mysticism is interpreted to include personal theism. Eckhart, however, combines these more closely than Śaṅkara. For example, Otto writes:

> Thus, we realize close resemblances between Śaṅkara and Meister Eckhart. In both men mysticism rises above a personal theism. The interpenetration of the theist and the mystic is much more marked in Eckhart than in Śaṅkara. Yet the greatest mystic of India is himself a witness that theism is not an accident of Western development, but somehow arises out of the deep necessity of mankind in general. In the language of religion he also attests to that statement of Paul's in Acts 14:17:
>
> He left not himself without witness.[24]

In the tradition of Vedānta philosophy, Otto's interpretation of Śaṅkara is rather close to the theory of transformation as the realistic development (*pariṇāma-vāda*). This is based on the theory that the effect is substantially identical with the cause, and really pre-exists in the cause (*satkārya-vāda*). From his theistic conceptual framework, Otto attempted to incorporate such ideas as "nescience" (*avidyā*) and "illusion" (*māyā*) into his monotheistic interpretation, but he was not successful in doing so. According to Otto, the main concern of Vedānta philosophy, whether Śaṅkara's or Rāmānuja's, was not to build a sophisticated philosophical system, but to save those who actually suffered from reincarnation. Daniel H.H. Ingalls (1916–99), a distinguished scholar of Indian philosophy, points out that Śaṅkara's attitude toward the truth was not philosophically strict but rather more psychological and religious. Thus, from the perspectives of Indian philosophy, it is possible to see Otto's theistic interpretation of the Vedānta philosophy as quite reasonable.[25] Until recently, religious studies have generally used the concepts and frameworks of religion, constructed in Western social and cultural contexts. Otto's study of Vedānta suggests that one should reconsider the approach to the History of Religions by taking into account the Hindu social and cultural context.

Here, I would like to reexamine the meaning of the religious concept of Bhakti-religion as a case study.[26] As Otto says, Bhakti-religion may be regarded as Hindu mysticism. Since the latter part of the nineteenth century, the theme of mysticism in the History of Religions has been a dominant part of the study of Indian religions. The application of the Western concept of mysticism to Indian religions has led to its being interpreted as representing Indian types of mysticism. Thus, Bhakti-religion was also understood as a theistic type of Hindu mysticism. However, one must pay attention to the fact that *bhakti* has often been interpreted as "faith." In his book *Die Gnadenreligion Indiens und das Christentum*, Otto compared *bhakti* with Christian faith. For Otto, Indian religious thought was neither metaphysics nor philosophical speculation, but a "theology" (*Glaubenslehre*) or a "doctrine of salvation" (*Heilslehre*), based on experiences of *the holy*. Otto regarded Vaiṣṇavism as a "religion of grace" (*Gnadenreligion*) in the Indian religious context. It is evident that Otto considers *bhakti* as similar to faith. In Wilfred C. Smith's words, "Bhakti is definitely one of the Hindu forms of faith."[27] In that case, one must question the extent to which Bhakti-religion is a Hindu form of mysticism.

The nature of *bhakti* varies according to an adherent's psychological attitudes and practices. The *bhakti* of the Vaiṣṇava tradition, which Otto studied, includes a broad range of religious commitment, varying from a popular Hindu's dimension of faith to that of mysticism. Although the meanings of Bhakti-religion and mysticism overlap to a fair extent in Hindu religious tradition, it is noteworthy that from the semantic perspectives of religion, the aspect of Bhakti-religion naturally shifts from that of mysticism in the light of the reality of Hindu religious tradition.

8

Toward the Semantic Understanding of Religions

For hundreds of years, religions including Christianity, Islam, Judaism, and Buddhism have coexisted in our world; interreligious dialogues have been increasingly undertaken. Religious "pluralism" is increasingly important in understanding contemporary world situations. This places emphasis on recognizing the values of different religions. Christian theology of religions has sought to clarify Christianity's relationship with other religions. Since the Second Vatican Council (1962–5), the Catholic Church, accepting some truths in other religions, has been actively engaged in religious dialogues. These efforts by Christian scholars have provided opportunities to reconsider the study of religion in the world and its methodology. The History of Religions, which discontinued its confessional ties with Christian theology, has been widely accepted as a research field for exploring the meaning of religion in human life; it attempts to understand the historical development of various world religions by clarifying the nature of religious phenomena. Today, however, with the rapid progress of the IT revolution, the world is entering a new era of globalization; paradigms of the past are changing at various speeds and on different levels. In the contemporary world, human beings are increasingly interconnected, as evidenced by environmental issues and the recent COVID-19 pandemic. Faced with such global situations, the History of Religions, like other sciences, has reached a major turning point, regardless of its Eastern or Western geographical orientation.

Rudolf Otto contributed to laying the foundation of the History of Religions; his theories still exert some influence on the study of religion, although less than before. Noting the characteristics of the modern study of religion, and using Otto's theory of religion, I will explore the contemporary significance of the study of religion and related important tasks of the History of Religions.

1 Trends in Understanding Religions in the Contemporary Study of Religion

Here, I will note the relation of Otto's religious theory to developments in the World Congresses of the IAHR (International Association for the History of Religions). This Association for the study of religion was established in 1950; it is the largest international association of religious studies in the world and meets once every five years. In August 2000, the 18th IAHR World Congress was held in Durban, South Africa, 100 years after the first conference in Paris in 1900. Since it was a commemorative conference, the overall theme was "History of Religions: Origins and Visions" and various panels reviewed the results of conventional religious studies. In March 2005, the 19th IAHR World Congress was held in Tokyo under the theme of "Religion: Conflict and Peace," with about 700 participants from overseas. In August 2010, the 20th IAHR World Congress was held at the University of Toronto in Toronto, Canada, under the convention theme of "Religion: A Human Phenomenon." In August 2015, at the University of Erfurt in Erfurt, Germany, the 21st IAHR World Congress was held with the theme of "Dynamics of Religion: Past and Present." These IAHR World Congresses explored approaches to understanding religion as a human activity within a range of conceptual frameworks from the humanities to the natural sciences, based on the theories and methods of religious studies.[1] The 22nd IAHR World Congress was scheduled to be held at the University of Otago in New Zealand in August 2020 under the theme of "Centres and Peripheries." Unfortunately, this conference was cancelled due to the pandemic spread of the COVID-19 infection.

The Science of Religions (*Religionswissenschaft*) was established in the modern West. In Germany, this was first related to Christian theology. In France, however, studies were more secular. Today, the previous frameworks and concepts of religious studies are being reexamined, as suggested by the convention themes of the IAHR World Congress. In the current era of religious pluralism, it is important to consider how the study of religion can go beyond the traditional Western conceptual framework to encompass world religions. From the latter half of the nineteenth century to the beginning of the twentieth century, the History of Religions became gradually independent of Christian theology and the philosophy of religion and was promoted as an "objective" or value-free discipline. The comparative study of religions was not always "apologetic" to Christianity. In certain cases, however, its rationalist studies undermined the absoluteness of a particular religion. While the History of Religions has gradually become recognized as a discipline based on its comparative framework, it brought about research results that differed from Christian theology.

One can point out the two main different lines of development in the modern History of Religions: (1) the approaches of comparative religion made by Christian theologians, which recognize both similarities and differences between religions with an attempt to demonstrate the superiority of Christianity; (2) secular approaches such as the sociology of religion, the anthropology of religion, and the psychology of religion, that attempt to elucidate the natures and characteristics of religions from their respective scientific perspectives. One also has to pay attention to non-Western scholars' approaches that attempt to clarify the characteristics of religions by introducing insights from non-Western religions. These are important interactions in the contemporary study of religion.

It is noteworthy that today, the History of Religions is often traditionally placed within the study of Christian theology in universities in Europe and the United States. For example, at German universities, Catholic and Protestant theologies are taught, as well as Islamic and Jewish theologies, not as secular studies. The use of a Western concept of "religion" is not always effective in understanding non-Western religious phenomena that reflect diverse cultural contexts. The American historian of religions Jonathan Z. Smith explains the process by which the term "religion" became widely used all over the world suggests this problem.[2] Thus, it is necessary to reexamine the concepts and frameworks of religious studies that have relied on Western religious traditions in the contemporary situation of religious pluralism.

In order to reconsider these important issues of the History of Religions, we must first recognize that the establishment and development of the History of Religions was based on the academic study of religious traditions by Western Christian scholars. In his article, "The History of Religions in America" (1962), Joseph M. Kitagawa (1915–92), a colleague of Mircea Eliade at the University of Chicago, discussed the research issues in the History of Religions. Kitagawa pointed out that the "History of Religions" was deeply influenced by Western historical and cultural traditions in its research methods and attitudes. He held that Western scholars of religion tend to think analytically, while Eastern scholars tend to directly intuit reality or experience the essence of ultimate reality. As Kitagawa says:

> The difficulty is that the assumptions and methodology of *Religionswissenschaft* are also products of Western historical culture. There is no denying that in practice the history of religions has acted too often as though there were such an objective frame of reference. Even those concerned with Eastern religions have

> asked, unconsciously if not consciously, "Western" questions and have expected Easterners to structure their religions in a way which was meaningful to Westerners. Admittedly, the Eastern emphasis on an immediate apprehension of the totality or essence of Ultimate Reality has been also conditioned by the Eastern historical communities. But the fact remains that the Western historians of religions, with their preoccupation with "conceptualization," have tended to interpret non-Western religious phenomena and attempted to fit them into their logical non-regional abstract systems of *Religionswissenschaft*.[3]

This issue, which Kitagawa already pointed out in the 1960s, suggests what is still an important task that scholars of the History of Religions need to undertake today. There is a need for a hermeneutical attitude in understanding religious phenomena on the basis of the accurate recognition of their concrete aspects. What I call "hermeneutical attitude" is an attempt to understand the meaning of religious phenomena by an interpretation that gradually illumines their meanings. In this context, this "hermeneutical attitude" is synonymous with the "sympathetic" understanding of faith, to which the historian of religion Wilfred C. Smith (1916–2000) refers. As Smith repeatedly emphasized, the understanding of religion involves the sympathetic understanding of the commitments of the adherent's faiths. In his essay, "Comparative Religion: Whither—and Why?," Smith says:

> The externals of religion—symbols, institutions, doctrines, practices—can be examined separately; and this is largely what in fact was happening until quite recently, perhaps particularly in European scholarship. But these things are not in themselves religion, which lies rather in the area of what these mean to those that are involved.[4]

For Smith, the "externals of religion" are not in themselves religion; religion lies in the area of what its "externals" mean to its adherents. There is no doubt that the study of religion must be academically valued if they are academic studies, but at the same time, its results must also be accepted by adherents of the traditions. When the author of this book attended Smith's lectures and graduate seminars on the study of religion at Harvard University about forty years ago, Smith emphasized these points to his students. The study of religion at the Center for the Study of World Religions, Harvard University, has aimed at a hermeneutical or "sympathetic" understanding of religion as Smith called it. In fact, although Smith's "sympathetic" attitude of understanding religion has been criticized as having an unclear relationship with the normative theological research, the hermeneutical issue of "understanding" religions in the context of contemporary religious pluralism is becoming increasingly important in the contemporary study of religion.

In the hermeneutical issue of the "understanding" of religion, one has to recognize that concrete religious phenomena consist of complex and diverse cultural phenomena and that in the increasingly complex contemporary world, it is more and more difficult to delineate them as solid research subjects. This fact implies that it is difficult to clearly distinguish religious phenomena from other cultural phenomena. In such situations, in order to understand religion, such methodologies of the History of Religions as the historical study of religion, the phenomenology of religion, the anthropology of religion, the sociology of religion, and the psychology of religion were sub-divided and independently created as the specific disciplines of religion. Various aspects of religious phenomena have been studied from different perspectives. On the basis of analysis by the historian of religions Ninian Smart, (1927–2001), it is possible to summarize the modern religious research in the following five points.[5]

First and foremost, the study of religion is necessarily "plural," or "cross-cultural." Thus, the theory of religion needs to be examined across cultures. We live in a pluralistic world, and religious studies naturally reflect the situations of that world. Second, the study of religion uses methods from many disciplines; it is "multidisciplinary" or "polymethodic." For example, historical perspectives and methods are needed to discuss Paul, Buddha, Wang Yang-ming, and others. In order to understand religion in relation to the modern urbanization, the viewpoints and methods of sociology and anthropology are necessary. Moreover, phenomenological perspectives and methods are required to consider the similarities and differences between Sufism and Advaita Vedānta philosophy. Various research methods are used to study religion, focusing on the historical development of religion and the relationship between religion and society/culture or the relationship with individuals.

Third, the study of religion is a "culture-bound" discipline. Religion is so closely linked to culture that one cannot clearly separate religion from other cultural phenomena. Therefore, the study of religion cannot be treated as separate from other disciplines; it does not have clear boundaries with other disciplines. Fourth, the study of religion deals with one specific aspect of human life, i.e., the religious aspect. Thus, it is "aspectual," like political science and economics. Finally, as a fifth characteristic, the study of religion, directed to the history and description of religious phenomena, raises the reflective questions that philosophy and theology deal with, i.e., normative questions. In other words, this fact means that although the descriptive study of religion is theoretically distinguished from the normative one, in actual religious studies, they are not clearly separated.

These five characteristics summarize the contemporary study of religion and, at the same time, they show the tasks of the History of Religions. They are also related to the questions as to whether religion is characterized by a "uniqueness" (*sui generis*) that cannot be reduced to society and culture and whether the History of Religions is a discipline with its own method of research. Such scholars of religion as Rudolf Otto, Gerardus van der Leeuw, and Mircea Eliade, who promoted the so-called phenomenological approach to religion, especially claimed the uniqueness of religion. In regard to this issue, lively discussions have been developed since the 1980s. The phenomenology of religion follows approaches distinct from such other disciplines as history, sociology, anthropology, and psychology. As the Japanese historian of religions Noriyoshi Tamaru points out, however, such disciplines of religions as the "history of religions" (*Religionsgeschichte*) and the anthropology of religion, which have been treated as the subdivisions of the History of Religions, consist of parts of such disciplines as the study of history and anthropology. One can say that the History of Religions is "a discipline defined by the common object of religion" rather than that based on a specific methodology.[6] It is true that the History of Religions has not always presented satisfactory theories for specific issues that are closely related to these fundamental problems. In recent years, there has been a tendency to study religious phenomena, inspired by cognitive sciences and cultural studies. Thus, it is difficult to regard the History of Religions as a particular discipline with its own specific methodology.

2 The Concept of "Holiness" and Its Implication

Here, I would like to examine Otto's concept of *the holy* and its meaning as a clue for examining the problems in the History of Religions. Otto lived in Germany at about the same time as Durkheim in France, who regarded the sacred as the deeper power behind society. In *Das Heilige*, Otto emphasized the centrality of *the numinous* in religion. This book emphasized the non-rational side of religion, based on his Christian theological interpretation. While devoting himself throughout his life to studying religions in the East, especially Indian religious thoughts, along with his Christian theology and the philosophy of religion, Otto explored the essence and meaning of *the holy* in religions. Otto explored the essence of religion at a deep dimension of religious experience, arguing that the nature of religion cannot be reduced to anything else, such as society, culture, or the human mind. From the depth of religious experience, Otto attempted to capture the essence of religion. This conclusion was his important methodological contribution to the History of Religions, especially to the phenomenology of religion.[7]

As discussed above, Otto invented the term, *the numinous* (*das Numinöse*), in attempting to describe the non-rational meaning of *the holy* in religions. The content of *the numinous* can only be felt in one's own religious experience. Even though one can discuss and argue about it, one cannot make it understood using only words. For everyday language or conceptualizing, it simply remains hidden and is the non-rational "wholly other" (*das ganz Andere*). According to Otto, the feeling of *the numinous* is at the heart of the religious phenomena; *the numinous* is the essence of religion, which is completely impossible to grasp conceptually and which fundamentally refuses to be interpreted. Based on the above-described perception of *the holy*, Otto was not interested in the exclusiveness of the doctrines of religion although he did not always disregard them. By paying attention to the feeling of *the numinous*, which constituted the basis of the doctrine, Otto turned his interest to the "lived religion" (*gelebte Religion*).[8] The doctrine or religious thought in religion is the rationalization or ethicalization of the non-rational elements of religious experience, the feeling of *the numinous* (*sensus numinous*), by theological or philosophical speculation. Otto called this process of rationalization the "schematization" (*Schematisierung*) of religion.[9] The non-rational nature of religious experience underlies rational concepts in the doctrines of religion; the doctrines produce the religious ideas of the attributes of God or of the absolute reality. Otto argues, however, from the primordial perspectives of *the holy*, that doctrines are secondary and derivative.

Otto conceives of *the holy* in religion as a complex category of intimately combined non-rational and rational elements and captures the essence of such religions in the world, whether in Christianity or in other religions. He argues that "a uniform and constant function of human psychology" is hidden behind various religions as "the underlying factor" of religion.[10] Otto says that all human beings share the same common religious feelings. However, from the standpoint of Christian theology, whether or not the non-rational and rational elements of religion are in good harmony indicates the superiority of that particular religion. On this basis, Otto emphasizes that Christianity is absolutely superior to other religions. As Robert F. Davidson also points out, it is noteworthy that consistently in his study of religion in India, Otto emphasizes the "greater maturity and profoundness of the Christian concepts of holiness, sin and salvation."[11] In his above-mentioned theory of religion, one finds fundamental characteristics of his Christian theological perspectives.

3 Parallel Development in the History of Religions

In his lecture, "Parallelisms in the Development of Religion East and West," delivered at the Asiatic Society of Japan during his visit to Japan in 1912, Otto took into account religious pluralism in the East and West. From his view of the "parallelism" of religions, he attempted his own interpretation of the world history of religions.[12] In the contemporary study of religion, Otto's view still provides value in considering current religious pluralism. The framework of his later interpretation of religions can be seen in his lecture, "Parallelisms in the Development of Religion East and West." In this lecture, mainly comparing Judeo-Christianity with Buddhism, Otto points out that although religions in the East and West developed almost completely independently, there are similarities between them, which are rooted in "common religious feelings."[13] As symbolically expressed in the words, "East is West, West is East," Otto believes that the religious phenomena of mysticism are always the same, regardless of time and space. He is convinced that there were significant similarities among religions that once existed or are still extant in the world. Otto attempted to capture them in the parallelism of religions, which he argued are not found in the world by chance, but exist as a universal fact.

From a comparative religious view of *the holy*, Otto investigated the characteristics of Christian thought, comparing it with Vedānta philosophy, through the feeling of *the numinous*. Otto considered that both Hindu and Christian thoughts are not merely a metaphysics, but are also a "soteriology" (*Heilslehre*) or a "theology" (*Glaubenslehre*), rooted in the experience of *the holy*. In short, they represent the "way" (*Weg*) to salvation. For example, Rāmānuja's thought, which Otto was the first Westerner to study, is one of the well-known Vedānta philosophies. According to Otto, what matters to Rāmānuja is not the "philosophy" (*Filosofie*), but the "apologetics" (*Apologetik*) of religious experience.[14] Moreover, Otto says, fundamental "mystical intuition" (*intuitus mysticus*) exists at the root of the ideas of Śaṅkara and Eckhart. According to Otto, however, "both veil this fact by their dialectic," which, as he notes, is also another kind of parallel between the two.[15]

In the depth of these two systems of thought, Otto says, there are the dimensions of "mystical intuition, or the completely non-rational *numinous*, rather than the rational ontology or the metaphysical logic. For the two teachers, Eckhart and Śaṅkara, pure "existence" (Sein), that is, Śaṅkara's *sat* (the higher Brahman) and Eckhart's *Esse*, is as close as reason can get to the essence of reality. However, it does not reach that essence, and results in being just the rational "scheme" of *the numinous*.[16] In regard to the mystical sentences in the Upaniṣads, which assert the identity of the supreme Brahman with Ātman (the essence of the individual human), namely, *tat tvam asi* or *ahaṃ brahmāsmi*, Otto says that "Each of them is rather perceptible [*fühlbar*]," and is totally different from the rational statement that "I became the pure being; I am the very being." This is exactly the same as Eckhart's reference to the "noble man" (*homo nobilis*), i.e., the "deified man" (*vergotteter Mensch*). This case is also more than a person who became the "true Being" (*Esse*). None of the concepts are of any use."[17]

One of the important characteristics of Otto's religious theory is that he regards the language that expresses the experience of *the numinous*, especially religious doctrine, as a "concept" or a rational "scheme." According to Otto, every statement, as long as it consists of words, tries to convey a concept.[18] Therefore, although rational understanding comes to the foreground, it does not exhaust the essence of *the holy*, for that relates to the non-rational. The essence of Otto's *numinous* is non-rational. In his words, "the nature of the numinous can only be suggested by means of the special way in which it is reflected in the mind in terms of feeling."[19]

The holy is an *a priori* category composed of rational and non-rational components. As Otto says, *the holy* is experienced as "objective and outside the self." Historian of religion Robert A. Orsi argues that it is known as "objectively real, not as delusion or fantasy" for those experiencing it; the experience of *the holy*, which is "relational" and "intersubjective," is "really real" to those who experience it. From the phenomenological or semantic viewpoint of religion, we may reinterpret it as a *meaning* for them.[20] While the rational in *the holy* belongs to the concepts with which we are familiar and which can be defined in words, the non-rational can only be experienced by pre-conceptual or trans-conceptual feelings, not by conceptual reflections. Rational words cannot exhaust the nature of *the holy*, for a religious experience is "non-rational." However, when the tendency of "rationalization" which unilaterally rationalizes the idea of God appears in the foreground, it seems as if the rational concept may be everything.

From the semantic viewpoint of religion, we can argue that the fact that *the holy* is "really real" for those who experience it implies that, though it remains existentially present for them, it is constructed as a *meaning*, consisting of the relationship of the non-rational with the rational. In other words, *the holy* is characterized by a multilayered structure of meaning; it is semantically categorized into the two: its semantic dimension constructed in its derivative sense and that in its original sense. *The holy* constructed as the meaning in its ordinary and derivative sense is accompanied by a rational or moral element. On the other hand, *numinous* is an explanatory word that Otto himself coined to express *the holy* in its original sense, or *the holy* with the rational, moral, and ethical elements subtracted. By talking about the non-rational component of religion, as Otto emphasizes, one can feel it to some extent. In short, from the semantic perspective of religion, we can reinterpret *the holy* as constituting a multilayered structure of meaning: the non-rational itself and the rational with moral elements. Accordingly, *the holy* can be understood as consisting of the deep dimension of the non-rational meaning and the superficial dimension of the rational meaning in ordinary language. When *the holy* is understood on the social and cultural surface, its meaning naturally becomes conceptual. For adherents living in religious faiths, however, *the holy* cannot always be conceptually expressed, for it contains plural meanings which suggest the depth of *the numinous*. Thus, when one semantically reinterprets Otto's religious theory, one can say that Otto's views of *the holy* provide important suggestions for the contemporary study of religion.

4 The Semantic Dimension of Holiness and Its Multi-Structures: Through the "Ideogram"

In order to understand the depth of *the holy*, which escapes the structure of the ordinary empirical meaning and which is disclosed by the experience of *the numinous*, I would like to consider Otto's "ideogram" (*Ideogramm*) from the semantic perspective of religion. In Otto's religious theory, *the holy* is first intuited in feeling. Ideograms are employed to express the intuitive divination and become the essential aspect of human ideas of transcendent reality. In the contemporary study of religion, although Otto's theory of religion has been variously discussed, to the best of the author's knowledge, Otto's interpretation of "ideogram" seems not yet seriously discussed.

Otto recognizes the linguistic level of meaning called "ideogram" in a way that overlaps the two semantic dimensions. At first glance, Otto's "ideogram" seems to be a concept of *the holy*, but it is by no means a "concept." It is nothing more than appearing "similar to a concept." It contains analogical characteristics.

For example, it suggests what is conceptually difficult to express and moves the human mind and causes "passion." However, Otto says, "natural" (*natürlich*) or ordinary human beings, who live in the world of everyday meaning and who have no idea of *the holy*, easily mistake the ideogram as a "natural concept" at the level of everyday meaning. Customarily, when a word is symbolically coded, its "meaning" becomes conceptual. When the depth of faith cannot be intuited, only the everyday meaning is grasped conceptually or rationally.

In order to understand *the numinous*, which is beyond the linguistic world of daily experience, Otto's "ideogram" functions between the deep and the superficial meanings. From an everyday viewpoint, an ideogram may appear to be rational, but it points to a deeper dimension of *the holy* conveyed by the feeling of *the numinous*. But as Otto says, it is *never* a concept, but "what is similar to a concept;" it is borrowed from the "area of emotion" (*Gemütsbereiche*). It usually has a "simply analogical characteristic" (*der bloß analogische Charakter*) in expressing numinous experience or the depth of reality. Through an ideogram, however, one can properly feel the genuine and non-rational nature of *the numinous*; in this way, religion is protected against a rationalistic interpretation (*Rationalisierung*). For Otto, an ideogram is a kind of illustrative substitute for a concept. As Davidson points out, in contrast to ordinary artistic symbols, an ideogram is "a kind of conceptual symbol, that is, a concept drawn from ordinary sense-experience and rational thought to represent and suggest the transcendent meaning of numinous feeling of which no exact conceptual interpretation is possible."[21] Otto emphasizes that an ideogram suggests the fluid or unarticulated depth of meaning beyond ordinary language.

As examples of ideogram in Eastern religious traditions, Otto mentions the terms "nothingness" (*wu*; *mu*) and "emptiness" (*śūnyatā*), each of which is an ideogram of the "wholly other" (*das ganz Andere*), that is, the "wonder"(*mirum*) by itself. "Wonder" as the "wholly other" cannot be grasped or understood by ordinary language. In Otto's discussion of *the numinous*, the term *mysterium* is its ideogram that resists or eludes conceptualization. Its positive content, however, is composed of a peculiar "contrast-harmony" (*Kontrast-harmonie*) in the entire history of religion.[22] As Todd Gooch points out, this "contrast-harmony" consists of "the simultaneous presence of two antithetical tendencies" in reactions to which *the numinous* gives rise: *the numinous* is both terrifying and fascinating.[23] Thus, Otto regards an ideogram as a non-conceptual pointer toward *the holy*. However, Otto did not elucidate the meaning of an ideogram more clearly in religious language and thus did not clarify the differences between the language of scripture and that of ordinary life. Perhaps, Otto's interpretation of any ideogram is so vague that it has not been well understood. Scholars of religious studies are presented with this task.

It is important for the historians of religions to understand that from Otto's viewpoint, there is no meaning of "holiness" or sacredness in an object or action, although they may be easily misunderstood as "sacred" in religious traditions. According to Otto, as Todd Gooch also points out, "Religious feeling is structurally determined by its intentional relationship to a religious object." Thus, Otto's strategy of understanding religion is to shed light on "the nature of that object by means of an analysis of the feeling-act in which it is given." In short, Otto's primary interest is in "the object toward which religious feeling is directed."[24] In ordinary life, an object, even though it is called "religious" and may be regarded as "sacred" in a religious community, it may be "profane" for non-adherents. For the faithful, it is meaningful only when it reflects their *numinous* experiences. The language of scripture does not consist of "rational" concept. It becomes a sacred or holy language that suggests the depth of reality and meaning when it is derived from religious experiences.

When one reconceptualizes Otto's view of *numinous* experience from the semantic perspective of religion, one can regard it as consisting of both the deep or unarticulated and the superficial or articulated dimension of meaning. For example, as one of the ideograms, Otto discusses the meaning of the word "salvation." Salvation may be "something whose meaning is often very little apparent" and "wholly obscure" to ordinary or "natural" (*natürlich*) human beings, who do not understand the word's depth of meaning. On the contrary, so far as they understand only its superficial meaning, they tend to find "salvation" highly tedious and uninteresting. According to Otto, so far as "natural" human beings understand merely the superficial meaning of salvation, they fail to understand its deep meaning. Since they do not have the "inward teacher" (*inwendiger Lehrer*) who could guide them to its depth of meaning, they easily misunderstand the word "salvation" as a "natural" concept which expresses the superficial dimension of meaning, not as a "mere ideogram of what is felt" (*das bloße Ideogramm des Gefühles*), which implies the deep experience of salvation. Thus, Otto emphasizes the significance of an ideogram for understanding the depth of meaning, i.e., *the numinous*.[25]

Like the linguistic concepts or doctrines of *the holy*, the words in scriptures are in a certain sense the "natural" expressions of *the numinous*. Otto acknowledges that they also hold important roles in the scriptures. By using a language common to the ordinary world of meaning, the depth of meanings hidden in that language are suggested. In the hermeneutical theory of Paul Ricoeur (1913–2005), who regards the task of the phenomenology of religion as an interpretation of "symbol," symbolic language is understood as an indispensable path to transcendence. He defines the symbol as a double-meaning expression, characterized by literal and figurative meanings; it is polysemic and virtually inexhaustible in depth. In his argument of "the phenomenology of the sacred," he introduces Otto's book *The Idea of the Holy*, in which "the sacred" is regarded as being "experienced as awesome, as powerful, as overwhelming." According to Ricoeur, the *numinous* element of the sacred does not initially have something to do with language, even if it may become so to a certain extent subsequently. "To speak of 'power' is to speak of something other than 'speech,' even if the power of speaking is thereby implied."[26] Thus, he argues that in order to understand the depth of the sacred, one should recognize the hidden meanings of the symbolic language describing it. In this regard, Ricoeur and Otto semantically share a common philosophical point of view.

Concrete examples given by Otto are the words "Yahweh's wrath" (*orgḗ*) in the Old Testament and "God's wrath" (*orgè theoŷ*) in the New Testament, which cause *numious* awe. For those whose faith is in Judaism or Christianity, "God's wrath" is by no means a "decrease" (*Minderung*) of holiness, but rather a "natural expression and element of 'holiness' itself." This "wrath" (*ira*) is nothing but "fear" (*tremendum*) itself. "Fear" which is wholly non-rational in itself, is "understood and expressed in the Old Testament by a simple analogy from the natural realm, that is, from the emotional life of man." Moreover, this analogy is so prominent and appropriate that it cannot be avoided at all when it comes to preserving its value and expressing religious feeling today. The word "God's wrath" is not an "original rational concept" but an "ideogram" or the pure "interpretative sign" (*Deute-Zeichen*) that being similar to a concept, implies a unique emotional element in religious experience.[27] "God's wrath" in the Bible is essentially "unnatural, that is, *numinous* wrath," and not the "natural" wrath which one may misunderstand at its rational or ethical dimension of meaning. In the Bible, it combines the original and the supernatural with the subsequent meanings. The non-rational element is revealed in "God's wrath," causing fear that cannot be caused by natural wrath.

Otto notes such terms as "nothing" and "emptiness" (*śūnyatā*), which characterize Buddhist philosophy, as specific examples of ideograms. They express the "wholly other," the "wonder" (*mirum*). At the same time, they are "paradoxical" and "antinomic."[28] The "wonder" as the "wholly other" cannot be grasped or understood; it is "beyond the category" of ordinary language. Thus, it cannot be conceptualized. In this way, Otto uses the term "ideogram" as the *word* for non-conceptual cognition between *the numinous* itself and its conceptual cognition. However, he does not make a clear analysis in regard to the language of the scriptures, theology, or philosophical thought.

In the world of many religions, for a scholar studying a religion other than his or her own, it is very important to note that scriptural language is poetically or mythically woven by "ideograms" that express experiences of *the numinous*, to which Otto refers. Scriptural language is not composed of "rationalized" concepts, or the feeling of *the numinous*. It is a fundamental language that verbalizes the sense of *the numinous*. The non-rational aspect of religion is fundamentally *holy*, and if it is lacking, religion is no longer a religion. When it is conceptualized, a theological or philosophical system is established. Otto's "rationalizing tendency" is found not only in Christian theology but also in the study of myths and other religions.

It is also noteworthy that Otto himself traveled to North Africa, Jerusalem, India, Burma, China and Japan, where he encountered the living faiths of non-Western religions, which he described in his travel letters and diaries. They reflect his "fieldwork." Otto focused on religious traditions in which faith was verbally expressed and attempted as much as possible to understand the meaning of words and actions of those faiths. By personal observation, he could intuit their depth, including aspects that cannot be understood by the study of scriptures, doctrines, and religious ideas. When Otto heard the chanting of the "Holy, Holy, Holy" at the Moroccan synagogue in 1911, this experience became the core of his understanding of *the holy*. Otto traveled many times, and as for modern scholars, direct exposure to religious traditions complemented his understanding of religious literature and the deeper meaning of religion.

Otto's theory of religion was further developed by Eliade, who critically inherited Otto's concept of "holiness" and applied it to a wider study of religious phenomena. Based on Otto's conception of *the holy*, Eliade regarded the history of religions as being made up of various manifestations of *the holy*, i.e., "hierophanies," from the manifestations of such forms as sacred stones and trees to the manifestation of God in different cultures. All religious phenomena express the same structure of reality. For Eliade, humans are not only "humans who make full use of symbols" (*homo symbolicus*), but also "religious humans" (*homo religiosus*). When humans are associated with *the holy*, the symbol becomes a "hierophany," revealing the meanings of *the holy* in everyday mundane space and time. Manifestations of the sacred differ in various cultures but are equivalent as long as they express the sacred. In all religions, Eliade argues that manifestations of the sacred and their dialectics are structurally identical.

The holy in religion has been superficially understood as a given historical "fact." Historians of religions tend to grasp various religious phenomena in their "inner horizons" of the cultures in which they were born and raised, leaving out the contexts of specific religious phenomena. In the context of contemporary religious pluralism, one needs to go beyond a superficial dimension of understanding religions to a deeper dimension of understanding religious phenomena. Today, historians of religions need to understand what lies behind religious phenomena. Moreover, Otto gives an example of how a philosopher understands; the philosophers' "god" is a "simply rational speculation and definition," but philosophers always consider the ideogram to be "anthropomorphism." However, philosophers' reflection would be inappropriate unless the true non-rational element of *the numinous* is properly perceived.

The depth of meaning in religious thought and faith is not just an intellectually understood horizontal world of meaning. It is a vertical dimension of meaning that is gradually cultivated when the social institutional fixed orientation of meaning is suppressed and the understanding of religious phenomena is deepened. It is illuminated only by the light of "deep knowledge," unlike the superficial meaning of religion, grasped by rational and conceptual knowledge.

In the contemporary History of Religions, the concept of *the holy* is widely acknowledged, although discussions on its details are ongoing. In religions rooted in an experience of *the holy*, historians of religions comprehend not only Judeo-Christianity but also other religions in this sense. Otto was a pioneer in the History of Religions. Of particular note in his approach is recognizing the dual meaning of religious language rooted in the experience of *the holy*. When one focuses only on the literal meaning of a religious language, one loses sight of the depth of meaning. Ricoeur also insists on a double meaning of symbolic language. In our rapidly globalizing contemporary world, one can find an important direction for the History of Religions, by further developing Otto's theory of *the holy*.

5 A Semantic Understanding of *the Numinous* in Religion

According to Otto, religion is "perfectly *sui generis* and irreducible." This means that *numinous* experience cannot be reduced by any socio-historical condition. When Otto uses the term *numinous* in order to "stand for 'the holy' *minus* its moral factor or 'moment', and, ... minus its 'rational' aspect altogether," he suggests that *numinous* experience cannot be strictly defined by any concept. It is beyond the ordinary or rational dimension of reality. Otto says that there is "only one way to help another to an understanding of it." "It can only be evoked, awakened in the mind."[29] In other words, one can understand the *numinous* experience only by awakening this consciousness inside the human mind. Moreover, in order to clarify this experience, one has to elicit it in the mind of another. For Otto, the fact that the faithful have religious experience points to the existence of an extraordinary religious dimension.

From the semantic perspective of religion, one can interpret Otto's theory of religion, especially the *numinous* experience. According to the philosophical semantic theory of the Japanese philosopher Toshihiko Izutsu (1914–93), the holiness of a *numinous* experience in a specific context, to which Otto refers, may not be an *a priori* attribute of religious experience, but a historical response in the religious commitment of the faithful. In Izutsu's words, the *numinous* experience by itself is "the primordial unity of the psychic and the metaphysical in their ultimate undifferentiation;" it is "the zero-point of consciousness," from which all forms of consciousness emerge, and at the same time, "the zero-point of Being" from which all forms of Being emerge. Otto's *numinous* experience or "the field of consciousness in its entirety" is "focused upon itself with no focal point anywhere."[30] Thus, it is true that the *numinous* experience itself, "unarticulated" by language, is *a priori* and an essential attribute of religious experience, but the "holiness" of the *numinous* experience, accompanied by its moral and rational aspect in a specific context, is not an *a priori* attribute of religious experience. It is "a particular articulated form" of *the numinous*, which is absolutely unarticulated. A particular form of holiness may be different among religious traditions.

For Otto, *the holy* certainly consists of the complex combination of the rational factor and the non-rational one. As he clearly mentions in the subtitle of his work *Das Heilige*, his study of the holy represents "an inquiry into the non-rational factor in the idea of the divine and its relation to the rational." His concept of holiness implies that in religion, both the rational and the non-rational aspects are closely combined. This means that *the holy* constitutes a double structure of reality and experience: *the holy* in its essential sense and that in its secondary sense, accompanied by the rational or moral aspect of religion. In other words, from the semantic perspective of religion, when one interprets the existence of *the holy* as a "meaning" for the adherents, it constitutes a double structure of meaning; while the non-rational aspect of *the holy* is recognized as the deep dimension of meaning, its rational one is the superficial dimension of meaning. The rational or moral dimension of meaning in *the holy* can be expressed with the concepts which one can rationally or logically understand in daily life, while the non-rational one cannot be grasped with any conceptualization. In regard to the non-rational factor of *the holy*, one can experience it only with emotions that are before or beyond concept. Otto emphasizes that the sense of *the numinous* is shared by humankind although its specific forms may be different in time and space. Especially in regard to the non-rational dimension of *the holy*, that is, the *numinous* experience, he emphasizes that it cannot be expressed in ordinary language; it is called "the wholly other" (*das ganz Andere*). In any case, Otto's concern is with "lived religion" (*gelebted Religion*), returning to the sense of *the numinous* which underlies the doctrinal basis of religion.

From the semantic religious perspective, one can say, Otto's idea of *the numinous* suggests the depth of reality, or the depth of religious experience which is still unarticulated by language, being before or beyond ordinary language. As the American historian of religions Gregory Alles points out, numinous feeling or *sensus numinis* is "fundamentally disconnected from the mental systems responsible for normal, conscious cognition."[31] Thus, it is not something to do with "normal, conscious cognition" in the ordinary language, although it may become so subsequently. According to the Swiss linguist Ferdinand de Saussure (1857–1913), language is a system of signs, whose structure consists of a signifier (*signifiant*) and a signified (*signifié*). In regard to the *numinous* experience, it is noteworthy that in Saussure's words, an imbalance often occurs between a signifier and a signified. Needless to say, the ordinary dimension of meaning in linguistic consciousness is completely controlled with socially established words. In one's daily life, all verbal meanings, which constitute the result of a social act of agreement, are by nature conventional. Once the meaning of a word is established, it turns into a linguistic custom. The unalterability of the relation is supported by linguistic customs in ordinary life-world. Thus, the life-world, which is reflected in a human mind, articulated with the established meanings of language, is one's "reality." The whole life-world is semantically classified into an ontological hierarchy of reality.

Once one's eyes are religiously or spiritually opened toward the depth of linguistic consciousness characterized by the *numinous* experience, the order of reality comes to be changed completely. From the semantic view of religion, the dimension of *numinous* experience to which Otto refers corresponds to the depth of reality or the depth of meaning beyond ordinary language. In the Taoist philosophy of Lao-tzŭ and Chuang-tzŭ, for example, Izutsu argues that the depth of meaning in human reality can only be reached through the mystical or *numinous* experience. In his words, "The reality of things as conceived by

Lao-tzŭ and Chuang-tzŭ is based on an extraordinary vision obtained in a peculiar kind of mystical experience."[32] Moreover, Izutsu continues:

> The world of Being as it appears to their spiritual eyes is a vast and boundless space where things exist in an amorphous, dream-like mode of existence, freely merging into one another and being constantly transformed into one another. It is not a usual world where things are clearly distinguishable from one another, each being definitely and unalterably delineated and determined. In this amorphous and dream-like world, nothing is rigidly fixed by the so-called "essence" or "quiddity." Ontological fluidity—that is the most salient feature of the world.[33]

According to Izutsu, this view of reality does not only constitute the central and fundamental characteristic of Taoist ontology; it also represents the essence of the mystical or *numinous* experience in Taoist religious tradition. In this tradition, the dimension of *numinous* experience may be "a vast and boundless space where things exist in an amorphous, dreamlike mode of existence." Thus, the *numinous* experience at the depth of reality is inexpressible in ordinary language that clearly distinguishes things, definitely and unalterably delineating and determining them. Semantically speaking, *numinous* experience may represent the deep dimension of reality or the absolutely unarticulated level of meaning, while the ordinary experience represents the superficial or the specifically articulated level of meaning. At the deep dimension of reality or at the unarticulated level of meaning beyond a superficial signified, there lies the vast space of a deep signified. At the depth of linguistic consciousness, there exists an amorphous mode of reality, i.e., *the numinous*, which is not combined with a definite signifier. Since it has no definite meaning, there is no doubt that it is inexpressible in ordinary language. In short, from the semantic view of religion, the concept of *the holy* in Otto's religious theory consists of a double structure of meaning: the superficial or articulated dimension of meaning, characterized by the rational and moral aspect of reality, and the deep or unarticulated dimension of meaning, suggested by the non-rational aspect of reality, or *the numinous* which has no semantic articulation by language.

In the study of religion, there has been a tendency to make the "facts" of religion the main focus. This means that religion has been conceptually or superficially understood without paying attention to its deep dimension of meaning or the depth of reality, derived from the *numinous* experience. In order to understand religion more accurately as it is in reality, one needs to understand it at the deep or unarticulated dimension of meaning, not only at the superficial or articulated dimension of meaning. In other words, one needs to be sympathetic to the semantic or hermeneutical perspective, suggested by the ideograms. In order to open a path toward the hidden meaning of religion, implied by the *numinous* experience, one has to focus on the "dimension of the depth" in *the holy*, going beyond rational or objective understanding. The depth of meaning in religion is not understood in the horizontal dimension of meaning conceptually or intellectually, but in the vertical dimension intuitively. By focusing on *the holy*, various religious phenomena can be regarded as indicating meaning derived from the *numinous* experiences. From Otto's perspective of religion, it is noteworthy that unlike in ordinary language, there may also be religious language, based on *numinous* experiences. They both essentially constitute one and the same language.

As the philosophy of language and the humanities of recent years have revealed, language is the basis of culture and cognition. From the perspective of semantic hermeneutics, both language and culture have a deep semantic structure hidden below the socially superficial level of meaning. In its deep semantic structure, the meaning of language is fluid and floating, and essentially unfixed. From the depth of the meaning, hidden in the bottom of linguistic consciousness, we attempt to clarify the deep meaning of various aspects of language and culture that have ambiguous and symbolic meanings. In this way, religious phenomena can be seen as the complex phenomena of "meaning," or the world of "meaning," conveyed through experiences of *the numinous*. Thus, it is possible to understand religious phenomena, based on the involvement of the adherents of religions.

In considering the methods of the History of Religions in the contemporary context of religious pluralism, there is no doubt that the empirical scientific understanding of various religions or religious phenomena remains very important. Bearing this in mind, scholars of religion must also attempt to understand religious phenomena in the depth of human reality. Their deep dimension of meaning can only be understood in their contexts. From such compound-eye perspectives, religion can be understood in the double dimensions of meaning in regard to *the holy*: the ordinary dimension of meaning and the deep one. One can say that the study of religion from the perspective of semantic hermeneutics will be more and more important in the future.

Conclusion

In this book, by examining Otto's study of religion through his comparison of Christianity with other religions within the framework of his Protestant Lutheran theology, I have attempted to consider the whole of his work as much as possible. As a philosopher of religion, he attempted to clarify the relationship between non-rational and rational elements of religion by developing the concept of *the numinous*. Otto compared Christianity with other religions, with a particular interest in Indian religious thought. Simultaneously, Otto was a Lutheran theologian, a philosopher of religion, and a scholar of comparative religion. We can say that Otto had three "faces" as a scholar.

These three "faces" were never separate; they merge in the "face" of a Lutheran theologian who believed in the absolute truth of Christianity. We need a widely encompassing perspective to understand his breadth and depth. In his theological reflection, *the holy* cannot be conceptually captured and expressed in words. Thus, he coined the word *numinous* to capture the non-rational aspect of *the holy*. Otto's exploration of the depth of faith hidden in *the holy* was fundamentally rooted in Luther's Christian theology. Since Otto was familiar with Luther's theological terms, he used them to develop his own theological reflections. For example, Luther's terminology was used to describe one aspect of *the numinous* as "tremendum" and "majestas."[1] This is important in understanding the essence of Otto's religious theory.

Otto's Lutheran-based theology included the philosophical and comparative perspectives of religion. While intuiting the essence of religion and attempting to clarify its uniqueness, Otto explored the religious experience that underpins religion. The research method that Otto considered "theological" (*theologisch*) is today understood by some scholars to be "phenomenological." For them, *Das Heilige* is the beginning of the phenomenology of religion. The understanding of Otto as a phenomenologist of religion was rooted in the way he was interpreted by Husserl and Scheler. Although Scheler was critical of Otto's view of *the holy* as an *a priori* emotional ability, he highly appreciated Otto's view of *the holy* as the way to lead to "phenomenological intuition."[2] However, Otto himself considered his study to be theological; his primary quest was for Christian truth. His Christian theological study contained broad perspectives and insights beyond the framework of the phenomenology of religion.

Since the late 1980s, issues of religious uniqueness, non-rationality, and mysticism, which Otto emphasized, have been re-examined by historians of religions. In post-Eliade studies of religion, there has been criticism of Otto's and Eliade's approach presupposing the uniqueness and non-rationality of religion. Eliade, influenced by Otto, attempted to capture the whole of religion in the relationship between the sacred and the profane. At that time, however, the discussion proceeded on the premise of the uniqueness of religion; the theological assumptions behind their perspectives were severely criticized. The issue of whether religious phenomena have a quality that can or cannot be reduced to social or psychological phenomena raises a fundamental question regarding the essential characteristic of the History of Religions.

All scholars of religion aiming for a systematic study of religion, including the phenomenologists of religion, have their own methodological approach. From the semantic viewpoint of religion, Otto's theory of religion can be considered a new interpretation. His concept of *the holy* represents a complex category in which the non-rational and the rational elements are inextricably combined. We can reinterpret the combination of the non-rational and rational as the multilayered meaning of "holy." In other words, it can be understood as a relationship between the rational or superficial meaning and the non-rational or deep meaning. Thus, although the viewpoint is not limited to a rational meaning of religion, its range is extended to the horizon of the non-rational. Thus, by reconsidering Otto's theory of religion semantically, religion or *the holy* can be understood as having multilayered dimensions of meaning.

Among the multilayered dimensions of meaning in *the holy*, we can understand the experience of *the numinous* through the "ideogram." The "ideogram" Otto refers to is an "interpretive sign" (*Deute-Zeichen*) that expresses a unique religious element of religion by the overlapping of everyday linguistic meaning and a deep one. But a "natural" (*natürlich*) person, who lives in an ordinary life with no experience of *the holy*, misunderstands the ideogram as a "natural concept" in the everyday semantic sense. When a word is symbolically coded to reflect social institutional meaning, the meaning is naturally regarded as conceptual. From the religious standpoint of semantic hermeneutics, however, Otto's "ideogram" is similar to the concept of *the holy*, but not entirely. It is used for things and events which are conceptually difficult to express and has an "analogical characteristic" which moves the human mind and causes passion. The ideogram suggests a deep dimension of meaning, hidden in the everyday or ordinary dimension of meaning, that is, the depth of meaning characterized by *the numinous*. Historians of religions seeking to understand the religion of others should keep in mind that the language of religious scriptures is expressed in ideograms. Through the multiple perspectives on religion, suggested by Otto's religious theory, religion can be understood not only from the everyday linguistic relationship, but also from the depth of the meaning, hidden in everyday linguistic consciousness. Accordingly, Otto's theory of religion has the potentiality to open up new horizons in the study of religion.

Otto's three "faces" eventually merge into the "face" of a Lutheran theologian when his writings are scrutinized. He explored the truth of Christianity, taking other religions into account, while rooted in his Lutheran faith. Otto explored the truth of Christianity, taking into account the thoughts of other religions, while rooting in his Lutheran faith. His study of Christian theology has the breadth and depth that also includes the perspectives of the philosophy of religion and comparative religion. Delving into Christian faith and teachings, he made a philosophical examination of the experience of *the holy* and attempted a hermeneutical study of Indian religious thought. Through his encounters with people in different religions and cultures, especially in India, and by translating Indian Sanskrit literature into German, he attempted to understand as deeply as possible the religious reflection of Hindu theologians.

From the twentieth century to this current century, interreligious dialogues that transcend religious differences have become increasingly significant. It is noteworthy that Otto engaged in dialogues that led to the realization of the "Religious League of Humanity" (*Religiöser Menschheitsbund*). Through his religious studies and practices, Otto sought to gain a deeper understanding of Christian truth, and from this position, attempted to understand Indian religious thought. For this reason, his research did not always produce the results that Hindus and Buddhists could accept. Thus, there was a limit in his approach to understanding other faiths. From the nineteenth to the twentieth century, however, when the History of Religions was about to separate and become independent of Christian theology as a discipline, Otto's study of religion was truly pioneering. From the view of modern religious studies, we may conclude that his research made a strong contribution to the foundation of the academic discipline of the "History of Religions."

Notes

Preface

1 Robert A. Orsi, "The Problem of the Holy," in *The Cambridge Companion to Religious Studies*, edited by Robert A. Orsi. New York: Cambridge University Press, 2012, pp. 96–7. Cf. Gavin Flood, "Politics, Experience, and the Languages of Holiness," *Numen* 67, 2020, p. 142.

2 Heinrich Frick, "Rudolf Otto innerhalb der theologischen Situation," *Zeitschrift für Theologie und Kirche* 19, 1938, S. 14. Moreover, Martin Kraatz (the former director of Religionskundliche Sammlung) says that in his letter to his friend Jacob Wilhelm Hauer (May 23, 1933), Otto described himself as "a modernistic and pietistic Lutheran with certain Quaker-tendencies." Cf. Martin Kraatz, "... meine stellung als 'modernistischer pietistisch angehauchter lutheraner mit gewissen quakerneigungen' ist eigen [...]'—Bio- und Epistolographisches zu Rudolf Otto," in Jörg Lauster, et al., *Rudolf Otto: Theologie-Religionsphilosophie-Religionsgeschichte*, Berlin: De Gruyter, 2014, S. 13–14. Behind the fact that Otto described himself as having "certain Quaker-tendencies" in this letter, there was also the fact that he was personally interested in the "silent worship" of the Quakers. He was eager to introduce this form of worship to all Protestant denominations, not just the Lutheran denomination. According to Kraatz, Otto helped his best friend, Swedish church historian Emanuel Lindeholm (1872–1937), to create a new form of worship. In 1920, Otto published an article on Quaker worship, "Silent Worship" (Schweigender Dienst), in the journal *Die Christliche Welt*. In any case, this article was renamed "Sakramentales Schweigen" in Otto's book *Sünde und Urschuld* (1932). Cf. Rudolf Otto, "Schweigender Dienst," *Die Christliche Welt* 36, 561–5, 1920; "Sakramentales Schweigen," *Sünde und Urschuld und andere Aufsätze zur Theologie*, München: Verlag C.H. Beck, 1932, S. 185–9. Moreover, in her book *Rudolf Ottos Liturgik*, Katharina Wiefel-Jenner (1958–), a scholar of Christian liturgy, states that it was not a coincidence that he was interested in the worship of the Quakers, which is understood as the "religion of experience" (Religion der Erfahrung). For the main content of faith for Quakers, is not revealed through doctrine, but only through experience. Cf. Katharina Wiefel-Jenner, "Der Schweigende Dienst," in *Rudolf Ottos Liturgik* (Göttingen: Vandenhoeck & Ruprecht, 1997), S. 190–203. In fact, as Jeong Hwa Choi points out, Quakers visited Otto in Marburg in September 1920 and participated in the first international conference of the RMB (Religiöser Menschheitbund), held in 1922. Cf. Jeong Hwa Choi, *Religion*

als "Weltgewissen:" Rudolf Ottos Religiöser Menschheitbund und das Zusammenspiel von Religionsforschung und Religionsbegegnung nach dem Ersten Weltkrieg (Zürich: LIT Verlag, 2013).

3 Rudolf Otto, *Das Heilige* (1917; München: Verlag C.H. Beck, 1963), S. 122–3. Rudolf Otto, *The Idea of the Holy*, translated by John W. Harvey (London: Oxford University Press, 1923), pp. 99–100.

4 For the origin of the Eranos Conference, see Rudolf Ritsema, "The Origins and Opus of Eranos: Reflections at the 55th Conference," *Eranos Jahrbuch*, vol. 56 (Frankfurt am Main: Insel Verlag, 1987). After Rudolf Ritsema declared the conference in 1988 as the last one, he started a new type of meeting with a small group of people being very interested in the *I-Ching*. Some years later, in 2006, a new Eranos Conference was founded; in the course of time, the character and people responsible for this conference changed. Since 2015 to the present, the president of this Eranos Conference has been the psychologist Armin Morich, the director of the C.G. Jung Institute in Dresden.

5 William Jones, "The Third Anniversary Discourse, on the Hindus," in *The Works of Sir William Jones*, vol. 3, London: printed for John Stockdale and John Walker, 1807, p. 34.

6 Toshihiko Izutsu, *God and Man in the Koran: Semantics of the Koranic Weltanschauung* (Tokyo: Keio University Press, 2015), pp. 2–4.

Introduction

1 In regards to the relationship between modern Europe and India, see Knut A. Jacobsen ed., *Brill's Encyclopedia of Hinduism*, vol. IV (Leiden: Brill, 2012); A.L. Basham, *The Wonder That Was India* (New York: Grove Press, 1977); Gavin Flood, *An Introduction to Hinduism* (Cambridge: Cambridge University Press, 1996), pp. 250–73.

2 Cf. Rudolf Otto, *Die Gnadenreligion Indiens und das Christentum: Vergleich und Unterscheidung* (Gotha: L. Klotz, 1930); Rudolf Otto, *India's Religion of Grace and Christianity Compared and Contrasted* (London: Student Christian Movement Press, 1930; New York: Macmillan, 1930).

3 Philip C. Almond, *Rudolf Otto: An Introduction to His Philosophical Theology* (Chapel Hill: The University of North Carolina Press, 1984), p. 123. Cf. Rudolf Otto, "Rāmānuja," *Die Religion in Geschichte und Gegenwart* 4, 1930.

4 Rudolf Otto, *Vischnu-Nārāyana: Texte zur indischen Gottesmystik* (Jena: E. Diederich, 1917), S. 1–4. Regarding his encounter with Vaiṣṇava faith during his first trip to India in 1911, Otto also mentions it at the beginning of the following article. Cf. Rudolf Otto, "Parallelen und Konvergenzen in der Religionsgeschichte," in: *Das Gefühl des Überweltlichen: Sensus numinis* (Munich: C. H. Beck, 1931), S. 1–2.

5 Hans Rollmann, "Rudolf Otto and India," *Religious Studies Review* 5, 1979, p. 199.

6 Joachim Wach, *Types of Religious Experience: Christian and Non-Christian* (Chicago: The University of Chicago Press, 1951), p. 215. For Ernst Troeltsch's perspectives on Christian theology, see his book, *Zur religiösen Lage, Religionsphilosophie und Ethik*, Gesammelte Schriften II (Tübingen: J. C. B. Mohr, 1922). Especially, in regard to Christian theology which incorporated the perspectives of the "religionsgeschichtliche Schule," see Troeltsch's article, "Die Dogmatik der "religionsgeschichtlichen Schule," in Ernst Troeltsch, *Zur religiösen Lage, Religionsphilosophie und Ethik*, Gesammelte Schriften II, S. 500–24. Moreover, in regard to his views of the relationship between Christian theology and the history of religions, see his article, "Wesen der Religion und der Religionswissenschaft," in Ernst Troeltsch, Gesammelte Schriften II, S. 452–99. In order to understand the Christian theological situations in the nineteenth century, see Ernst Troeltsch, "Rückblick auf ein halbes Jahrhundert der theologischen Wissenschaft," Gesammelte Schriften II, S. 193–26.

7 Jonathan Z. Smith, *Imagining Religion: From Babylon to Jonestown* (Chicago: The University of Chicago Press, 1982), p. xi.

8 John B. Carman, *Majesty and Meekness: A Comparative Study of Contrast and Harmony in the Concept of God* (Michigan: William B. Eerdmans Publishing Company, 1994), pp. 35–6.

9 Cf. Gustav Mensching, "Rudolf Otto und die Religionsgeschichte," in: *Rudolf Ottos Bedeutung für die Religionswissenschaft und Theologie heute* (Leiden: Brill, 1971), S. 49–69. Noriyoshi Tamaru, *The History and Task of the History of Religions* [in Japanese, *Shūkyōgaku no rekishi to kadai*] (Yamamoto Shoten, 1987), pp. 250–1. Moreover, Gustav Mensching's main work is *Die Religion: Erscheinungsformen, Strukturtypen und Lebensgesetze* (Wilhelm Goldmann, GmbH, 1984).

10 Friedrich Heiler's main work is *Das Gebet: Eine religionsgeschichtliche und religionspsychologische Untersuchung*, 5. Auflage (1923), München: Ernst Reinhardt Verlag, 1969.

11 Cf. Joachim Wach, edited with an Introduction by Joseph M. Kitagawa, *The Comparative Study of Religions* (New York: Columbia University Press, 1958), pp. xxi–xxii. Regarding Otto's History of Religions, see Wach's article, "Rudolf Otto and the Idea of the Holy," in: Joachim Wach, *Types of Religious Experience: Christian and Non-Christian* (Chicago: The University of Chicago Press, 1951), pp. 209–27.

12 In this regard, see Mircea Eliade, translated from the French by Willard R. Trask, *The Sacred and the Profane: the Nature of Religion* (New York: A Harvest Book, Harcourt, Brace & World, Inc., 1959), p. 10.

13 The international conference on Rudolf Otto, "Rudolf Otto: Theologie-Religionsphilosophie-Religionsgeschichte," was organized by Professor Jörg Lauster (1966–), who was the professor of Systematic Theology at Marburg University at

that time and a professor of München University at present. At the beginning of this conference, two scholars delivered the keynote speeches; one was Dr. Martin Kraatz, the former director of Marburg Religionskundliche Sammlung, editing Otto's letters, and the other was Professor Gregory D. Alles, author of *Rudolf Otto: Autobiographical and Social Essays* (1996). The result of this international conference was published as *Rudolf Otto: Theologie-Religionsphilosophie-Religionsgeschichte* (Berlin: De Gruyter, 2014).

14 Yoshitsugu Sawai, "Rudolf Otto's View of Indian Religious Thought," in Jörg Lauster, et al., *Rudolf Otto: Theologie-Religionsphilosophie-Religionsgeschichte* (Berlin: De Gruyter, 2014), S. 539–50.

15 This AAR panel, "Genealogies of the Numinous," was organized by Gregory D. Alles, a professor of McDaniel College. In this panel, I presented the paper, "Rudolf Otto's Perspective of Indian Religious Thought as a Type of Mysticism."

16 Wolfgang Gantke und Vladislav Serikov hrsg., *100 Jahre "Das Heilige:" Beiträge zu Rudolf Ottos Grundlagenwerk*, Theion: Studien zur Religionskultur, Band 32 (Frankfurt am Main: Peter Lang GmbH, 2017).

17 Rudolf Otto, *Das Heilige: Über das Irrationale in der Idee des Göttlichen und sein Verhältnis zum Rationalen*, mit einer Einführung zu Leben und Werk Rudolf Ottos von Jörg Lauster und Peter Schüz und einem Nachwort von Hans Joas (München: C.H. Beck, 2014). Cf. Hans Joas, Nachwort: "Säkulare Heiligkeit: Wie aktuell ist Rudolf Otto?" p. 257.

18 Philip C. Almond, *Rudolf Otto: An Introduction to His Philosophical Theology* (Chapel Hill: The University of North Carolina Press, 1984), p. ix.

19 Gregory D. Alles, *Rudolf Otto: Autobiographical and Social Essays* (Berlin: Mouton de Gruyter, 1996), p. 1. Cf. Gregory D. Alles, "Rudolf Otto and the Politics of Utopia," *Religion* vol. 21, 1991, pp. 235–56.

20 Todd A. Gooch, *The Numinous and Modernity: An Interpretation of Rudolf Otto's Philosophy of Religion* (Berlin: Walter de Gruyter, 2000), p. 27.

21 Melissa Raphael, *Rudolf Otto and the Concept of Holiness* (Oxford: Clarendon Press, 1997), p. 17.

22 S.P. Dubey, *Rudolf Otto and Hinduism* (Varanasi: Bharatiya Vidya Prakashan, 1969), p. 4.

23 Here, I would like to mention only the main works on Rudolf Otto in contemporary Japan: Toshimaro Hanazono, *Introduction to the Phenomenology of Religion* [in Japanese, *Shūkyō-genshōgaku nyūmon*, Tokyo: Heibon-sha, 2016]; Tsuyoshi Maeda, *The Ground of Holiness: Traveling Otto* [in Japanese, *Sei no daichi: tabisuru Otto*, Tokyo: Kokusho-kankōkai, 2016]; Toshihiko Kimura, *Rudolf Otto and Zen* [in Japanese, *Rudolf otto to zen*, Daitō-shuppansha, 2011]; Satoko Fujiwara, *The Concept of "Holiness" and Modernity: Toward a Critical Study of Comparative Religion* [in Japanese, *'Sei'-gainen to kindai: hihanteki hikaku-shūkyōgaku ni mukete*, Taishō-

daigaku-shuppankai, 2005]; Chie Warashina, "Between Theology and the History of Religions: on R. Otto, Das Heilige" [in Japanese, *Shingaku to shūkyōgaku no hazama de: R. Otto, Seinarumono o megutte*, the Doctoral dissertation, submitted to Tokyo University of Foreign Studies, 2017].

Chapter 1

1 Eric J. Sharpe, *Comparative Religion: A History* (Illinois: Open Court, second edition: 1986), p. 167.
2 Robert A. Orsi, "The Problem of the Holy," in Robert A. Orsi ed., *The Cambridge Companion to Religious Studies* (New York: Cambridge University Press, 2012), pp. 96–7.
3 R. Otto, "Vita for the First Examination in Theology," in Gregory D. Alles ed., *Rudolf Otto: Autobiographical and Social Essays* (Berlin: Mouton de Gruyter, 1996), p. 51.
4 Ibid., p. 54. Cf. Philip C. Almond, *Rudolf Otto*, p. 11.
5 Gregory D. Alles ed., *Rudolf Otto: Autobiographical and Social Essays*, p. 54. Friedrich Schleiermacher, *Über die Religion: Reden an die Gebildeten unter ihren Verächtern*, ed. Rudolf Otto (Göttingen: Vandenhoeck & Ruprecht, [1799] 1899).
6 Rudolf Otto, *Die Anschauung vom heiligen Geiste bei Luther: Eine historisch-dogmatische Untersuchung* (Göttingen: Vandenhoeck & Ruprecht, 1898). Cf. Joachim Wach, "Rudolf Otto and the Idea of the Holy," in: Joachim Wach, *Types of Religious Experience: Christian and Non-Christian*, 1951, p. 213.
7 Rudolf Otto, *Leben und Wirken Jesu nach historisch-kritische Auffassung* (Göttingen: Vandenhoeck & Ruprecht, 1902), S. 5; Rudolf Otto (tr. Henry James Whitby), *Life and Ministry of Jesus According to the Historical and Critical Method* (Chicago: The Open Court Publishing Co., 1908), Preface. Cf. Friedrich Heiler, "The Experience of the Divine," *Journal of the Liberal Ministry*, vol. I, no. 1, 1961, p. 3.
8 When he was in an unstable position as a Privatdozent, Otto was worried about the future of his career. At that time, he sent a letter to Ernst Troeltsch in Heidelberg for consultation. Then, Troeltsch sent a letter of encouragement to him and invited him to Heidelberg. In his letter to Otto, dated January 17, 1904, according to Almond's quotation, Troeltsch wrote:

> You must now, above all, pull yourself together, and call to mind the views that you hold for yourself as a man, quite apart from any and every theology. You must have views that are for your own personal use. What you do with theology, we will want to look further into . . . If it doesn't go well, then you will just have to begin something different. For the moment, attend in general only to peace of mind and the strength of the inner man.

Cf. Philip C. Almond, *Rudolf Otto*, pp. 15–16. Cf. HS. 797/800. Troeltsch an Otto. November 17, 1904.

9 Robert F. Davidson, *Rudolf Otto's Interpretation of Religion* (Princeton: Princeton University Press, 1947), p. 134.

10 In regard to his decline of the invitation to the Gifford Lectures, see Gregory D. Alles ed., Rudolf Otto: Autobiographical and Social Essays (Berlin: Mouton de Gruyter, 1996), p. 253. Regarding the decline of the invitation from the University of Calcutta, see Friedrich Heiler, "The Experience of the Divine," *Journal of the Liberal Ministry*, vol. I, no. 1, 1961, p. 3.

11 "Rudolf Otto, National Liberal candidate (1913)," Gregory D. Alles ed., *Rudolf Otto*, pp. 115–28.

12 Rudolf Otto, "Towards the Reform of Divine Service," *The Hibbert Journal*, vol. 29, no. 1, p. 2. This article is included in Otto's *Religious Essays* with the title of "Towards a Liturgical Reform." Cf. Rudolf Otto, *Zur Erneuerung und Ausgestaltung des Gottesdienstes* (Gießen: Alfred Döpelmann, 1925).

13 Robert F. Davidson, *Rudolf Otto's Interpretation of Religion*, 1947, p. 5. Cf. Rudolf Otto, "Towards the Reform of Divine Service," p. 1.

14 HS. (Handschriften Otto-Nachlaβ Universitäts-Bibliothek, Marburg) 797/178. Cf. Philip C. Almond, *Rudolf Otto*, p. 25.

15 Philip C. Almond, *Rudolf Otto*, p. 25, 147 (note 85).

16 HS. 797/170, 171. Cf. Philip C. Almond, *Rudolf Otto*, p. 25.

17 Rudolf Otto, *Kantisch-Fries'sche Religionsphilosophie und ihre Anwendung auf die Theologie*, S. 195; *The Philosophy of Religion Based on Kant and Fries*, 1931, p. 225.

18 Rudolf Otto, *Religious Essays: A Supplement to "The Idea of the Holy"* (London: Oxford University Press, 1931), p. 30.

19 Rudolf Otto, *Kantisch-Fries'sche Religionsphilosophie und ihre Anwendung auf die Theologie*, S. 192.

20 Rudolf Otto, *Vischnu-Nārāyana: Texte zur indischen Gottesmystik* (Jena: E. Diederich, 1917), S. 7.

21 Kurt Rudolph, "Religionsgeschichtliche Schule," *Encyclopedia of Religion*, edited by Mircea Eliade, vol. XII (New York: Macmillan, 1987), pp. 294–5.

22 Hiroshi Kubota, "The Religiousness of the 'History of Religions:' the Religionsgeschichtliche Schule as a religious movement and its strategy of 'mission'" [in Japanese, *'Shūkyō-shi' no shūkyō-sei: shūkyō-undō toshiteno shūkyōshi-gakuha to sono 'fukyō' senryaku*], in *What is the History of Religion* [in Japanese, *Shūkyō-shi towa nani ka*], edited by Hiroshi Ichikawa, Kazuo Matsumura, and Kazuko Watanabe, vol. 1 (Tokyo: Lithon, 2008), pp. 69–70. Moreover, in regard to the development of the Religionsgeschichtliche Schule and its characteristics, see Kurt Rudolph, "Religionsgeschichtliche Schule," *Encyclopedia of Religion*, vol. XII, pp. 293–6.

23 Ibid., p. 70.

24 Rudolf Otto, *Die Gnadenreligion Indiens und das Christentum: Vergleich und Unterscheidung* (Gotha: L. Klotz, 1930), S. 42–3; Rudolf Otto, *India's Religion of Grace and Christianity, Compared and Contrasted* (London: Student Christian Movement Press; New York: Macmillan, 1930), p. 61.

25 Adolf von Harnack, "Die Aufgabe der theologischen Fakultäten und die allgemeine Religionsgeschichte," (Berlin: Gistav Scjade (Otto Francke), 1901). Cf. Kurt Nowak ed., *Adolf von Harnack als Zeitgenosse: Reden und Schriften aus den Jahren des Kaiserreichs und der Weimarer Republik*, vol. 1 (Berlin: de Gruyter, 1996), S. 797–815. Cf. Eric J. Sharpe, *Comparative Religion: A History* (Illinois: Open Court, Second edition: 1986), pp. 127–8.

26 Hiroshi Kubota, "Among Politics, Religion, and Scholarship: 'Religionswissenschaft' in Germany under Naziism" [in Japanese, *Seiji-shūkyō-gakumon no hazamade: nachizumu-ki doitsu no shūkyōgaku*] in *Talking Religion Again: rethinking of the modern categories* [in Japanese, *Shūkyō o katari-naosu: kindaiteki kategorī no saikō*], edited by Junichi Isomae and Talal Asad (Tokyo: Misuzu-shobō, 2006), pp. 58–9.

27 Adolf von Harnack, "Die Bedeutung der theologischen Fakultäten," Kurt Nowak ed., *Adolf von Harnack als Zeitgenosse*, vol. 1, S. 856–74.

28 Hiroshi Kubota, "Among Politics, Religion, and Scholarship," pp. 59–60.

29 Rudolf Otto, *Das Gefühl des Überweltlichen: Sensus numinis* (München: C.H. Beck, 1932), S. 58.

30 Noriyoshi Tamaru, *The History and Task of the History of Religions* [in Japanese, *Shūkyōgaku no rekishi to kadai*], p. 239.

31 Friedrich Heiler, "The Experience of the Divine," *Journal of the Liberal Ministry*, vol. I, no. 1, 1961, pp. 4–5.

32 Rudolf Otto, *Kantisch-Fries'sche Religionsphilosophie und ihre Anwendung auf die Theologie*, S. 83.

33 Jakob Friedrich Fries, *Wissen, Glaube und Ahndung* (Jena, 1805; Göttingen: Verlag "Öffentliches Leben," 1931), S. 176. Especially for the relationships among knowledge, faith, and intuitive apprehension, see Ibid., S. 61–76.

34 Ibid., S. 76.

35 Ibid., S. 176–7.

36 Rudolf Otto, *Kantisch-Fries'sche Religionsphilosophie und ihre Anwendung auf die Theologie*, S. 8–9.

37 Chie Warashina, "Between Theology and the History of Religions: on R. Otto, Das Heilige" [in Japanese, *Shingaku to shūkyōgaku no hazama de: R. Otto, Seinarumono o megutte*], 2017, pp. 117–20, 156.

38 Tsuyoshi Maeda, *The Ground of Holiness: Traveling Otto* [in Japanese, *Sei no daichi: tabisuru Otto*], 2016, pp. 139–40.

39 Todd A. Gooch, *The Numinous and Modernity: An Interpretation of Rudolf Otto's Philosophy of Religion* (Berlin: Walter de Gruyter, 2000), p. 54. Cf. J. Wendland, "Neufriesianismus," *Die Religion in Geschichte und Gegenwart*, 2nd ed., vol. IV (Tübingen: Mohr/Siebeck, 1930), columns 499–500.

40 Nathan Söderblom, "Holiness," J. Hastings ed., *Encyclopaedia of Religion and Ethics*, VI, 1913, p. 740, 731. Cf. Eric J. Sharpe, *Comparative Religion: A History*, pp.159–60; Eric J. Sharpe, *Nathan Söderblom and the Study of Religion* (Chapel Hill: The University of North Carolina Press, 1990), pp. 168–70.

41 Joachim Wach, "Rudolf Otto and the Idea of the Holy," in: Joachim Wach, *Types of Religious Experience: Christian and Non-Christian*, 1951, p. 213.

42 Hugh Nicholson, *Comparative Theology and the Problem of Religious Rivalry* (Oxford: Oxford University Press, 2011), pp. xiv–xv. In regard to the perspectives of "comparative theology," see Francis X. Clooney S.J., *Comparative Theology: Deep Learning Across Religious Borders* (Chichester: Wiley-Blackwell, 2010); Francis X. Clooney S.J. ed., *The New Comparative Theology: Interreligious Insights from the Next Generation* (London: T & T Clark International, 2010).

43 Ibid., pp. 110–11.

Chapter 2

1 Regarding the detailed content of his trips, see Tsuyoshi Maeda, *The Ground of Holiness: Traveling Otto* [in Japanese, *Sei no daichi: tabisuru Otto*] (Tokyo: Kokusho kankōkai, 2016). Hans-Jürgen Greschat, a scholar of religious studies at Marburg University, remarks that it is noteworthy that in the Christian theological world of Germany, Otto went on journeys to collect research materials. Cf. Hans-Jürgen Greschat, "On Rudolf Otto the Traveller," *Religious Studies in Dialogue: Essays in Honour of Albert C. Moore*, edited by Maurice Andrew, Peter Matheson and Simon Rae (Faculty of Theology, University of Otago, Dunedin, New Zealand, 1991), pp. 1–8.

2 Reinhard Shinzer, "Rudolf Otto—Entwurf einer Biographie," *Rudolf Otto's Bedeutung für die Religionswiss*enschaft und die Theologie Heute, hrsg. von Ernst Benz (Leiden: Brill, 1971), S. 3.

3 Tsuyoshi Maeda, "The Fundamental Ground of Holiness" [in Japanese, *Sei no genkyō*], *Journal of Religious Studies* [in Japanese, *Shūkyō kenkyū*], no. 314, 1997, p. 2.

4 Philip C. Almond, *Rudolf Otto*, pp. 18–19. This passage originally appeared in *Die christliche Welt* 25 (1911), S. 709. No date is given in his travel letter, but May 20 and 27 in 1911 were Saturdays.

5 HS. 797/572, 19. Otto an Johanne Ottmer. Nov. 7. 1911. Johanne Ottmer, who was born in 1861, studied medicine and married a doctor of medicine, Ernst Ottmer. She became a widow in 1904 upon her husband's death, and then lived in a small

apartment with her only daughter, Margarete Ottmer. After Otto's mother died, however, the sister and daughter moved into Otto's apartment and lived with him until 1937 when he passed away.

6 OA. (Rudolf-Otto-Archiv, Marburg) 379. S. 8f. Quotation from Tsuyoshi Maeda, *The Ground of Holiness: Traveling Otto*, p. 193.

7 Rudolf Otto, *The Original Gītā: The Song of the Supreme Exalted One*, translated and edited by J.E. Turner (London: George Allen and Unwin Ltd, 1939, p. 9. In regard to Otto's translation of *Bhagavadgītā*, there are the following three works; *Die Urgestalt der Bhagavad-Gītā*, Tübingen: J.C.B. Mohr, 1934; *Der Sang des Hehr-Erhabenen: Die Bhagavad-Gītā*, Stuttgart: W. Kohlhammer, 1934; *Die Lehrtraktate der Bhagavad-Gītā*, Tübingen: J.C.B. Mohr, 1934. Although the English translation of *Bhagavadgītā* was published after his death in 1939, he wrote the "Author's Preface" of this book in 1935 before he passed away.

8 Ibid., p. 10.

9 Ibid., p. 14.

10 Eric J. Sharpe, *Comparative Religion: A History* (London: Gerald Duckworth & Co. Ltd., 1975), p. 167, note 50. Franklin Edgerton, *The Bhagavadgītā* (Cambridge: Harvard University Press, 1944), pp. xiii–xiv.

11 In regard to Garbe's theory, see the introduction of his German translation of the *Bhagavadgītā*. Cf. Richard Garbe, *Die Bhagavadgītā* (Leipzig: H. Haessel Verlag, 1905), pp. 6–18. Cf. Rudolf Otto, *Die Gnadenreligion Indiens und das Christentum: Vergleich und Unterscheidung* (Gotha: L. Klotz, 1930), S. 16; *India's Religion of Grace and Christianity, Compared and Contrasted*, pp. 18–19. Moreover, in regard to the responses from the scholars of Indian philosophy at that time, see Franklin Edgerton, *The Bhagavadgītā* (Cambridge: Harvard University Press, 1944), pp. xiii–xiv; S. Radhakrishnan, "Introductory Essay," *The Bhagavadgītā* (New York: Harper & Row, 1948), pp. 14–15. For example, in the note of his English translation of the *Bhagavadgītā*, F. Edgerton says: "A pupil of Garbe's, the late Rudolf Otto, has more recently carried dissection of the Gītā to a far greater extreme. I consider his work negligible." In regard to Otto's German translation of *The Bhagavadgītā*, S.P. Dubey argues in detail. Cf. S.P. Dubey, *Rudolf Otto and Hinduism* (Varanasi: Bharatiya Vidya Prakashan, 1969). In addition, according to Angelika Malinar, a professor of Indian studies at the University of Zurich, Garbe's translation and interpretation of the *Bhagavadgītā* marked the beginning of the most productive period of research on the *Bhagavadgītā;* Garbe's view incited new attempts to reconstruct the different text layers that make up the *Bhagavadgītā*. Cf. Angelika Malinar, "Bhagavadgītā," *Brill's Encyclopedia of Hinduism*, vol. II: *Sacred Texts and Languages, Ritual Traditions, Arts, Concepts* (Leiden: Brill, 2010), pp. 104–5.

12 Rudolf Otto, *Das Heilige*, 1917; München, 1963, S. 170–1; *The Idea of the Holy*, translated by John W. Harvey (London: Oxford University Press, 1923), pp. 141–2.

13 Rudolf Otto, *Sünde und Urschuld und andere Aufsätze zur Theologie* (München: C.H. Beck'sche Verlagsbuchhandlung, 1932), S. 61.

14 Rudolf Otto, *Vischnu-Nārāyana: Texte zur indischen Gottesmystik* (Jena: E. Diederich, 1917), S. 7.

15 *Roku-dai shinpō* (literally in English, "six great news"), no. 445, April 7, 1912, p. 90.

16 In regard to Otto's visit to Mt. Kōya, see *Roku-dai shinpō*, no. 452, May 26, 1912.

17 Rudolf Otto, "Numinoses Erlebnis im Zazen," in *Das Gefühl des Überweltlichen*, 1932, S. 243. In regard to Otto's description that he visited a Zen Buddhist temple in Tokyo, it seems that he may have visited it in Kyoto, not in Tokyo.

18 Toshihiko Kimura, *Rudolf Otto and Zen* [in Japanese, *Rudolf otto to zen*] (Tokyo: Daitō-shuppan-sha, 2011), p. 17. As Kimura points out, Otto obtained detailed information about Zen from D.T. Suzuki's article, "The Meditation Hall and the Monkish Discipline," *The Eastern Buddhist*, vol. II, 1–2, 1922. In any case, Kimura confirms that a Zen master, whom Otto met in Kyoto, was Mokurai Takeda at the Kenninji Temple of Rinzai Buddhist Sect; it is clear from the fact that in December 1930 when Mokurai Takeda passed away, his successor Ekijū Takeda presented his relic (Andenken) to Marburg. For details, refer to his book, p. 27.

19 Schûej Ôhasama, *Zen: Der lebendige Buddhismus in Japan* (Gotha: Leopold Klotz Verlag, 1925).

20 In this regard, see Jeong Hwa Choi, *Religion als "Weltgewissen:" Rudolf Ottos Religiöser Menschheitsbund und das Zusammenspiel von Religionsforschung und Religionsbegegnung nach dem Ersten Weltkrieg*. Studien und Dokumentationen zur praktischen Religionswissenschaft, vol. 5 (Zürich: Lit Verlag, 2013).

21 Martin Kraatz, "Wirkungsstätten der Religionswissenschaft: die Religionskundliche Sammlung in Marburg," *Deutsche Vereinigung für Religionsgeschichte* 12, Mitteilungsblatt, 1979, S. 3. In order to clarify the importance of materiality for understanding religion, I discussed it while comparing the Tenri University Sankōkan Museum, founded by Shōzen Nakayama, i.e., the second Shinbashira of Tenrikyo, with the Marburger Religionskundliche Sammlung, founded by Rudolf Otto. Cf. Yoshitsugu Sawai, "The Significance of Materiality for Religious Studies," in Saburo S. Morishita ed., *Materiality in Religion and Culture: Tenri University-Marburg University Joint Research Project* (Zürich: LIT Verlag, 2016), pp. 15–24.

22 Martin Kraatz, "Religionskundliche Sammlung 60 Jahre alt," *Universität Zeitung*, Nr.191, Nov. 12, 1987.

23 Tsuyoshi Maeda, *The Ground of Holiness: Traveling Otto* [in Japanese, *Sei no daichi: tabisuru Otto*], p. 268.

24 Gregory D. Alles, "The Rebirth of Cultural Colonialism as Religionswissenschaft: Rudolf Otto's Import House," *Temenos*, vol. 43, no. 1, The Finnish Society for the Study of Religion, 2007, p. 34; Gregory D. Alles ed., *Rudolf Otto: Autobiographical and Social Essays*, p. 128. The first three volumes, co-opted into the *Quellen der*

Religionsgeschichte from an earlier series, the *Religionsurkunden der Völker*, are as follows:

1. Johannes Warneck, *Die Religion der Batak: ein Paradigma für die animistischen Religionen des Indischen Archipels* (Göttingen: Vandenhoeck & Ruprecht, 1909).
2. Hans Haas, "*Amida Buddha unsere Zuflucht: Urkunden zum Verständnis des japanischen Sukhāvatī-Buddhismus* (Göttingen: Vandenhoeck & Ruprecht, 1910).
3. Jakob Spieth, *Die Religion der Eweer in Süd-Togo* (Göttingen: Vandenhoeck & Ruprecht, 1911).

25 Rudolf Otto, *Das Gefühl des Überweltlichen: Sensus numinis* (München: C.H. Beck, 1932), S. 58.

26 Philip C. Almond, *Rudolf Otto*, p. 5. Ernst Benz, "Rudolf Otto als Theologe und Persönlichkeit," in: *Rudolf Otto's Bedeutung für die Religionswissenschaft und die Theologie Heute*, herausgegeben von Ernst Benz (Leiden: E.J. Brill, 1971.), S. 32–3.

27 David Morgan ed., *Religion and Material Culture: The Matter of Belief* (London: Routledge, 2010), p. 8. In his article, Morgan denotes five discrete, but clearly interrelated themes in the recent study of religion: (1) the felt-life of belief, (2) embodiment, (3) space and ritual, (4) performance and practice, and (5) aesthetics. Cf. David Morgan, "Materiality, Social Analysis, and the Study of Religions," in *Religion and Material Culture*, pp. 55–74.

28 Elisabeth Arweck and William Keenan ed., *Materializing Religion: Expression, Performance and Ritual* (London: Ashgate, 2006), p. 1.

29 Cf. Yoshitsugu Sawai, "The Significance of Materiality for Religious Studies," in *Materiality in Religion and Culture: Tenri University-Marburg University Joint Research Project*, edited by Saburo S. Morishita (Zürich: LIT Verlag, 2016), pp. 15–24.

30 Rudolf Otto, "Ist eine Universalreligion wünschenswert und möglich? Und wenn, wie kann man sie erreichen?" *Die Christliche Welt*, Jg. 27. 1913. Sp. 1237–43.

31 Rudolf Otto, "Menschheitsbund, Religiöser" in *Die Religion in Geschichte und Gegenwart*, Zweite Auflage, Dritter Band (1929), S. 2122–3. Cf. Philip C. Almond, *Rudolf Otto*, pp. 20–1; Gregory D. Alles, "Rudolf Otto and the Politics of Utopia," *Religion*, no. 21, pp. 235–56.

32 "Von Celon zum Himalaya von Birger Forell," Uppsala, 1929; aus dem Schwedischen übertragen von Ursula Lorenz, 1987. *Report* from Dr. Rudolf Otto and Rev. Birger Forell on their work for the Universal Religious Peace Conference, 1927, HS.797/725. Cf. Tsuyoshi Maeda, *The Ground of Holiness* [in Japanese, *Sei no daichi*], pp. 220–31. In regard to the life of Birger Forell who accompanied Otto's trip, see Martin Kraatz's lecture in Berlin on July 7, 2008. Cf. Martin Kraatz, "Birger Forell: Der Mensch—in seinen Marburger Wurzeln und in dem, was daraus wuchs" (Berlin, Vaterunser-

Kirchengemeinde, 7. Juli 2008); Martin Kraatz, "Birger Forell 1893–1993," *Alma Mater Philippina* (Marburger Universitätsbund e.V., Sommersemester 1994), S. 4–8.

33 Rudolf Otto, "An Inter-Religious League," *The Hibbert Journal*, vol. 29, no. 4, 1931, pp. 588–9.

34 Ibid., pp. 588, 593.

35 Cf. Eric J. Sharpe, *Nathan Söderblom and the Study of Religion* (Chapel Hill: The University of North Carolina Press, 1990).

36 Francis X. Clooney, S. J., *Comparative Theology: Deep Learning Across Religious Borders* (Chichester: Wiley-Blackwell, 2010), p. 19. Hugh Nicholson, "The New Comparative Theology and the Problem of Theological Hegemonism," in *The New Comparative Theology: Interreligious Insights from the Next Generation*, edited by Francis X. Clooney, S.J. (London: T & T Clark International, 2010), p. 52. In regard to his term "comparative theology," Francis X. Clooney, S.J. says on page 19 of his *Comparative Theology*:

> I found the term "comparative theology" to be useful in my decades of teaching in the Theology Department at Boston College, a Catholic and Jesuit institution. When I arrived there in 1984, some were still of the view that theology and religious studies were disciplines separate and at cross-purposes; the study of world religions was of course part of the latter, not the former, so interest in other religions was a sure sign that one was not a theologian. Given my background and expertise, I knew I was both a theologian and a scholar of Hinduism, and firmly believed that these distinctive disciplines were mutually enriching. To commit myself to theology and a double learning, I began describing my work as "comparative theology."

Chapter 3

1 Cf. Joachim Ritter ed., "Heilig," *Historisches Wörterbuch der Philosophie*, Bd. 3 (Basel/Stuttgart: Schwabe & Co. Verlag, 1974).

2 Friedrich Heiler, "The Experience of the Divine," *Journal of the Liberal Ministry*, vol. I, no. 1, 1961, p. 4.

3 Ernst Troeltsch, *Die Absolutheit des Christentums und die Religionsgeschichte* (Tübingen: J.C.B. Mohr, 1912). Friedrich Heiler, "The Experience of the Divine," *Journal of the Liberal Ministry*, vol. I, no. 1, 1961, p. 3.

4 The first Japanese translation of *Das Heilige* was published in 1927 by Idea-shoin (later, Iwanami-bunko); its revised edition was published from Iwanami-bunko in 1968. Since then, two new translations have been published; one from Sōgen-sha in 2005 and the other from Iwanami-bunko in 2010.

5 Toshimaro Hanazono, *Introduction to the Phenomenology of Religion* [in Japanese, *Shūkyō-genshōgaku nyūmon*, 2016], p. 43. Warashina also points out that for Otto himself, *Das Heilige* was certainly a Christian theological work. Cf. Chie Warashina, "Between Theology and the History of Religions: on R. Otto, Das Heilige" [in Japanese, *Shingaku to shūkyōgaku no hazama de: R. Otto, Seinarumono o megutte*, 2017], p. 240.
6 In relation to why Otto was regarded as one of the pioneers of the phenomenology of religion, Hanazono says it was probably derived from Max Scheler's influences. Cf. Toshimaro Hanazono, ibid., p. 44.
7 HS. (Handschriften Otto-Nachlaβ Universitäts-Bibliothek, Marburg) 797/794: Edmund Husserl, Brief an Rudolf Otto (5.3.1919). H. W. Schütte, *Religion und Christentum in der Theologie Rudolf Ottos* (Berlin: de Gruyter, 1969), S. 139–42. Tsuyoshi Maeda, ibid., pp. 272–3.
8 Max Scheler, *Vom Ewigen im Menschen*, 1921, Gesammelte Werke Band 5 (Bern, 1954), S. 141.
9 Rudolf Otto, *The Idea of the Holy*, translated by John W. Harvey, 1923 (Oxford: Oxford University Press, 1977), p. 7; *Das Heilige*, 1917 (München: Verlag C.H. Beck, 1963), S. 7.
10 Max Scheler, *Vom Ewigen im Menschen*, Maria Scheler (ed.), *Gesammelte Werke V* (Bern: Francke Verlag, 1954), S. 141, 167.
11 Douglas Allen, *Structure and Creativity in Religion* (The Hague: Mouton Publishers, 1978), p. 60.
12 Kurt Rudolf, *Die Religionswissenschaft an der Leipziger Universität*, Leipzig, 1962, S. 55f.; "Die Problematik der Religionswissenschaft als akademisches Lehrfach," *Kairos* 9, S. 34.
13 Robert F. Davidson, *Rudolf Otto's Interpretation of Religion* (Princeton: Princeton University Press, 1947), p. 9.
14 Noriyoshi Tamaru, *The History and Task of History of Religions* [in Japanese, Shūkyōgaku no rekishi to kadai, 1987], p. 238.
15 Robert F. Davidson, *Rudolf Otto's Interpretation of Religion*, pp. 10–11.
16 Philip Almond, "Rudolf Otto and the Kantian Tradition," *Neue Zeitschrift für Systematicsche Theologie und Religionsphilosophie* 25, 1983, pp. 52–3. Almond notes that it has been said that there is a sharp break between the first half of *Das Heilige* (a phenomenological analysis up to Chapter 13 in the English translation of *The Idea of the Holy*) and the second half of the same book (a philosophical analysis starting from Chapter 14 in the English translation of the same work). Cf. P. Seifert, *Die Religionsphilosophie bei Rudolf Otto* (Düsseldorf: C.H. Nolte, 1936), pp. 90f.
17 Rudolf Otto, "Foreword by the Author," *The Idea of the Holy* (London: Oxford University Press, 1923), p. xxi. Cf. Rudolf Otto, *Sünde und Urschuld* (München: C.H. Beck, 1932), S. 190.

18 Mircea Eliade, *The Sacred and the Profane: The Nature of Religion*, translated by Willard R. Trask (New York: Harcourt, Brace & World, 1959), pp. 8–10.

19 R. Otto, *Das Heilige*, S. 5; *The Idea of the Holy*, p. 5.

20 R. Otto, *Das Heilige*, S. 6; *The Idea of the Holy*, p. 6.

21 R. Otto, *Das Heilige*, S. 6–7; *The Idea of the Holy*, p. 7.

22 R. Otto, *Das Heilige*, S. 13; *The Idea of the Holy*, p. 12.

23 R. Otto, *Das Heilige*, S. 11; *The Idea of the Holy*, pp.10–11.

24 R. Otto, *Das Heilige*, S.11; R. Otto, *Das Gefühl des Überweltlichen: sensus numinis*, 1932, S. 327. Cf. Robert F. Davidson, *Rudolf Otto's Interpretation of Religion*, pp. 22–3.

25 R. Otto, "Foreword by the Author," *The Idea of the Holy*, p. xxi. Cf. R. Otto, Introduction, *Religious Essays*, p. vi.

26 R. Otto, *Das Heilige*, S.1; *The Idea of the Holy*, p. 1.

27 Ibid.

28 R. Otto, *Das Heilige*, S.1–2; *The Idea of the Holy*, pp. 1–2.

29 Ibid.

30 Jörg Lauster, "Religion as Feeling: Schleiermacher's Program as a Task for Theology," Dietrich Korsch and Amber L. Griffioen eds., *Interpreting Religion: The Significance of Friedrich Schleiermacher's Reden über die Religion for Religious Studies and Theology* (Tübingen: Mohr Siebeck, 2011), p. 81.

31 R. Otto, *Das Heilige*, S. 10; *The Idea of the Holy*, p. 9.

32 R. Otto, *Das Heilige*, S. 12; *The Idea of the Holy*, p. 11.

33 Jakob Friedrich Fries, *Wissen, Glaube und Ahndung* (Göttingen: Öffentliches Leben, 1931), S. 175, 235; Rudolf Otto, *Kantisch-Fries'sche Religionsphilosophie und ihre Anwendung auf die Theologie* (Tübingen: J.C.B. Mohr, 1921), S. 111–13. As Almond points out, the word "feeling" (*Ahndung*) is a classic term of the modern German word *Ahnung*. In his *Kantisch-Fries'sche Religionsphilosophie und ihre Anwendung auf die Theologie*, Otto uses the word *Ahnung*, but in *Das Heilige* and his later writings, he uses the word *Ahndung*. Cf. Philip C. Almond, "Rudolf Otto and the Kantian Tradition," p. 57.

34 Philip C. Almond, "Rudolf Otto and the Kantian Tradition," *Neue Zeitschrift für Systematicsche Theologie und Religionsphilosophie* 25, p. 58.

35 R. Otto, Rudolf Otto, *Das Heilige*, S. 42; *The Idea of the Holy*, p. 31.

36 R. Otto, *Das Heilige*, S. 42; *The Idea of the Holy*, p. 31.

37 R. Otto, *Das Heilige*, S. 16; *The Idea of the Holy*, pp.14–15.

38 R. Otto, *Das Gefühl des Überweltlichen: sensus numinis*, S. 203.

39 Toshimaro Hanazono, *Introduction to the Phenomenology of Religion* [in Japanese, *Shūkyō-genshōgaku nyūmon*, 2016], p. 77.

40 R. Otto, *Das Heilige*, S. 29; *The Idea of the Holy*, pp. 25–6.

41 R. Otto, *Das Heilige*, S. 31; *The Idea of the Holy*, p. 26.

42 R. Otto, *Das Heilige*, S. 122–3; *The Idea of the Holy*, pp. 99–100.

43 R. Otto, *Das Heilige*, S. 59–60; *The Idea of the Holy*, p. 44.
44 R. Otto, *Das Heilige*, S. 138; *The Idea of the Holy*, p. 113.
45 Toshimaro Hanazono, *Introduction to the Phenomenology of Religion*, p. 58. In regard to Otto's theory of "*a priori*," the historian of religions Michael Pye mentions that in *Das Heilige*, Otto attempted to argue in an "un-Kantian" way that the numinous feeling is "an irrational *a priori*." In this regard, Pye points out that it is different from Troeltsch's view that the *a priori* laws that construct religious ideas exist in reason. Cf. Michael Pye, "Troeltsch and the Science of Religion," in *Ernst Troeltsch: Writings on Theology and Religion*, translated and edited by Robert Morgan and Michael Pye (Atlanta: John Knox Press, 1977), p. 241.
46 Philip C. Almond, "Rudolf Otto and the Kantian Tradition," *Neue Zeitschrift für Systematicsche Theologie und Religionsphilosophie* 25, p. 63.
47 Bernard Häring, "'Das Heilige' Rudolf Ottos in der neueren Kritik," *Geist und Leben*, vol. 24, 1951, p. 66; Philip C. Almond, "Rudolf Otto and the Kantian Tradition," p. 63. In regard to the criticism of Otto's "schematization," see the following works; Philip C. Almond, *Rudolf Otto: An Introduction to His Philosophical Theology* (Chapel Hill: The University of North Carolina Press, 1984), pp. 97–102; Robert F. Davidson, *Rudolf Otto's Interpretation of Religion* (Princeton: Princeton University Press, 1947), pp. 187–92; Melissa Raphael, *Rudolf Otto and the Concept of Holiness* (Oxford: Clarendon Press, 1997), pp. 121–6.
48 Rudolf Otto, *Das Heilige*, S. 61; *The Idea of the Holy*, pp. 45–6.
49 Rudolf Otto, *Das Heilige*, S. 61; *The Idea of the Holy*, pp. 45–6.
50 Robert F. Davidson, *Rudolf Otto's Interpretation of Religion*, p. 187. Cf. Rudolf Otto, *The Idea of the Holy*, pp.144–5; Rudolf Otto, *Das Heilige*, S. 173–4.
51 Joachim Wach, "Rudolf Otto and the Idea of the Holy," in *Types of Religious Experience: Christian and Non-Christian* (Chicago: The University of Chicago Press, 1951), p. 222.
52 Robert F. Davidson, *Rudolf Otto's Interpretation of Religion*, p. 155.
53 Philip C. Almond, "Rudolf Otto and the Kantian Tradition," *Neue Zeitschrift für Systematicsche Theologie und Religionsphilosophie* 25, pp. 66–7. Robert F. Davidson, *Rudolf Otto's Interpretation of Religion*, pp. 155–6.

Chapter 4

1 Kurt Rudolph, "Religionsgeschichtliche Schule," *Encyclopedia of Religion*, edited by Mircea Eliade, vol. XII (New York: Macmillan, 1987), pp. 294–5.
2 Hiroshi Kubota, "The Religiousness of 'the History of Religions:' the History-of-Religions School as a Religious Movement and Its Strategy of 'Mission'" [in Japanese, *Shūkyō-shi no shūkyōsei: shūkyō-undō to shite no shūkyōshi-gakuha to sono 'fukyō'*

senryaku], in: Hiroshi Ichikawa, Kazuo Matsumura, and Kazuko Watanabe ed., *What is the History of Religions* [in Japanese, *Shūkyō-shi to wa nani ka*], vol. 1 (Tokyo: Rithon, 2008), pp. 69–70.
In regard to the development of the History-of-Religions School and its characteristics, see Kurt Rudolph, "Religionsgeschichtliche Schule," *Encyclopedia of Religion*, vol. XII, pp. 293–6.

3 R. Otto, *Das Gefühl des Überweltlichen* (1932), S. 58. Cf. Robert F. Davidson, *Rudolf Otto's Interpretation of Religion* (Princeton: Princeton University Press, 1947), p. 10.

4 In regard to the detailed discussion, see Chapter 6 of this book.

5 Rudolf Otto, *Naturalistische und religiöse Weltansicht* (Tübingen: J. C. B. Mohr, 1904), S. 30.

6 Ibid., S. 212–78.

7 Rudolf Otto, *Kantisch-Fries'sche Religionsphilosophie und ihre Anwendung auf die Theologie* (Tübingen: J. C. B. Mohr, 1909), S. 197.

8 Ibid., S. 195. For example, in his book, *Die Absolutheit des Christentums und die Religionsgeschichte* (Tübingen: JCB Mohr, 1902), E. Troeltsch compares the relationship between Christianity and other religions. Though he considers it from the viewpoint of the comparative study of religions, he essentially asserts the absoluteness of Christianity.

9 Rudolf Otto, "Parallels and Convergences in the History of Religion," in Rudolf Otto, *Religious Essays: A Supplement to "The Idea of the Holy"* (London: Oxford University Press. 1931), p. 107; Rudolf Otto, "Parallelen und Konvergenzen in der Religionsgeschichte," in Rudolf Otto, *Das Gefühl des Überweltlichen (Sensus Numinis)* (München: C.H. Beck'sche Verlag, 1932), S. 296.

10 Rudolf Otto, "Parallels and Convergences in the History of Religion," p. 108. Cf. Rudolf Otto, "Parallelen und Konvergenzen in der Religionsgeschichte," S. 297.

11 Ibid., pp. 108–9. Cf. Rudolf Otto, "Parallelen und Konvergenzen in der Religionsgeschichte," S. 298.

12 Noriyoshi Tamaru, *The History of Religions: Its History and Task* [in Japanese, *Shūkyōgaku no rekishi to kadai*, 1987], pp. 134–6.

13 Ibid., p. 246.

14 Rudolf Otto, "Parallels and Convergences in the History of Religion," p. 96. Cf. Rudolf Otto, "Parallelen und Konvergenzen in der Religionsgeschichte," S. 284. Moreover, see Chapter 17 in Otto, *Das Heilige*, 1917; München, 1963.

15 R. Otto, "Parallels and Convergences in the History of Religion," pp. 99–100. Cf. R. Otto, "Parallelen und Konvergenzen in der Religionsgeschichte," S. 287.

16 R. Otto, "Parallels and Convergences in the History of Religion," p. 103. Cf. R. Otto, "Parallelen und Konvergenzen in der Religionsgeschichte," S. 291.

17 Rudolf Otto, *Siddhānta des Rāmānuja: Ein Text zur indischen Gottesmystik* (Jena: E. Diederich, 1917), S. 2.

18 Rudolf Otto, *Die Gnadenreligion Indiens und das Christentum* (Gotha: L. Klotz, 1930), S. 6; *India's Religion of Grace and Christianity, Compared and Contrasted*, p. 17.

19 Rudolf Otto, *Kantisch-Fries'sche Religionsphilosophie und ihre Anwendung auf die Theologie*, S. 195. Cf. Wilhelm Haubold, *Die Bedeutung der Religionsgeschichte für die Theologie Rudolf Ottos* (Leipzig: Leopold Klotz Verlag, 1940), S. 60.

20 Rudolf Otto, "Parallels and Convergences in the History of Religion," p. 95. Cf. Noriyoshi Tamaru, *The History of Religions: Its History and Task*, pp. 134–5.

21 Philip C. Almond, "Rudolf Otto and Buddhism," in Peter Masefield and Donald Wiebe ed., *Aspects of Religion: Essays in Honour of Ninian Smart* (New York: Peter Lang, 1994), pp. 60–1.

22 Rudolf Otto, "Parallelisms in the Development of Religion East and West," *The Transactions of the Asiatic Society of Japan* 40, 1912, pp. 153–8.

23 Dietz Lange ed., *Nathan Söderblom: Brev-Lettres-Briefe-Letters, A Selection from His Correspondence* (Göttingen: Vandenhoeck & Ruprecht, 2006), p. 425. Cf. Rudolf Otto, *Die Gnadenreligion Indiens und das Christentum: Vergleich und Unterscheidung*, Vorwort, S. iii.

24 Friedrich Heiler, "Die Bedeutung Rudolf Ottos für die vergleichende Religionsgeschichte," in Birger Forell, Heinrich Frick, Friedrich Heiler, *Religionswissenschaft in neuer Sicht* (Marburg: N.G. Elwert, 1951), S. 15–16.

25 Rudolf Otto, "Briefe Rudolf Ottos von seiner Fahrt nach Indien und Ägypten," *Die christliche Welt* 52, no. 24 (1958), cols. 986–7. Cf. *Rudolf Otto: Autobiographical and Social Essays*, translated and edited by Gregory D. Alles (Berlin: Mouton de Bruyter, 1996), pp. 94–6.

Otto's niece, Margarete Ottmer, was the daughter of his sister, Johanne Ottmer. After the death of his sister, Margarete was single for the rest of her life and lived with Otto until his death in 1937.

26 *Report from Dr. Rudolf Otto and Rev. Birger Forell on their work for the Universal Religious Peace Conference*, HS. 797/725, pp. 6, 8 (Marburg University, 1927). Cf. Rudolf Otto, *Die Gnadenreligion Indiens und das Christentum: Vergleich und Unterscheidung*, S. iv; *India's Religion of Grace and Christianity, Compared and Contrasted*, pp. 7–8.

27 Rudolf Otto, *Die Gnadenreligion Indiens und das Christentum*, S. 10; *India's Religion of Grace and Christianity, Compared and Contrasted*, pp. 21–2.

28 When Otto stayed in Mysore, Alcondavilli Govindācārya, who was eighty years old at the time, taught Otto about Rāmānuja's thought. In his *Report*, "From Ceylon to the Himalayas," Birger Forell, who accompanied Otto during his trip, writes:

> What was the most interesting was the encounter with Govinda Charya Swamin of 80 years old. He has written about Hindu theology and corresponded with Professor Otto on Rāmānuja for many years. We [Otto and Forell] looked forward to this encounter with excitement.

Birger Forell, "Von Celon zum Himalaya," aus dem Schwedischen übertragen von Ursula Lerenz, 1987 (Rudolf Otto-Archiv), S. 31.

In regard to Otto's book, *Die Gnadenreligion Indiens und das Christentum*, based on his Christian perspectives, the historian of religion John B. Carman, who is well known for his works on Rāmānuja's thought, says:

> In fact, this book of Otto's had a number of Hindu readers from the devotional movements. They were gratified by his very positive appreciation of devotional Hinduism, which up to that point had rarely occurred among European scholars, but they were disappointed by what seemed to them very negative conclusions.

Cf. John B. Carman, *Majesty and Meekness: A Comparative Study of Contrast and Harmony in the Concept of God* (Wm. B. Eerdmans-Lightning Source, 1994), pp. 34–5.

29 Cf. William Graham, *Beyond the Written Word: Oral Aspects of Scripture in the History of Religion* (Cambridge: Cambridge University Press, 1987).

30 Wilfred Cantwell Smith, "Comparative Religion: Whither—and Why?" in: *The History of Religions: Essays in Methodology*, edited by Mircea Eliade and Joseph M. Kitagawa (Chicago: The University of Chicago Press, 1959), pp. 31–58.

31 Yoshitsugu Sawai, "Rudolf Otto's View of Indian Religious Thought," in Jörg Lauster, et al., *Rudolf Otto: Theologie-Religionsphilosophie-Religionsgeschichte*, S. 549–50.

Chapter 5

1 John B. Carman, "Conceiving Hindu'Bhakti' as Theistic Mysticism," *Mysticism and Religious Traditions*, edited by Steven T. Katz (New York: Oxford University Press, 1983), p. 194.

2 Leigh Eric Schmidt, "The Making of Modern 'Mysticism,'" *Journal of the American Academy of Religion*, vol. 71, 2003, pp. 276–7.

3 Ibid., pp. 289–90.

4 Hidetaka Fukazawa, "The Birth of 'Religion:' The Creation and Curse of the Modern Concept of Religion" [in Japanese, *Shūkyō no seitan: kindai shūkyō gainen no seisei to jubaku*], in *What is Religion?* [in Japanese, *Shūkyō towa nani ka*] (Tokyo: Iwanami-shoten, 2003), pp. 41–2.

5 Louis Bouyer, "Mysticism: An Essay on the History of the Word," *Understanding Mysticism*, edited by Richard Woods (New York: A Division of Doubleday & Company, Inc., 1980), p. 43.

6 Margaret Smith, "The Nature and Meaning of Mysticism," *Understanding Mysticism*, edited by Richard Woods, p. 20.

7 Leigh Eric Schmidt, "The Making of Modern 'Mysticism,'" p. 283. Cf. Robert Alfred Vaughan, *Hours with the Mystics: A Contribution to the History of Religious Opinion*, 2 vols (London: Slark, 1856; 5th edition, 1888).
8 Philip C. Almond, *Mystical Experience and Religious Doctrine: An Investigation of the Study of Mysticism in World Religions* (Berlin: Walter de Gruyter & Co., 1982), p. 120.
9 Margaret Smith, "The Nature and Meaning of Mysticism," p. 20.
10 Steven T. Katz ed., *Mysticism and Philosophical Analysis* (New York: Oxford University Press, 1978). Wayne Proudfoot, *Religious Experience* (Berkeley: University of California Press, 1985).
11 Hans H. Penner, "The Mystical Illusion," *Mysticism and Religious Traditions*, edited by Steven T. Katz (Oxford: Oxford University Press, 1983), p. 89.
12 Ibid., pp. 90–1.
13 Ibid., pp. 92–3.
14 Grace M. Jantzen, *Power, Gender and Christian Mysticism* (Cambridge: Cambridge University Press, 1995), pp. 24–5.
15 Steven M. Wasserstrom, *Religion after Religion: Gershom Scholem, Mircea Eliade, and Henry Corbin at Eranos* (Princeton: Princeton University Press, 1999), pp. 239–41.
16 Rudolf Otto, *West-östliche Mystik*, S. viii; *Mysticism East and West*, p. 6 (author's translation). In regard to Otto's argument of Indian religious thought, the Indian religious scholar S.P. Dubey published his understanding of Otto's views. Cf. S.P. Dubey, *Rudolf Otto and Hinduism* (Varanasi: Bharatiya Vidya Prakashan, 1969).
17 Rudolf Otto, "Parallelisms in the Development of Religion East and West," *The Transactions of the Asiatic Society of Japan* 40, 1912, p. 154.
18 Ibid., p. 158.
19 Cf. Rudolf Otto, "Parallels and Convergences in the History of Religion," in: Rudolf Otto, *Religious Essays: A Supplement to "The Idea of the Holy"* (London: Oxford University Press, 1931).
20 Rudolf Otto, *Das Heilige* (München: 1917); reprint (München: Verlag C.H. Beck, 1963), S. 30–1. This English translation is mine.
21 Rudolf Otto, *West-östliche Mystik* (Gotha: L. Klotz, 1926; München: Verlag C.H. Beck, Dritte Auflage, 1971), S. 162; *Mysticism East and West* (New York: The Macmillan Company, 1932), pp. 157–8.
22 For a detailed discussion on this point, see Chapter 7 of this book.
23 R. Otto, *West-östliche Mystik*, S. 163; *Mysticism East and West*, pp. 158–9.
24 R. Otto, *West-östliche Mystik*, S. 2; *Mysticism East and West*, p. 14. In regard to a comparative theological study on the "aim and the method of Otto's apologetic—namely, the vindication of Eckhart and the use of Śaṅkara as a foil" in *Mysticism East and West*, see Hugh Nicholson, *Comparative Theology and the Problem of Religious Rivalry* (Oxford: Oxford University Press, 2011).
25 R. Otto, *West-östliche Mystik*, S. 3; *Mysticism East and West*, p. 15.

26 R. Otto, *West-östliche Mystik*, S. 7; *Mysticism East and West*, p. 20.
27 R. Otto, *West-östliche Mystik*, S. 6–7; *Mysticism East and West*, pp. 20–1.
28 R. Otto, *West-östliche Mystik*, S. 8–9; *Mysticism East and West*, pp. 21–2. Cf. Robert F. Davidson, *Rudolf Otto's Interpretation of Religion*, p. 129.
29 R. Otto, *West-östliche Mystik*, S. 9–10; *Mysticism East and West*, pp. 22–4.
30 R. Otto, *West-östliche Mystik*, S. 31–2; *Mysticism East and West*, pp. 44–5.
31 R. Otto, *West-östliche Mystik*, S. 43–60; *Mysticism East and West*, pp. 57–72.
32 R. Otto, *West-östliche Mystik*, S. 60; *Mysticism East and West*, p. 72. (The English translation is mine.)
33 For religious phenomena centered on the Śṛṅgeri Monastery, whose founder is traditionally believed to be Śaṅkara, see my book, *Thoughts and Faiths of Śaṅkaran Tradition* [in Japanese, *Shankara-ha no shisō to shinkō*] (Tokyo: Keio University Press, 2016).
34 R. Otto, *West-östliche Mystik*, S. 60; *Mysticism East and West*, p. 72.
35 S.P. Dubey, *Rudolf Otto and Hinduism*, p. 64.
36 In regard to the detail discussion of the faith and thought in Śaṅkaran religious tradition, see my book, *The Faith of Ascetics and Lay Smārtas: A Study of the Śaṅkaran Tradition of Śṛṅgeri* (Vienna: Sammlung de Nobili, 1992).
37 R. Otto, *West-östliche Mystik*, S. 35; *Mysticism East and West*, p. 48. The English translation is mine.
38 Rudolf Otto, *Die Gnadenreligion Indiens und das Christentum*, S. 52; *India's Religion of Grace and Christianity, Compared and Contrasted*, pp. 72–3.
39 R. Otto, *Die Gnadenreligion Indiens und das Christentum*, S. 52; *India's Religion of Grace and Christianity*, p. 73. Cf. Yoshitsugu Sawai, "Reflections on Bhakti as a Type of Indian Mysticism," in *The Historical Development of the Bhakti Movement in India: Theory and Practice*, edited by Iwao Shima et al., Japanese Studies on South Asia no. 8 (New Delhi: Manohar, 2010), pp. 19–33.
40 R. Otto, *Die Gnadenreligion Indiens und das Christentum*, S. 52–3; *India's Religion of Grace and Christianity*, p. 73.
41 R. Otto, *Die Gnadenreligion Indiens und das Christentum*, S. 53–4; *India's Religion of Grace and Christianity*, p. 74.
42 R. Otto, *Die Gnadenreligion Indiens und das Christentum*, S. 54; *India's Religion of Grace and Christianity*, p. 75.
43 R. Otto, *Die Gnadenreligion Indiens und das Christentum*, S. 64–5; *India's Religion of Grace and Christianity*, pp. 86–7.
44 R. Otto, *Die Gnadenreligion Indiens und das Christentum*, S. 56–7; *India's Religion of Grace and Christianity*, pp. 77–8.
45 R. Otto, *Die Gnadenreligion Indiens und das Christentum*, S. 71; *India's Religion of Grace and Christianity*, p. 94.
46 R. Otto, *Die Gnadenreligion Indiens und das Christentum*, S. 71; *India's Religion of Grace and Christianity*, pp. 94–5.

47 R. Otto, *West-östliche Mystik*, S. 1; *Mysticism East and West*, p. 13.
48 R. Otto, *West-östliche Mystik*, S. 1–2; *Mysticism East and West*, p. 13.
49 In regard to the view of *avidyā* in Śaṅkara's philosophy, see Hajime Nakamura, *Śaṅkara's Thought* [in Japanese, *Shankara no shisō*] (Tokyo: Iwanami-shoten, 1989), pp. 534–43; Sengaku Mayeda, *A Thousand Teachings: The Upadeśasāhasrī of Śaṅkara* (Tokyo: University of Tokyo Press, 1979), pp. 76–84.

Chapter 6

1 Hidetaka Fukazawa, "The Birth of 'Religion:' The Creation and Curse of the Modern Concept of Religion" [in Japanese, "Shūkyō no seitan: kindai shūkyō gainen no seisei to jubaku"], in *What is Religion?* [in Japanese, *Shūkyō towa nani ka*], pp. 24–5.
2 Rudolf Otto, "The 'Wholly Other' in Religious History and Theology," in Rudolf Otto, *Religious Essays: A Supplement to "The Idea of the Holy"* (London: Oxford University Press, 1931), p. 78.
3 Friedrich Heiler, "Die Absolutheit des Christentums im Lichte der allgemeinen Religionsgeschichte," *Das Wesen des Katholizismus: Sechs Vorträge, gehalten im Herbst in Schweden* (München: Verlag von Ernst Reinhardt, 1920), S. 119.
4 Tsuyoshi Maeda clarifies this point through his detailed analysis of Otto's travel notes and diaries. For details, see Tsuyoshi Maeda's book, *The Ground of Holiness: Traveling Otto*, 2016.
5 Rudolf Otto, *Das Heilige*, S. 170–1; *The Idea of the Holy*, pp. 141–2.
6 Rudolf Otto, *Das Heilige*, S. 31; *The Idea of the Holy*, p. 26.
7 Rudolf Otto, "The 'Wholly Other' in Religious History and Theology," p. 78.
8 Ibid., p. 92, note 1.
9 Rudolf Otto, "Das Ganz-Andere in Ausserchristlicher und in Christlicher Theologie und Spekulation," in Rudolf Otto, *Das Gefühl des Überweltlichen (Sensus Numinis)* (München: C.H. Beck'sche Verlag, 1932), S. 231.
10 In regard to Otto's viewpoint, Noriyoshi Tamaru accurately points out as follows:

> In my opinion, it [Otto's research] was an effort to clarify the peculiar meaning of religion in general, and of Christianity in particular. To that extent, one can say that his position was basically apologetic and theological. This was quite natural when we consider his academic position as a professor of systematic theology. It is also one of the points that were often overlooked.

Cf. Noriyoshi Tamaru, *The History of Religions: Its History and Task*, 1987, p. 237.
11 Yoshitsugu Sawai, "Polytheism and Monotheism in Hinduism" (in Japanese, *Hindūkyō ni okeru tashinsei to isshinsei*), *G-TEN*, edited by Tenri Yamato Cultural Congress, vol. 53, 1990, pp. 43–7.

12 Masaaki Hattori, *The Mystical Thought of Ancient India* (in Japanese, *Kodai indo no shinpi shisō*) (Tokyo: Kodansha, 1979), pp. 14–30. Kana Tomizawa, "British Gentlemen's Indian Controversy: The Understanding of India and Religion by 'Orientalists' at the End of the 18th Century" (in Japanese, *Igirisu shinshi no indo ronsō: 18 seiki-matsu 'orientarisuto' no indo-rikai to shūkyō-rikai*), in Susumu Shimazono and Yoshio Tsuruoka ed., *Reconsidering "Religion"* (in Japanese, *Shūkyō saikō*) (Tokyo: Perikan-sha, 2004), pp. 298–300. Cf. Richard King, *Orientalism and Religion: Postcolonial Theory, India and the "Mystic East"* (London, New York: Routledge, 1999), pp. 122–3.

13 John B. Carman, *Majesty and Meekness: A Comparative Study of Contrast and Harmony in the Concept of God* (Michigan: William B. Eerdmans Publishing Company, 1994), pp. 34–5. C.A.F. Rhys Davids, "Book Review: Rudolf Otto, *India's Religion of Grace and Christianity Compared and Contrasted*." *The Hibbert Journal*, vol. 29, no. 4, 1931, p. 744.

14 Rudolf Otto, *Die Gnadenreligion Indiens und das Christentum*, S. 6–7; *India's Religion of Grace and Christianity, Compared and Contrasted*, pp. 17–18.

15 R. Otto, *Die Gnadenreligion Indiens und das Christentum*, S. 6; *India's Religion of Grace and Christianity, Compared and Contrasted*, p. 17.

16 R. Otto, *Das Heilige*, S. 164; *The Idea of the Holy*, p. 135.

17 R. Otto, *Das Gefühl des Überweltlichen*, S. 261.

18 R. Otto, *Das Heilige*, S. 79; *The Idea of the Holy*, p. 60.

19 R. Otto, *Das Gefühl des Überweltlichen*, S. 261.

20 R. Otto, *Das Heilige*, S. 116; *The Idea of the Holy*, p. 94.

21 *Bhagavadgītābhāṣya with Śāṅkarabhāṣya.* Works of Śaṅkarācārya in Original Sanskrit, vol. II (Poona: Motilal Banarsidass, 1929; reprint ed., Delhi: Motilal Banarsidass, 1978), II. 29, p. 24.

22 R. Otto, *Das Gefühl des Überweltlichen*, S. 263.

23 Ibid., S. 262.

24 Ibid., S. 264. This English translation of the *Kena Upaniṣad* (4:30) is from Otto's German translation.

25 Robert F. Davidson, *Rudolf Otto's Interpretation of Religion*, p. 107.

26 Cf. William Graham, *Beyond the Written Word: Oral Aspects of Scripture in the History of Religion* (Cambridge: Cambridge University Press, 1987).

Chapter 7

1 Rudolf Otto, *West-östliche Mystik* (Gotha: L. Klotz, 1926; München: Verlag C.H. Beck, Dritte Auflage, 1971). Rudolf Otto, *Die Gnadenreligion Indiens und das Christentum*, Gotha: L. Klotz, 1930. In regard to Otto's study of Indian religions, see the list of Indian religious thought studies in Chapter 2 of this book.

2 Rudolf Otto, *West-östliche Mystik*, S.VIII. 3; Rudolf Otto, "Parallelisms in the Development of Religion East and West," 1912, p. 154. Cf. *The Transactions of the Asiatic Society of Japan* 40 [in Japanese, *Nihon ajia kyōkai kiyō*] (Reprinted Volumes 39 and 40, 1964.)
4 Rudolf Otto, "Parallels and Convergences in the History of Religion," in: Rudolf Otto, *Religious Essays: A Supplement to "The Idea of The Holy"* (London: Oxford University Press, 1931); "Parallelen und Konvergenzen in der Religionsgeschichte," in: Rudolf Otto, *Das Gefühl des Überweltlichen*, 1932.
5 Rudolf Otto, "Parallels and Convergences in the History of Religion," *Religious Essays*, pp.108–9.
6 R. Otto, *West-östliche Mystik*, S. 162; *Mysticism East and West*, p. 158.
7 R. Otto, *West-östliche Mystik*, S. 163; *Mysticism East and West*, p. 158.
8 R. Otto, *West-östliche Mystik*, S. 163; *Mysticism East and West*, p. 159.
9 R. Otto, *West-östliche Mystik*, S. 163; *Mysticism East and West*, pp. 158–9.
10 R. Otto, *West-östliche Mystik*, S. 164–5; *Mysticism East and West*, pp. 159–61.
11 R. Otto, *West-östliche Mystik*, S. 43–60; *Mysticism East and West*, pp. 57–72.
12 R. Otto, *West-östliche Mystik*, S. 167–8; *Mysticism East and West*, pp. 162.
13 R. Otto, *West-östliche Mystik*, S. 169; *Mysticism East and West*, p. 163.
14 R. Otto, *West-östliche Mystik*, S. 171–2; *Mysticism East and West*, p. 165.
15 R. Otto, *Das Heilige*, S. 60–5; *The Idea of the Holy*, pp. 45–9.
16 R. Otto, *West-östliche Mystik*, S. 120; *Mysticism East and West*, p. 122.
17 R. Otto, *West-östliche Mystik*, S. 35; *Mysticism East and West*, p. 48.
18 R. Otto, *West-östliche Mystik*, S. 177–8; *Mysticism East and West*, pp. 169–70. See this author's discussion of the characteristics of Rāmānuja's interpretation of the Upaniṣads scriptures in comparison with Śaṅkara's thought. Cf. Yoshitsugu Sawai, "Rāmānuja's Hermeneutics of the Upaniṣads in Comparison with Śaṅkara's Interpretation," *Journal of Indian Philosophy* (Dordrecht: Kluwer Academic Publishers, 1991), vol. 19, no. 1.
19 John B. Carman, *Majesty and Meekness: A Comparative Study of Contrast and Harmony in the Concept of God* (Michigan: William B. Eerdmans Publishing Company, 1994), p. 34.
20 Rudolf Otto, *Die Gnadenreligion Indiens und das Christentum*, S. 18; *India's Religion of Grace and Christianity*, pp. 31–2.
21 R. Otto, *Das Heilige*, S. 170–1; *The Idea of The Holy*, pp. 141–2.
22 R. Otto, *West-östliche Mystik*, S. 184; *Mysticism East and West*, p. 175.
23 R. Otto, *West-östliche Mystik*, S. 182; *Mysticism East and West*, pp. 173–4.
24 R. Otto, *West-östliche Mystik*, S. 143; *Mysticism East and West*, p. 140.
25 Daniel H.H. Ingalls, "Śaṁkara on the Question: Whose is Avidyā?," *Philosophy East and West*, vol. 3, no. 4, 1953, p. 72.
26 In regard to the meaning of the Hindu concept of bhakti, see Yoshitsugu Sawai, "Reflections on Bhakti as a Type of Indian Mysticism," in Iwao Shima et al., *The*

Historical Development of the Bhakti Movement in India: Theory and Practice. Japanese Studies on South Asia no. 8 (New Delhi: Manohar, 2011), pp. 19–33.

27 Wilfred C. Smith, *Faith and Belief* (Princeton: Princeton University Press, 1979), p. 219.

Chapter 8

1 In regard to the IAHR World Congress (Tokyo Convention), held in Tokyo in 2005, its contents are summarized in Gerrie ter Haar and Yoshio Tsuruoka ed., *Religion and Society: An Agenda for the 21st Century* (Leiden/Boston: Brill, 2007).

2 Jonathan Z. Smith, "Religion, Religions, Religious," in: *Critical Terms for Religious Studies*, ed. by Mark C. Taylor (Chicago and London: The University of Chicago Press, 1998), pp. 269–84.

3 Joseph W. Kitagawa, "The History of Religions in America," in: *The History of Religions: Essays in Methodology*, ed. by Mircea Eliade and Joseph M. Kitagawa (Chicago: The University of Chicago Press, 1959), p. 22.

4 Wilfred Cantwell Smith, *The Meaning and End of Religion*, New York: Harper & Row, 1962; W.C. Smith, "Comparative Religion: Whither—and Why?" in: *The History of Religions: Essays in Methodology*, ed. by Mircea Eliade and Joseph M. Kitagawa, p. 35.

5 Ninian Smart, *Reflections in the Mirror of Religion*, edited by John P. Burris (London: Macmillan Press, 1997), pp. 175–6.

6 Noriyoshi Tamaru, *The History of Religions: Its History and Task* [in Japanese, *Shūkyōgaku no rekishi to kadai*, 1987], p. 84.

7 Douglas Allen, *Structure and Creativity in Religion* (The Hague: Mouton Publishers, 1978), p. 60.

8 Cf. Rudolf Otto, *Die Gnadenreligion Indiens und das Christentum* (Gotha: Leopold Klotz Verlag, 1930), S. 29. Although Otto emphasizes the non-rational element of religion, I would like to reaffirm here again that he never downplays the rational element of religion. In this regard, as the subtitle of *Das Heilige* suggests, Otto would like to clarify the relationship between the non-rational and rational elements in religion.

9 Rudolf Otto, *Das Heilige*, S. 60–5, 165–71; *The Idea of the Holy*, pp. 45–9, 136–42.

10 Rudolf Otto, "Parallels and Convergences in the History of Religion," in: R. Otto, *Religious Essays* (Oxford University Press, 1931), p. 96.

11 Robert F. Davidson, *Rudolf Otto's Interpretation of Religion*, p. 107. Cf. R. Otto, *Das Heilige*, S. 170–1.

12 R. Otto, "Parallelen und Konvergenzen in der Religionsgeschichte," in: R. Otto, *Das Gefühl des Überweltlichen* (München: C.H. Beck'sche Verlagsbuchhandlung, 1932), S. 282.

13 R. Otto, "Parallelisms in the Development of Religion East and West," *The Transactions of the Asiatic Society of Japan* 40, pp. 153–8.
14 R. Otto, *Die Gnadenreligion Indiens und das Christentum*, S. 18; *India's Religion of Grace and Christianity*, pp. 31–2.
15 R. Otto, *West-östliche Mystik*, S.41; *Mysticism East and West*, p. 53.
16 R. Otto, *West-östliche Mystik*, S. 31–2; *Mysticism East and West*, pp. 44–5.
17 R. Otto, *West-östliche Mystik*, S. 32; *Mysticism East and West*, pp. 44–5.
18 R. Otto, *Das Heilige*, S. 2; *The Idea of the Holy*, p. 2.
19 R. Otto, *Das Heilige*, S. 13; *The Idea of the Holy*, p. 12.
20 Robert A. Orsi, "The Problem of the Holy," in *The Cambridge Companion to Religious Studies*, edited by Robert A. Orsi (New York: Cambridge University Press, 2012), pp. 102–4. As another phrase for the holy, Orsi suggests the "2 + 2 = 5 of holiness" here.
21 Ibid., S. 27–8. Cf. Robert F. Davidson, *Rudolf Otto's Interpretation of Religion*, p. 114.
22 Ibid., S. 56–7.
23 Todd A. Gooch, *The Numinous and Modernity: An Interpretation of Rudolf Otto's Philosophy of Religion* (Berlin: Walter de Gruyter, 2000), p. 113.
24 Ibid., p. 112.
25 R. Otto, *Das Heilige*, S. 47–8; *The Idea of the Holy*, p. 35.
26 Paul Ricoeur, *La symbolique du mal*, Paris: Aubier, 1960. For Ricoeur, this book became his turning point into hermeneutics. Since then, the interpretation of symbols with a double meaning became his main concern. In regard to Otto's religious theory in Ricoeur's argument of "the phenomenology of the sacred," see his article, "Manifestation and Proclamation," *Blaisdell Institute Journal* 11, 1978, pp. 13–35; reprinted in Paul Ricoeur, *Figuring the Sacred: Religion, Narrative, and Imagination*, edited by Mark I. Wallace and translated by David Pellauer (Minneapolis: Fortless Press, 1995), pp. 48–67.
27 R. Otto, *Das Heilige*, S. 21; *The Idea of the Holy*, pp. 18–19.
28 R. Otto, *Das Heilige*, S. 35; *The Idea of the Holy*, p. 30.
29 Rudolf Otto, *Das Heilige*, S. 5–7; *The Idea of the Holy*, pp. 5–7.
30 Toshihiko Izutsu, *The Structure of Oriental Philosophy: Collected Papers of the Eranos Conference*, vol. 1 (Tokyo: Keio University Press, 2008), pp. 146–7. Cf. Yoshitsugu Sawai, "A Semantic Perspective on Otto's Theory of Religion," *Tenri Journal of Religion*, no. 45 (Tenri: Tenri University Press, 2017), pp. 1–11.
31 Gregory D. Alles, "Rudolf Otto and the Cognitive Science of Religion," in Jörg Lauster et al., *Rudolf Otto: Theologie–Religionsphilosophie–Religionsgeschichte*, p. 25.
32 Toshihiko Izutsu, *The Structure of Oriental Philosophy*, vol. 1, p. 18. In regard to Izutsu's philosophical semantic theory, see Yoshitsugu Sawai, "The Structure of Reality in Izutsu's Oriental Philosophy," in Anis Malik Thoha ed., *Japanese Contribution to Islamic Studies: The Legacy of Toshihiko Izutsu Interpreted* (Kuala Lumpur: International Islamic University Malaysia, 2010), pp. 1–15; "Editor's Essay,"

i.e., "Izutsu's Creative 'Reading' of Oriental Thought and Its Development," in Toshihiko Izutsu, *The Structure of Oriental Philosophy*, vol. 2 (Tokyo: Keio University Press, 2008), pp. 215–23.

33 Toshihiko Izutsu, *The Structure of Oriental Philosophy*, vol. 1, p. 18.

Conclusion

1 Rudolf Otto, *Das Heilige*, S. 122–3; *The Idea of the Holy*, pp. 99–100.

2 Max Scheler, *Vom Ewigen im Menschen*, 1921, Gesammelte Werke Band 5 (Bern, 1954), S. 141.

Bibliography

Rudolf Otto's Main Works

1898

Die Anschauung vom heiligen Geiste bei Luther: Eine historisch-dogmatische Untersuchung. Göttingen: Vandenhoeck & Ruprecht.

1899

Über die Religion: Reden an die Gebildeten under ihren Verächtern. Von Friedrich Schleiermacher. Neu hrsg. von Rudolf Otto. Göttingen.

1902

Leben und Wirken Jesu nach historisch-kritische Auffassung. Göttingen: Vandenhoeck & Ruprecht.

Life and Ministry of Jesus According to the Historical and Critical Method. Translated by Henry James Whitby. Chicago: The Open Court Publishing Co., 1908.

1904

Naturalistische und religiöse Weltansicht. Tübingen: J. C. B. Mohr, 1904.

Naturalism and Religion. Translated by J. Arthur Thomson, Margaret R. Thomson. Edited by W.D. Morrison. London: Williams & Norgate Ltd., 1907.

1909

Kantisch-Fries'sche Religionsphilosophie und Ihre Anwendung auf die Theologie. Tübingen: J.C.B. Mohr, 1921.

1912

"Parallelisms in the Development of Religion East and West." *The Transactions of the Asiatic Society of Japan* 40.

1913

"Parallelen der Religionsentwicklung." *Frankfurter Zeitung*, April 1.

"Ist eine Universalreligion wünschenswert und möglich? Und wenn, wie kann man sie erreichen?" *Die Christliche Welt*, Jg. 27.

1916

Dīpikā des Nivāsa: Eine indische Heilslehre. Tübingen: J.C.B. Mohr.

"Aller Meister Lehren, aus dem Sanskrit." *Zeitschrift für Missionskunde und Religionswissenschaft* 31.

"Artha-pañcaka oder die fünf Artikel." *Theologische Studien und Kritiken* 89.
"Von indischer Frömmigkeit." *Die Christliche Welt* 30.

1917

Das Heilige: Über das Irrationale in der Idee des Göttlichen und sein Verhältnis zum Rationalen. Munich: C.H. Beck, 1963; 2014.
The Idea of the Holy: An Inquiry into the Non-rational Factor in the Idea of the Divine and its Relation to the Rational. Translated by John W. Harvey. London: Oxford University Press, 1923.
Vischnu-Nārāyana: Texte zur indischen Gottesmystik. Jena: E. Diederich.
Siddhānta des Rāmānuja: Ein Text zur indischen Gottesmystik. Jena: E. Diederich.
"Bhakti-Hundertvers (Bhakti-Śatakam) von Rāma-Candra." *Zeitschrift für Missionskunde und Religionswissenschaft* 32.

1920

"Schweigender Dienst." *Die Christliche Welt* 36.

1922

"Aus Rabindranath Takkurs väterlicher Religion." *Die Christliche Welt* 36.
"Zum Verhältnisse von mystischer und gläubiger Frömmigkeit." *Zeitschrift für Theologie und Kirche* 3.

1923

Aufsätze das Numinose betreffend. Munich: C.H. Beck.

1923

"Östliche und westliche Mystik." *Logos* 13.

1925

Zur Erneuerung und Ausgestaltung des Gottesdienstes. Gießen: Alfred Döpelmann.
"Meister Eckhart's Mystik im Unterschiede von östlicher Mystik." *Zeitschrift für Theologie und Kirche* 6.
"Indischer Theismus." *Zeitschrift für Missionskunde und Religionswissenschaft* 40.

1926

West-östliche Mystik: Vergleich und Unterscheidung zur Wesensdeutung. Gotha: L. Klotz.

1928

"Zum Verständnis von Rabindranath Tagore: Ein Stück altindischer Theologie." *Die Hilfe* 34.
"Christianity and the Indian Religion of Grace: A Comparison." *National Christian Council Review*, New Series 6.

1929

"Menschheitsbund, Religiöser." *Die Religion in Geschichte und Gegenwart.* Zweite Auflage, Dritter Band.

Christianity and the Indian Religion of Grace. Madras: Christian Literature Society for India.

"Ein Stück indischer Theologie, Übertragen aus Yāmunamuni's 'Dreifacher Erweis.'" *Zeitschrift für Theologie und Kirche* 10.

"Bewusstseins-Phänomenologie des personalen Vedānta." *Logos* 18.

"Die Methoden des Erweises der Seele im personalen Vedānta." *Zeitschrift für Religionspsychologie* 2.

1930

Die Gnadenreligion Indiens und das Christentum: Vergleich und Unterscheidung. Gotha: L. Klotz.

India's Religion of Grace and Christianity Compared and Contrasted. London: Student Christian Movement Press; New York: Macmillan.

"Rāmānuja." *Die Religion in Geschichte und Gegenwart* 4.

"In Brahmas Tempel." *Münchener Neueste Nachrichten*, 1, April 7.

"Der verlorene Sohn in Indien? Ähnlichkeit und Unterschied indischer und christlicher Religion." *Münchener Neueste Nachrichten*, 3, October 9.

"Towards the Reform of Divine Service." *The Hibbert Journal*, vol. 29, no. 1.

1931

Rabindranath Tagore's Bekenntnis. Tübingen: J.C.B. Mohr.

"An Inter-Religious League." *The Hibbert Journal*, vol. 29, no. 4.

Religious Essays: A Supplement to "The Idea of the Holy." London: Oxford University Press.

"Parallels and Convergences in the History of Religion," in Rudolf Otto, *Religious Essays*. London: Oxford University Press.

"'Meine Religion' von Rabindranath Tagore." *Westermanns Monatshefte* 75.

1932

Gottheit und Gottheiten der Arier. Giessen: Alfred Topelmann.

Mysticism East and West: A Comparative Analysis of the Nature of Mysticism. New York: Macmillan.

Das Gefühl des Überweltlichen: sensus numinis. Munich: C.H. Beck.

"Parallelen und Konvergenzen in der Religionsgeschichte." *Das Gefühl des Überweltlichen: Sensus numinis*. Munich: C.H. Beck.

"Hymne an Varuna." *Die Christliche Welt*, 46.

Sünde und Urschuld und andere Aufsätze zur Theologie, Munich: C.H. Beck.

1934

Die Urgestalt der Bhagavad-Gītā. Tübingen: J.C.B. Mohr.

"Nārāyana, seine Herkunft und seine Synonyme." *Zeitschrift für Missionskunde und Religionswissenschaft* 49.

"Mystische und gläubige Frömmigkeit." *Commemoration Volume of the Science of Religion in Tokyo Imperial University*, Tokyo: Herald Press.

1935

Der Sang des Hehr-Erhabenen: Die Bhagavad-Gītā. Stuttgart: W. Kohlhammer.

Die Lehrtraktate der Bhagavad-Gītā. Tübingen: J.C.B. Mohr.

"Krishna's Lied." *Zeitschrift für Missionskunde und Religionswissenschaft* 50.

1936

Die Katha-Upanishad. Berlin: Alfred Topelmann.

"Die Katha-Upanishad in ihrer Urgestalt." *Zeitschrift für Missionskunde und Religionswissenschaft* 51.

"Vom Naturgott zur Brautmystik." *Zeitschrift für Missionskunde und Religionswissenschaft* 51.

Otto's Posthumous Publications

1938

"Briefe Rudolf Ottos von seiner Fahrt nach Indien und Ägypten." *Die Christliche Welt* 52.

1939

The Original Gītā: The Song of the Supreme Exalted One, translated and edited by J.E. Turner, London: Allen and Unwin.

1943

Varuna-Hymnen des Rig-Veda. Religionsgeschichtliche Texte, ed. Gustav Mensching, vol. 1. Bonn: Ludwig Röhrscheid.

1948

Varuna-Hymnen des Rig-Veda. Religionsgeschichtliche Texte, Heft 1.

1951

Mystique d'Orient et mystique d'Occident. Paris: Payot.

1958

"Briefe Rudolf Ottos von seiner Fahrt nach Indien und Ägypten." *Die Christliche Welt* 52, no. 24.

1981

Aufsätze zur Ethik. Hrsg. von Jack Stewart Boozer. Munich: C.H. Beck.

2014

Das Heilige: Über das Irrationale in der Idee des Göttlichen und sein Verhältnis zum Rationalen, mit einer Einführung zu Leben und Werk Rudolf Ottos von Jörg Lauster und Peter Schüz und einem Nachwort von Hans Joas. Munich: C.H. Beck.

Letters, Reports, and Newspapers in regard to Rudolf Otto

HS. (Handschriften Otto-Nachlaβ Universitäts-Bibliothek, Marburg) 797/800. Troeltsch an Otto. Nov. 17. 1904.

HS. 797/572, 19. Otto an Johanne Ottmer. Nov. 7. 1911.

OA. 379. October 12, 1911.

HS. 797/725. *Report* from Dr. Rudolf Otto and Rev. Birger Forell on their work for the Universal Religious Peace Conference, 1927.

HS. 797/794: Edmund Husserl, Brief an Rudolf Otto. March 5, 1919.

Birger Forell, "Von Celon zum Himalaya." Aus dem Schwedischen übertragen von Ursula Lerenz (Rudolf Otto-Archiv), 1987.

Roku-dai shinpō (in English, "six great news"), no. 445, April 7, 1912.

Roku-dai shinpō, no. 452, May 26, 1912.

References on Rudolf Otto

Allen, Douglas. *Structure and Creativity in Religion*. The Hague: Mouton Publishers, 1978.

Alles, Gregory D. ed. *Rudolf Otto: Autobiographical and Social Essays*. Berlin: Mouton de Gruyter, 1996.

Alles, Gregory D. "The Rebirth of Cultural Colonialism as Religionswissenschaft: Rudolf Otto's Import House," *Temenos*, vol. 43, no. 1, The Finnish Society for the Study of Religion, 2007.

Alles, Gregory D. "Rudolf Otto and the Politics of Utopia." *Religion*, no. 21, 2011.

Almond, Philip C. *Mystical Experience and Religious Doctrine: An Investigation of the Study of Mysticism in World Religions*. Berlin: Walter de Gruyter & Co., 1982.

Almond, Philip C. "Rudolf Otto and the Kantian Tradition." *Neue Zeitschrift für Systematicsche Theologie und Religionsphilosophie* 25, 1983.

Almond, Philip C. *Rudolf Otto: An Introduction to His Philosophical Theology*. Chapel Hill: The University of North Carolina Press, 1984.

Almond, Philip C. "Rudolf Otto and Buddhism." In Peter Masefield and Donald Wiebe ed., *Aspects of Religion: Essays in Honour of Ninian Smart*. New York: Peter Lang, 1994.

Arweck, Elisabeth; Keenan, William. Ed. *Materializing Religion: Expression, Performance and Ritual*. London: Ashgate, 2006.

Benz, Ernst. "Rudolf Otto als Theologe und Persönlichkeit." In: *Rudolf Otto's Bedeutung für die Religionswissenschaft und die Theologie Heute*, herausgegeben von Ernst Benz. Leiden: E.J. Brill, 1971.

Bhagavadgītābhāṣya with Śāṅkarabhāṣya. Works of Śaṅkarācārya in Original Sanskrit, vol. II. Poona: Motilal Banarsidass, 1929; reprint ed., Delhi: Motilal Banarsidass, 1978.

Bouyer, Louis. "Mysticism: An Essay on the History of the Word." *Understanding Mysticism*, edited by Richard Woods. New York: A Division of Doubleday & Company, Inc., 1980.

Carman, John B. "Conceiving Hindu 'Bhakti' as Theistic Mysticism." *Mysticism and Religious Traditions*, edited by Steven T. Katz. New York: Oxford University Press, 1983.

Carman, John B. *Majesty and Meekness: A Comparative Study of Contrast and Harmony in the Concept of God*. Michigan: William B. Eerdmans Publishing Company, 1994.

Choi, Jeong Hwa. *Religion als "Weltgewissen:" Rudolf Ottos Religiöser Menschheitbund und das Zusammenspiel von Religionsforschung und Religionsbegegnung nach dem Ersten Weltkrieg*. Zürich: LIT Verlag, 2013.

Clooney, S.J., Francis X. *Comparative Theology: Deep Learning Across Religious Borders*. Chichester: Wiley-Blackwell, 2010.

Clooney, S.J. Ed. *The New Comparative Theology: Interreligious Insights from the Next Generation*. London: T & T Clark International, 2010.

Davids, C.A.F. Rhys. "Book Review: Rudolf Otto, *India's Religion of Grace and Christianity Compared and Contrasted*." *The Hibbert Journal*, vol. 29, no. 4, 1931.

Davidson, Robert F. *Rudolf Otto's Interpretation of Religion*. Princeton: Princeton University Press, 1947.

Dubey, S.P. *Rudolf Otto and Hinduism*. Varanasi: Bharatiya Vidya Prakashan, 1969.

Edgerton, Franklin. *The Bhagavadgītā*. Cambridge: Harvard University Press, 1944.

Eliade, Mircea. *Das Heilige und das Profane*, Reinbeck: Rowohlt Taschenbuch, 1967. *The Sacred and the Profane: the Nature of Religion*. Translated from the French by Willard R. Trask. New York: A Harvest Book, Harcourt, Brace & World, Inc., 1959.

Eranos Jahrbuch, vol. 56. Frankfurt am Main: Insel Verlag, 1987.

Flood, Gavin. "Politics, Experience, and the Languages of Holiness." *Numen*. 67, 2020.

Forell, Birger. "Von Celon zum Himalaya von Birger Forell," Uppsala, 1929; aus dem Schwedischen übertragen von Ursula Lorenz, 1987.

Frick, Heinrich. "Rudolf Otto innerhalb der theologischen Situation." *Zeitschrift für Theologie und Kirche* 19, 1938.

Fries, Jakob Friedrich. *Wissen, Glaube und Ahndung*. Jena, 1805; Göttingen: Verlag "Öffentliches Leben," 1931.

Fujiwara, Satoko. *The Concept of "Holiness" and Modernity: Toward a Critical Study of Comparative Religion* [in Japanese, *'Sei'-gainen to kindai: hihanteki hikaku-shūkyōgaku ni mukete*], Tokyo: Taishō-daigaku-shuppankai, 2005.

Fukazawa, Hidetaka. "The Birth of 'Religion:' the Creation and Curse of the Modern Concept of Religion" [in Japanese, "Shūkyō no seitan: kindai shūkyō gainen no seisei to jubaku"], in *What is Religion?* [in Japanese, *Shūkyō towa nani ka*], Tokyo: Iwanami-shoten, 2003.

Gantke, Wolfgang und Serikov, Vladislav. hrsg. *100 Jahre "Das Heilige:" Beiträge zu Rudolf Ottos Grundlagenwerk*. Theion: Studien zur Religionskultur, Band 32. Frankfurt am Main: Peter Lang GmbH, 2017.

Garbe, Richard. *Die Bhagavadgītā*. Leipzig: H. Haessel Verlag, 1905.

Gooch, Todd A. *The Numinous and Modernity: An Interpretation of Rudolf Otto's Philosophy of Religion*. Berlin: Walter de Gruyter, 2000.

Graham, William. *Beyond the Written Word: Oral Aspects of Scripture in the History of Religion*. Cambridge: Cambridge University Press, 1987.

Greschat, Hans-Jürgen. "On Rudolf Otto the Traveller," *Religious Studies in Dialogue: Essays in Honour of Albert C. Moore*, edited by Maurice Andrew, Peter Matheson and Simon Rae. Faculty of Theology, University of Otago, Dunedin, New Zealand, 1991.

Hanazono, Toshimaro. *Introduction to the Phenomenology of Religion* [in Japanese, *Shūkyō-genshōgaku nyūmon*], Tokyo: Heibon-sha, 2016.

Häring, Bernard. "'Das Heilige' Rudolf Ottos in der neueren Kritik." *Geist und Leben*, vol. 24, 1951.

Harnack, Adolf von. "Die Aufgabe der theologischen Fakultäten und die allgemeine Religionsgeschichte." Berlin: Gistav Scjade (Otto Francke), 1901.

Harnack, Adolf von. "Die Bedeutung der theologischen Fakultäten," in Kurt Nowak ed., *Adolf von Harnack als Zeitgenosse*, vol. 1, 1996.

Hattori, Masaaki. *The Mystical Thought of Ancient India* (in Japanese, *Kodai indo no shinpi shisō*). Tokyo: Kodansha, 1979.

Haubold, Wilhelm. *Die Bedeutung der Religionsgeschichte für die Theologie Rudolf Ottos*. Leipzig: Leopold Klotz Verlag, 1940.

Heiler, Friedrich. "Die Absolutheit des Christentums im Lichte der allgemeinen Religionsgeschichte." *Das Wesen des Katholizismus: Sechs Vorträge, gehalten im Herbst in Schweden*. Munich: Verlag von Ernst Reinhardt, 1920.

Heiler, Friedrich. "Die Bedeutung Rudolf Ottos für die vergleichende Religionsgeschichte." In Birger Forell, Heinrich Frick, Friedrich Heiler, *Religionswissenschaft in neuer Sicht*. Marburg: N.G. Elwert, 1951.

Heiler, Friedrich. *Das Gebet: Eine religionsgeschichtliche und religionspsychologische Untersuchung*, 5. Auflage (1923), Munich: Ernst Reinhardt Verlag, 1969.

Heiler, Friedrich. "The Experience of the Divine." *Journal of the Liberal Ministry*, vol. I, no. 1, 1961.

Ingalls, Daniel H.H. "Śaṁkara on the Question: Whose Is Avidyā?" *Philosophy East and West*, vol. 3, no. 4, 1953.

Izutsu, Toshihiko. *The Structure of Oriental Philosophy: Collected Papers of the Eranos Conference*, vol. 1. Tokyo: Keio University Press, 2008.

Izutsu, Toshihiko. *God and Man in the Koran: Semantics of the Koranic Weltanschauung*. Tokyo: Keio University Press, 2015.

Jantzen, Grace M. *Power, Gender and Christian Mysticism*. Cambridge: Cambridge University Press, 1995.

Joas, Hans. Nachwort: "Säkulare Heiligkeit: Wie aktuell ist Rudolf Otto?" in Rudolf Otto, *Das Heilige: Über das Irrationale in der Idee des Göttlichen und sein Verhältnis zum Rationalen*, mit einer Einführung zu Leben und Werk Rudolf Ottos von Jörg Lauster und Peter Schüz. Munich: C.H. Beck, 2014.

Jones, William. "The Third Anniversary Discourse, on the Hindus," in *The Works of Sir William Jones*, vol. 3, London: printed for John Stockdale and John Walker, 1807.

Katz, Steven T. Ed. *Mysticism and Philosophical Analysis.* New York: Oxford University Press, 1978.

Kimura, Toshihiko. *Rudolf Otto and Zen* [in Japanese, *Rudolf Otto to zen*], Tokyo: Daitō-shuppansha, 2011.

King, Richard. *Orientalism and Religion: Postcolonial Theory, India and the "Mystic East."* London, New York: Routledge, 1999.

Kitagawa, Joseph W. "The History of Religions in America." In: *The History of Religions: Essays in Methodology*, ed. by Mircea Eliade and Joseph M. Kitagawa. Chicago: The University of Chicago Press, 1959.

Kraatz, Martin. "Wirkungsstätten der Religionswissenschaft: die Religionskundliche Sammlung in Marburg." *Deutsche Vereinigung für Religionsgeschichte* 12, Mitteilungsblatt, 1979.

Kraatz, Martin. "Religionskundliche Sammlung 60 Jahre alt." *Universität Zeitung*, Nr.191, Nov. 12, 1987.

Kraatz, Martin. "'. . . meine stellung als 'modernistischer pietistisch angehauchter lutheraner mit gewissen quakerneigungen' ist eigen . . .'—Bio- und Epistolographisches zu Rudolf Otto," in Jörg Lauster, et al., *Rudolf Otto: Theologie-Religionsphilosophie-Religionsgeschichte*, Berlin: De Gruyter, 2014.

Kraatz, Martin. "Birger Forell: Der Mensch – in seinen Marburger Wurzeln und in dem, was daraus wuchs." Berlin, Vaterunser-Kirchengemeinde, 7. Juli 2008.

Kubota, Hiroshi. "The Religiousness of the 'History of Religions:' the Religionsgeschichtliche Schule as a religious movement and its strategy of 'mission'" [in Japanese, "'Shūkyō-shi' no shūkyō-sei: shūkyō-undō toshiteno shūkyōshi-gakuha to sono 'fukyō' senryaku"], in *What is the History of Religion* [in Japanese, *Shūkyō-shi towa nani ka*], edited by Hiroshi Ichikawa, Kazuo Matsumura, and Kazuko Watanabe, vol. 1, Tokyo: Lithon, 2008.

Kubota, Hiroshi. "Among Politics, Religion, and Scholarship: 'Religionswissenschaft' in Germany of Naziism" [in Japanese, "Seiji-shūkyō-gakumon no hazamade: nachizumu-ki doitsu no 'shūkyōgaku"] in *Talking Religion Again: Rethinking of the Modern Categories* [in Japanese, *Shūkyō o katari-naosu: kindaiteki kategorī no saikō*], edited by Junichi Isomae and Talal Asad, Tokyo: Misuzu-shobō, 2006.

Lange, Dietz. Ed., *Nathan Söderblom: Brev-Lettres-Briefe-Letters, A Selection from His Correspondence.* Göttingen: Vandenhoeck & Ruprecht, 2006.

Lauster, Jörg. "Religion as Feeling: Schleiermacher's Program as a Task for Theology." In Dietrich Korsch and Amber L. Griffioen eds., *Interpreting Religion: The Significance of Friedrich Schleiermacher's Reden über die Religion for Religious Studies and Theology*. Tübingen: Mohr Siebeck, 2011.

Lauster, Jörg et al. *Rudolf Otto: Theologie-Religionsphilosophie-Religionsgeschichte.* Berlin: De Gruyter, 2014.

Maeda, Tsuyoshi. *The Ground of Holiness: Traveling Otto* [in Japanese, *Sei no daichi: tabisuru Otto*], Tokyo: Kokusho-kankōkai, 2016.
Maeda, Tsuyoshi. "The Fundamental Ground of Holiness" [in Japanese, "Sei no genkyō"], *Journal of Religious Studies* [in Japanese, *Shūkyō kenkyū*], no. 314, 1997.
Mayeda, Sengaku. *A Thousand Teachings: The Upadeśasāhasrī of Śaṅkara*, Tokyo: University of Tokyo Press, 1979.
Malinar, Angelika. "Bhagavadgītā." *Brill's Encyclopedia of Hinduism*, vol. II: Sacred Texts and Languages, Ritual Traditions, Arts, Concepts. Leiden: Brill, 2010.
Mensching, Gustav. "Rudolf Otto und die Religionsgeschichte." in: *Rudolf Ottos Bedeutung für die Religionswissenschaft und Theologie heute*, Leiden: Brill, 1971.
Mensching, Gustav. *Die Religion: Erscheinungsformen, Strukturtypen und Lebensgesetze*, Goldmann Wilhelm GmbH, 1984.
Morgan, David. Ed. *Religion and Material Culture: The Matter of Belief*. London: Routledge, 2010.
Morgan, David. "Materiality, Social Analysis, and the Study of Religions," in *Religion and Material Culture*, edited by David Morgan. London: Routledge, 2010.
Nakamura, Hajime. *Śaṅkara's Thought* [in Japanese, *Shankara no shisō*]. Tokyo: Iwanami-shoten, 1989.
Nicholson, Hugh. "The New Comparative Theology and the Problem of Theological Hegemonism," in *The New Comparative Theology: Interreligious Insights from the Next Generation*, edited by Francis X. Clooney, S.J. London: T & T Clark International, 2010.
Nicholson, Hugh. *Comparative Theology and the Problem of Religious Rivalry*. Oxford: Oxford University Press, 2011.
Nowak, Kurt. Ed. *Adolf von Harnack als Zeitgenosse: Reden und Schriften aus den Jahren des Kaiserreichs und der Weimarer Republik*, vol. 1, Berlin: de Gruyter, 1996.
Ôhasama, Schûej. *Zen: Der lebendige Buddhismus in Japan*, Gotha: Leopold Klotz Verlag, 1925.
Orsi, Robert A. "The Problem of the Holy." In *The Cambridge Companion to Religious Studies*, edited by Robert A. Orsi. New York: Cambridge University Press, 2012.
Orsi, Robert A. Ed. *The Cambridge Companion to Religious Studies*. New York: Cambridge University Press, 2012.
Penner, Hans H. "The Mystical Illusion." In *Mysticism and Religious Traditions*, edited by Steven T. Katz. Oxford: Oxford University Press, 1983.
Proudfoot, Wayne. *Religious Experience*. Berkeley: University of California Press, 1985.
Pye, Michael. "Troeltsch and the Science of Religion." In *Ernst Troeltsch: Writings on Theology and Religion*, translated and edited by Robert Morgan and Michael Pye. Atlanta: John Knox Press, 1977.
Radhakrishnan, S. "Introductory Essay." *The Bhagavadgītā*. New York: Harper & Row, 1948.
Raphael, Melissa. *Rudolf Otto and the Concept of Holiness*. Oxford: Clarendon Press, 1997.

Rennie, Bryan S. *Reconstructing Eliade: Making Sense of Religion*. Albany: State University of New York Press, 1996.

Ricoeur, Paul. *La symbolique du mal*. Paris: Aubier, 1960.

Ricoeur, Paul. "Manifestation and Proclamation." *Blaisdell Institute Journal* 11, 1978.

Ricoeur, Paul. *Figuring the Sacred: Religion, Narrative, and Imagination*. Edited by Mark I. Wallace, and translated by David Pellauer. Minneapolis: Fortless Press, 1995.

Ritter, Joachim. Ed., "Heilig." *Historisches Wörterbuch der Philosophie*. Bd. 3. Basel/Stuttgart: Schwabe & Co. Verlag, 1974.

Rollmann, Hans. "Rudolf Otto and India." *Religious Studies Review*, 5, 1979.

Rudolph, Kurt. *Die Religionswissenschaft an der Leipziger Universität*. Leipzig, 1962.

Rudolph, Kurt. "Die Problematik der Religionswissenschaft als akademisches Lehrfach," *Kairos* 9, 1967.

Rudolph, Kurt. "Religionsgeschichtliche Schule." *Encyclopedia of Religion*. Edited by Mircea Eliade, vol. XII, New York: Macmillan, 1987.

Sawai, Yoshitsugu. "Polytheism and Monotheism in Hinduism" [in Japanese, "Hindūkyō ni okeru tashinsei to isshinsei"], *G-TEN*. Edited by Tenri Yamato Cultural Congress, vol. 53, 1990.

Sawai, Yoshitsugu. "Rāmānuja's Hermeneutics of the Upaniṣads in Comparison with Śaṅkara's Interpretation." *Journal of Indian Philosophy*, vol. 19, no.1. Dordrecht: Kluwer Academic Publishers, 1991.

Sawai, Yoshitsugu. *The Faith of Ascetics and Lay Smārtas: A Study of the Śaṅkaran Tradition of Śṛṅgeri*. Vienna: Sammlung de Nobili, 1992.

Sawai, Yoshitsugu. "Izutsu's Creative 'Reading' of Oriental Thought and Its Development." Editor's essay in Toshihiko Izutsu, *The Structure of Oriental Philosophy*, vol. 2, Tokyo: Keio University Press, 2008.

Sawai, Yoshitsugu. "The Structure of Reality in Izutsu's Oriental Philosophy." In Anis Malik Thoha ed., *Japanese Contribution to Islamic Studies: The Legacy of Toshihiko Izutsu Interpreted*. Kuala Lumpur: International Islamic University Malaysia, 2010.

Sawai, Yoshitsugu. "Reflections on Bhakti as a Type of Indian Mysticism." In Iwao Shima et al., *The Historical Development of the Bhakti Movement in India: Theory and Practice*. Japanese Studies on South Asia, no. 8. New Delhi: Manohar, 2011.

Sawai, Yoshitsugu. "Rudolf Otto's View of Indian Religious Thought." in Jörg Lauster, et al., *Rudolf Otto: Theologie-Religionsphilosophie-Religionsgeschichte*. Berlin: De Gruyter, 2014.

Sawai, Yoshitsugu. "The Significance of Materiality for Religious Studies." In Saburo S. Morishita ed., *Materiality in Religion and Culture: Tenri University-Marburg University Joint Research Project*. Zürich: LIT Verlag, 2016.

Sawai, Yoshitsugu. *Thoughts and Faiths of Śaṅkaran Tradition* [in Japanese, *Shankara-ha no shisō to shinkō*]. Tokyo: Keio University Press, 2016.

Sawai, Yoshitsugu. "A Semantic Perspective on Otto's Theory of Religion," *Tenri Journal of Religion*, no. 45, Tenri University Press, 2017.

Sawai, Yoshitsugu. *Rudolf Otto: The Origin of the History of Religions* [in Japanese, *Rudolf Otto: shūkyōgaku no genten*]. Tokyo: Keio University Press, 2019.

Scheler, Max. *Vom Ewigen im Menschen.* 1921, Gesammelte Werke Band 5. Bern Francke Verlag, 1954.

Schleiermacher, Friedrich. *Über die Religion: Reden an die Gebildeten unter ihren Verächtern.* Edited by Rudolf Otto. Göttingen: Vandenhoeck & Ruprecht, [1799] 1899.

Schmidt, Leigh Eric. "The Making of Modern 'Mysticism.'" *Journal of the American Academy of Religion*, vol. 71, 2003.

Sharpe, Eric J. *Comparative Religion: A History.* Illinois: Open Court, Second edition: 1986.

Sharpe, Eric J. *Nathan Söderblom and the Study of Religion.* Chapel Hill: The University of North Carolina Press, 1990.

Seifert, P. *Die Religionsphilosophie bei Rudolf Otto.* Düsseldorf: C.H. Nolte, 1936.

Shinzer, Reinhard. "Rudolf Otto—Entwurf einer Biographie." *Rudolf Otto's Bedeutung für die Religionswissenschaft und die Theologie Heute.* Hrsg. von Ernst Benz. Leiden: Brill, 1971.

Schütte, H. W. *Religion und Christentum in der Theologie Rudolf Ottos.* Berlin: de Gruyter, 1969.

Smart, Ninian. *Reflections in the Mirror of Religion*, edited by John P. Burris. London: Macmillan Press, 1997.

Smith, Jonathan Z. *Imagining Religion: From Babylon to Jonestown.* Chicago: The University of Chicago Press, 1982.

Smith, Jonathan Z. "Religion, Religions, Religious." In: *Critical Terms for Religious Studies*, ed. by Mark C. Taylor. Chicago and London: The University of Chicago Press, 1998.

Smith, Margaret. "The Nature and Meaning of Mysticism." *Understanding Mysticism*, edited by Richard Woods. New York: A Division of Doubleday & Company, Inc., 1980.

Smith, Wilfred Cantwell. "Comparative Religion: Whither—and Why?" In: *The History of Religions: Essays in Methodology*, edited by Mircea Eliade and Joseph M. Kitagawa. Chicago: The University of Chicago Press, 1959.

Smith, Wilfred Cantwell. *The Meaning and End of Religion.* New York: Harper & Row, 1962.

Smith, Wilfred Cantwell. *Faith and Belief.* Princeton: Princeton University Press, 1979.

Söderblom, Nathan. "Holiness." J. Hastings ed., *Encyclopaedia of Religion and Ethics*, VI, 1913.

Suzuki, Daisetz Teitaro. "The Meditation Hall and the Monkish Discipline." *The Eastern Buddhist*, vol. II, 1–2, 1922.

Tamaru, Noriyoshi. *The History and Task of the History of Religions* [in Japanese, *Shūkyōgaku no rekishi to kadai*], Tokyo: Yamamoto Shoten, 1987.

Ter Haar, Gerrie and Tsuruoka, Yoshio. Ed., *Religion and Society: An Agenda for the 21th Century*. Leiden/Boston: Brill, 2007.

Thoha, Anis Malik ed., *Japanese Contribution to Islamic Studies: The Legacy of Toshihiko Izutsu Interpreted*. Kuala Lumpur: International Islamic University Malaysia, 2010.

Tomizawa, Kana. "British Gentlemen's Indian Controversy: The Understanding of India and Religion by "Orientalists" at the End of the 18th Century" (in Japanese, *Igirisu shinshi no indo ronsō: 18 seiki-matsu 'orientarisuto' no indo-rikai to shūkyō-rikai*), in Susumu Shimazono and Yoshio Tsuruoka ed., *Reconsidering 'Religion'* (in Japanese, *Shūkyō saikō*). Tokyo: Perikan-sha, 2004.

Troeltsch, Ernst. *Zur religiösen Lage, Religionsphilosophie und Ethik*. Gesammelte Schriften II. Tübingen: J.C.B. Mohr, 1922.

Troeltsch, Ernst. *Die Absolutheit des Christentums und die Religionsgeschichte*, Tübingen: J.C.B. Mohr, 1902.

Vaughan, Robert Alfred. *Hours with the Mystics: A Contribution to the History of Religious Opinion*, 2 vols. London: Slark, 1856; 5th edition, 1888.

Wach, Joachim. *Types of Religious Experience: Christian and Non-Christian*. Chicago: The University of Chicago Press, 1951.

Wach, Joachim. Edited with an Introduction by Joseph M. Kitagawa. *The Comparative Study of Religions*. New York: Columbia University Press, 1958.

Warashina, Chie. "Between Theology and the History of Religions: on R. Otto, Das Heilige" [in Japanese, *Shingaku to shūkyōgaku no hazama de: R. Otto, Seinarumono o megutte*, the Doctoral dissertation, submitted to Tokyo University of Foreign Studies], 2017.

Wasserstrom, Steven M. *Religion after Religion: Gershom Scholem, Mircea Eliade, and Henry Corbin at Eranos*. Princeton: Princeton University Press, 1999.

Wendland, J. "Neufriesianismus." *Die Religion in Geschichte und Gegenwart*. 2nd ed., vol. IV, Tübingen: Mohr/Siebeck, 1930.

Wiefel-Jenner, Katharina. "Der Schweigende Dienst," in *Rudolf Ottos Liturgik*. Göttingen: Vandenhoeck & Ruprecht, 1997.

Index

Abgeordnetenhaus (House of Representatives) 17
absolute superiority 63
absoluteness of Christianity 20, 30, 53, 56, 166 n.8
adherents of Śaṅkaran religious tradition (= *smārtas*) 95, 170 n.36
Advaita (non-dual) Vedānta philosophy 6, 119
Age of Discovery ix
Age of Enlightenment 4
ahaṃ brahmāsmi 135
Ahndung, Ahnung 63–4, 69, 164 n.33
  see intuitive apprehension
Alienum 65, 105
aliud valde 65, 105–6
Allen, Douglas 55
Alles, Gregory D. xii, 9–10, 48, 143
Allgemeine Religionsgeschichte (general history of religions) 22, 23, 157 n.25
Almond, Philip C. 3, 9, 10, 14, 16, 18, 67, 68, 69, 155 n.8, 163 n.16, 164 n.33
  rational religion 62
analogy (*Entsprechung*) 62, 90, 121, 139
anthropology of religion 129, 131, 132
anthropomorphism 141
anyad 65, 105–6
apologetics (*Apologetik*) 123, 134
a priori 6, 17, 53, 54, 57, 58, 61, 64, 66–9, 79, 123, 135, 142, 147, 165 n.45
Arweck, Elisabeth 47
Asiatic Society of Bengal ix, 2
Asiatic Society of Japan 33, 42, 79, 89, 116, 134
associated with the object (*Objekt-bezogen*) 61
Ātman 92, 93, 94, 95, 101, 105, 106, 111–12, 119, 120–1, 135
  Ātman-mysticism 94, 120
  individual Ātman 95
  see Brahman
ātman 6, 76–7, 93, 112, 121
  ātma-siddhi (realization of the self) 98
Aufsätze das Numinose Betreffend 43
awe vii, 64–6, 75, 76, 139

Barth, Karl 46
Being 92, 93, 135, 142, 144
Bhagavadgītā ix, 5, 11, 38–40, 49, 111, 112, 115, 122, 159 n.7, n.11
  Original Gītā 37, 39, 159 n.7
Bhāgavatas 38
bhakti (devotion) 3, 6, 38, 74, 77, 78, 81, 82, 83, 94, 95, 96, 97, 108, 109, 122, 125, 173 n.26
  bhakti-mārga (way of devotion) 96, 122
  Bhakti religion 11, 38, 39, 77, 80, 98, 99, 108–10, 123, 125
Bhakti-stotras (devotional hymns) 95
Bible 15, 20, 21, 22, 41, 71, 99, 139
  Biblical Christianity 15
  Biblical documents 21
  Book of Isaiah 19
Bleeker, Claas Jouco 55
Bousset, Wilhelm 25
Brahman 6, 38, 39, 76, 77, 92–5, 101, 105–6, 112, 120, 121, 122, 124, 135
  supreme Brahman 95, 106, 135
  with attributes (*saguṇa-brahman*) 95, 124
  without attributes (*nirguṇa-brahman*) 122, 124
Brahmanism 76
breakthrough (*Durchbruch*) 112
Buddha, Gautama 43, 76, 131
Buddhism 32, 44, 48, 72, 93, 108, 119, 127, 134
  Buddhist philosophy 139
  Buddhist traditions 5, 79
Buddhist Youth Association in Ceylon (YMBA) 48
Bultmann, Rudolf Karl 46–7
Breslau University 16, 29, 46, 53

Caitanya 77
Calvin 18
Carman, Ann 12
Carman, John B. xii, 5, 6, 11, 12, 85, 108, 123, 168 n.28
Catholic Church 23, 127
Center for the Study of World Religions (Harvard University) 11, 130
Choi, Jeong Hwa 151 n.2
Christian theologian vii, x, 1, 3, 11, 13–16, 19, 22–7, 30, 41, 50, 54, 55, 72, 73, 83, 115, 124, 129
Christian theology vi–ix, xii, 1, 3, 4–7, 8, 13, 14, 17, 19–22, 23, 29, 31, 38, 40–1, 46, 49, 50, 52–3, 56–8, 62, 71, 72, 73, 78, 83, 86, 115, 117, 127–9, 132, 133, 140, 147, 149, 153 n.6
Christian thought x, 1, 6, 33, 82, 96, 99, 106, 110, 122, 134
Christian truth 22, 52, 84, 147, 148, 149
Chuang-tzŭ 143–4
Clooney, Francis xii, 26, 50, 158 n.42, 162 n.36
common religious feeling 5, 89, 104, 116, 133, 134
Comparative History of Religions (*vergleichende Religionsgeschichte*) 7
comparative religion vii, viii, ix, xi, 2, 5, 17, 19, 26, 29ff., 57, 85, 93, 96, 103, 104, 115, 117, 129, 130, 147, 149
comparative study of religions 2, 10, 20, 21, 22, 41, 49, 57, 58, 71, 72, 73–5, 103, 128, 166 n.8
comparative theology 26–7, 50, 158 n.42, 162 n.36
comparison 5, 22, 23, 30, 50, 52, 71, 73, 74, 79, 80, 97, 99, 108, 116, 147, 173 n.18
compound-eye perspectives 145
Colebrooke, Henry Thomas ix, 2
concept of *the holy* 11, 31, 50, 51, 59, 60, 104, 132, 136, 141, 144, 148
concept of "religion" 60, 104
conceptual framework vi, 7, 59, 83, 95, 101, 104, 107, 110, 113, 119, 121, 124, 128
Confucius 76
contrast-harmony (*Kontrast-harmonie*) 64, 137
convergence (*Konvergenz*) 74, 75, 89, 116, 117
Corbin, Henry viii
cosmic 'illusion' of *avidyā* 96
creature-feeling (*Kreaturgefühl*) 63
crypto-theology (*Kryptotheologie*) 56

das ganz Andere vii, 6, 65, 83, 103, 104, 105, 106, 133, 137, 143
Das Gefühl des Überweltlichen 43, 61, 65
Das Heilige 147,vii, xi, 1, 4, 8, 9, 10, 11, 13, 15, 16, 17, 19, 20, 23, 25, 26, 34, 37, 40, 41, 44, 46, 51–69, 90, 105, 117, 122, 132, 142, 147, 162 n.4, 163 n.5; n.16, 164 n33, 165 n.45
Das Heilige und das Profane 8, 59
Davids, C. A. F. Rhys 108
Davidson, Robert F. 9, 17, 18, 56, 57, 61, 68, 69, 92, 112, 133, 137
deified man (*vergotteter Mensch*) 135
depth (*Tiefe*)
- of existence 110
- of meaning 137, 138, 141, 143, 145, 149; *see also* meaning
- of *the numinous* 105, 111, 112, 136
- of the *numinous* feeling 112
- of one's soul 94, 120
- of reality 60, 137, 138, 143, 144
- of religious experience 133, 143

De Servo Arbitrio vii, 66
Der Römerbrief 46
Deussen, Paul 3, 4, 107
development of religion 4, 5, 33, 42, 51, 60, 66, 75, 104, 107, 115–17, 131
dialectic of the sacred 59
dialectical theology 46
Die Anschauung vom heiligen Geiste bei Luther 15, 34, 66
Die christliche Welt 24, 31, 151 n.2
Die Gnadenreligion Indiens und das Christentum 5, 21, 38, 49, 57, 75, 77, 80, 82, 90, 107, 108, 115, 117, 122, 123, 125, 168 n.28
Die Religion in Geschichte und Gegenwart (2nd edition) 38
dimension
- of meaning, 138, 141–5, 149; *see also* meaning

of *numinous* experience 143, 144
of reality 142, 144
of religious experience 132
discourse of mystic experience 115ff.
disguised theology 56
dissimile 106
divina majestas vii, 66
divination (*Divination*) 17, 25, 136
divine majesty (*divina majestas*) 66
divinity (*Gottheit*) 62, 76, 86, 87, 91, 93, 118
Doctor of Theology (*Licentiatus theologiae*) 15
double structure of reality and experience 142
dualistic realism 39
Dubey, S.P. 9, 10, 11, 95, 159 n.11, 169 n.16
Durkheim, Émile 9, 11, 51, 132

East India Company ix
Eastern Buddhist Society 48
Eckhart, Meister 3, 6, 26, 27, 33, 38, 77, 87, 91–5, 96, 100, 107, 120, 124, 134, 135, 169 n.24
Edgerton, Franklin 39, 159 n.11
Eleatic philosophy 76
Elephanta Island 80
Eliade, Mircea vi, viii, 8, 59, 62, 84, 129, 132, 140, 148
emancipation 38
mokṣa 94, 95
nirvāṇa 93, 119
Emergency Association of German Science 33
emotion 11, 13, 15, 24, 25, 47, 54, 63, 64, 87, 91, 112, 122, 137, 143
emotional response in human awareness 61
emptiness (*śūnyatā*) 137, 139
Eranos Conference vii–viii, 152 n.4
Erlangen School of Neo-Lutheran Theology 15
esse 92, 135
"absolute, simple, and non-additional Being" (*Esse absolutum, simpliciter nullo addito*) 92
"pure and simple Being" (*esse purum et simpkex*) 92
essence of religion 7, 15, 21, 51, 56, 62, 72, 73, 78, 82, 85, 86, 87, 111, 115, 132, 133, 147
ethicalization 121, 133
evolution 4, 42, 51, 75, 110, 116
pluralistic evolutionary theory 75
single-line evolutionary theory of religion 75
theory of 4, 42, 51
"Evolution and Religion" 42
existence 16, 38, 53, 54, 87, 92, 98, 110, 135, 142, 144
existential philosophy 47
experience
of God 20, 41
of mystery" (*Erleben des Mysteriums*) 73
of mystical union 91, 118
nonrational experience 21
of ultimate reality 5, 6
Zen experience 43
externals of religion 130
Eynon, Matthew xiii

"face" ix, x, 147, 149
faith (*Glaube*) 24, 25, 78
in God 89, 108, 121, 122
in spiritual beings 78
false category 87
fantasy 65, 135
fear (*Furcht*) 64
feeling (*Gefühl*) 17, 24, 63, 73
of "absolute dependence" (*Gefühl der Abhängigkeit schlechthin*) 63, 73
of "dependence" (*das Gefühl der 'Abhängigkeit'*) 63
feeling-reaction (*Gefühls-reaktion*) 61, 63, 64
of *the numinous* 61, 67, 81, 85, 110, 111, 117, 121, 133, 134, 137, 140
of truth (*Wahrheitsgefühl*) 17, 68, 69
feministic perspective 88
Flood, Gavin xii, 151 n.1
Forell, Birger 18, 33, 48, 79, 161 n.32, 167 n.28
foundation of the soul (*Seelengrund*) 67
Frank, Franz Reinhold von 15

Fries, Jacob Friedrich 17, 24–5, 54, 57, 63–4, 67, 69, 73
Fröbe-Kapteyn, Olga viii
Fujiwara, Satoko 11
Fukazawa, Hidetaka 86
fundamental horror (*Urschauer*) 112

Garbe, Richard 39–40, 122, 159 n.11
Geist und Wort bei Luther 15
German Faith Movement (*Deutsche Glaubensbewegung*) 48
Gifford Lectures 17, 156 n.10
God
  apprehension of God 60, 92
  attributed Brahman 94
  cause of the world (*Ursache der Welt*) 122
  Deus 91, 92, 93, 118, 124
  immanent God 118
  īśvara (*Īśvara*) 6, 74, 93, 97, 99, 122, 124; *see* Lord *or* God
  kingdom of God 16
  non-rational and impersonal God 91, 118
  of salvation (*Heilsgott*) 82
  simplicity of God (*simplicitas Dei*) 6
  Supreme God (*parameśvara*) 6, 38, 122, 124
  transcendent God (*der transzendente Gott*) 91
  without modes (*Deus sine modis*) 91, 118
  wonder (*Wunder*) of God 91, 110, 111, 118; *see* wonder
  see īśvara or Lord
godless state (*Gottlosigkeit*) 120
Goethe, Johann Wolfgang von 2, 42
Gooch, Todd A. 9, 10, 137, 138
Gospel of John 40
Göttingen University 14, 29, 42
Govindācārya, Alcondavilli 167 n.28
grace (*prasāda*) 99
grace (*gratia*) 109
  gratia sola 77, 109
grace of God 68, 99, 101, 109, 121
Graham, William A. 83, 113
Greek thought 76
Gregory of Nyssa 110
ground of the soul (*Seelengrund*) 112

Haas, Hans 161
Hackmann, Heinrich Friedrich 79
hagios 60
Hakuin's *Wasan* 44
Hanazono, Toshimaro xii, 11, 154 n.23, 163 n.6
Häring, Bernhard 68
Häring, Theodor von 15
Harnack, Adolf von 22, 53
Haskell Lectures 29, 33
Hauer, Jakob Wilhelm 48, 49, 151 n.2
Hegel, Friedrich 4
Heidegger, Martin 46, 54
Heiler, Friedrich vi, 1, 7–8, 23–4, 52, 80, 104, 153 n.10
Heraclitus (Greek philosopher) 77, 78
hermeneutical 37, 83, 84, 101, 113, 130, 131, 138, 145, 149
hidden theology 59
hierophany 59, 140
Hillman, James viii
Hinduism 10, 27, 37, 41, 49, 50, 56, 72, 77, 78, 79, 80, 81–3, 103, 105, 106–8, 111, 113, 162 n.36, 168 n.28
historian of religions (*Religionswissenschaftler*) vii, viii, 3, 4, 7, 13, 23, 25, 30, 39, 45, 46, 47, 48, 49, 57, 75, 79, 80, 86, 87, 88, 129, 131, 143, 165 n.45
history
  abandonment of 75
  historical contextualization (*historische Kontextualisierung*) 9
  historical facts 21, 71
History of Religions vi, vii, viii, ix, x, xi, 1–7, 8, 11, 19, 20, 22, 23, 24, 41, 47, 51, 52, 54, 56, 59, 72, 80, 103, 104, 106, 110, 112, 117, 125, 127, 128–9, 130, 131, 132, 133, 141, 145, 148, 149, 153 n.6
History-of-Religions School 13, 15, 71ff., 165 n.2, 166 n.2
  see Religionsgeschichtliche Schule
holy, the vii, x, 1, 5, 6, 8, 10, 11, 17, 20, 26, 31, 32, 40, 41, 50, 51ff., 60–5, 66–9, 80, 81, 82, 99, 104, 106, 115, 122–5, 132, 133, 135, 136, 137, 138, 140, 141–5, 147, 148, 149

holy
ethical meaning 60
non-rational dimension 143
"holy word" of magical hymns 76
holiness (*Heiligkeit*) 7, 9, 10, 11, 25, 26, 31, 32, 51, 85, 98, 101, 113, 132–3, 136, 138, 139, 140, 142
see the holy
homo religiosus 140
homo symbolicus 140
"How Schleiermacher rediscovered religion" ("*Wie Schleiermacher die Religion wiederentdeckte*") 24
humanity (*Menschentum*) 47, 49, 65, 81, 87
Hume, David 4
Husserl, Edmund Gustav Albrecht 13, 54, 55, 72, 147

IAHR (International Association for the History of Religions) 128, 174 n.1
identity of *brahman* and *ātman* 6, 94, 95, 101, 105, 106, 120, 121, 135
see tat tvam asi or *ahaṃ brahmāsmi*
ideogram (*Ideogramm*) 13641, 145, 148, 149
illusion (*māyā*) 87, 96, 101, 125
incarnation of Śiva (*śivāvatāra*) 95
independence (*kaivalya*) 120
Indian philosophy 3, 6, 41, 94, 120, 122, 123, 125, 159 n.11
Indian religious thought viii, ix, xi, xii, 1, 3, 4, 6, 7, 8, 11, 13, 23, 24, 29, 32, 33, 34, 37, 38, 40, 41, 49, 50, 66, 84, 85, 97, 104, 105–8, 110, 115, 121, 122, 125, 132, 147, 149, 169 n.16, 172 n.1
India's religion of grace 3
Indian type of mysticism 115
Indo-European languages ix
Indology ix, 1, 2, 86, 107
Ingalls, Daniel H.H. 125
inner abyss (*innere Abgrund*) 112
inner affinity (*innerliche Verwandtschaft*) 92
inspiration (*Einfälle*) 25, 112
interpenetration 95, 124
interpretative sign (*Deute-Zeichen*) 139
interreligious cooperation 48
Introduction to the Science of Religion 2
intuition (*Anschauung, Intuition*) 15, 24, 25, 47, 63, 73, 91, 92, 94, 120, 134
and emotion 15, 25
phenomenological intuition (of the essence) 55, 148
intuitive apprehension (*Ahndung; Ahnung*) 17, 24, 25, 157 n.33
inward teacher (*inwendiger Lehrer*) 138
īśvara 6, 74, 93, 97, 99, 122, 124
see Lord *or* God
Izutsu, Toshihiko viii, x, 142, 143, 144, 175 n.32

Jacobi, Hermann G. 40
Jacobsohn, Hermann 18
Jagadguru 81–2, 95
Saccidānandaśivābhinavanṛsiṃhabhāratī (the thirty-third Jagadguru) 82
see Śaṅkara
Jahweh 76
James, William 9
Jantzen, Grace M. 88
JARS (Japanese Association for Religious Studies) xii
Jewish-Christian traditions 79
jñāna-mārga (the way of knowledge) 96
Joas, Hans 9
Jones, William ix, 2, 107
journey to the East 26, 32, 45, 48, 79, 83, 89, 104, 116
Jung, Carl Gustav viii, 152 n.4

Kahn, Albert 32
Kahn Foundation, the 32
Kant, Immanuel 16, 17, 25, 54, 63, 66, 67, 68, 69, 73, 86
transcendental idealism 69, 73
Kant-Fries's philosophy of religion 17
Kantisch-Fries'sche Religionsphilosophie und ihre Anwendung auf die Theologie (*The Philosophy of Religion Based on Kant and Fries*) xi, 17, 19, 20, 24, 34, 69, 73, 164 n.33
Katz, Steven T. 87
Keane, Webb 47
Keenan, William 47
Kenninji Temple 160 n.18
Kiba, Ryōhon 48
Kimura, Toshihiko 11, 160 n.18

Kipling, Rudyard 100
Kitagawa, Joseph M. 129–30
knowledge ix, 2, 4, 17, 24, 25, 26, 43, 56, 64, 66, 73, 76, 92, 115, 118, 141
jñāna 38, 94, 96, 112, 120, 121
Wissen 24, 25, 64, 157 n.33
Kōya, Mt. 42, 160 n.16
Kraatz, Margot xii
Kraatz, Martin xii, 9, 45, 151 n.2, 154 n.13, 161, n.32
Kristensen, William Brede xi
Kubota, Hiroshi 156 n.22, 165 n.2

language of scripture 137, 138
Lao-tzŭ 76, 143–4
Lauster, Jörg 9, 63, 151 n.2, 153 n.13
law of parallel lines of development 72, 74, 89, 104
League of Nations 48, 49
Leben und Wirken Jesu nach historisch-kritische Auffassung 16, 21
liberation 10, 98
liberal theology 21, 46, 71
līlā 97
lived religion (*gelebte Religion*) 133, 143
logos 76, 77
Lord 19, 31, 74, 77, 93, 97, 109
see īśvara or God
Luther, Martin vii, 15, 16, 18, 26, 60, 61, 64, 66, 77, 93, 96, 100, 122, 147
Lutheran Church 14, 16, 18
Lutheran theologian vii, viii, xi, 1, 5, 13, 14, 22, 26, 29, 30, 49, 53, 72, 79, 83, 93, 107, 115, 119, 147, 149
Lutheran theology 14, 15, 66, 147

Madhva 109
Dvaita (dual) Vedānta philosophy 109
Maeda, Tsuyoshi xii, 11, 30, 45, 46, 158 n.1, 171 n.4
magical hymns 76
majesty (*majestas*) 65, 66, 80, 81
Mahābhārata 38, 39
Mahāyāna Buddhist mysticism 43
Malinar, Angelika 159 n.11
Marburg University (Philipps-Universität Marburg) vi, vii, xi, xii, 1, 5, 7, 8, 9, 11, 19, 23, 29, 31, 44, 45, 46, 47, 52, 53, 56, 153 n.13, 158 n.1
Marburg Friedhof 19
Marburger Religionskundliche Sammlung xii, 9, 31, 44, 45, 80, 82, 160 n.21
MARBURGER Universitäts-Zeitung 45
marvel (*adbhuta*) 112
materiality 47, 160 n.21
expressions 43, 47, 106, 138
forms 18, 20, 23, 45, 47, 111, 140, 143
material 5, 30, 44, 46, 47, 54, 67, 80
māyā 96, 97, 125
meaning
deep dimension of the non-rational 136
double structure of 142, 144
dual meaning of religious language 141
fluid or unarticulated depth of 137
hidden 138, 139, 145, 149
multilayered structure of meaning 136
superficial dimension of the rational meaning 136
transcendent meaning of numinous feeling 137
unarticulated level of 144
Mensching, Gustav vi, 7, 49, 75, 153 n.9
metuenda voluntas vii, 66
mirum 65, 137, 139
monotheism 4, 10, 75, 78, 103, 105, 107
"Moral Law and the Will of God" (*Sittengesetz und Gottesville*) 17
Morgan, David 47, 161 n.27
Morich, Armin 152 n.4
Müller, Friedrich Max 2, 22, 103, 107
"My View of Japanese Religion" 42
Mysore king (Mahārāja) 81
mysteriosum 68
mysterious (*acintya*) 112
mysterious coincidence 78
union 40, 87, 90, 91, 93, 110, 117, 118, 119; *see unio mystica*
mystery (*mysterium*) 6, 31, 64, 65, 69, 73, 80, 90, 105
mysterium fascinans 64
mysterium tremendum 64
mystical intuition (*intuitus mysticus*) 91, 92, 94, 120, 134
mystical experiences 86, 91, 117
see intuition
mystical theology 86

mysticism (*Mystik*) 6, 8, 11, 26, 29, 38, 40, 43, 52, 56, 76, 77, 85ff., 103, 105, 107, 110, 111, 115–19, 120, 122, 124, 125, 134, 148, 169 n.24
All-One theopantistic 77
Ātman-mysticism 94, 120
bhakti-mysticism (*bhakti-Mystik*) 96, 97, 122
essence of a mysterious spiritual phenomenon 90
essential union or the essential unity with the divine 90
God-mysticism (*Gottesmystik*) 93, 94, 95, 96, 119, 120
Indian type of 116
of introspection (*Innenschau*) 93, 94, 119, 120
non-dualism 81
Oriental mysticism 93
Savior-mysticism (*Heilandsmystik*) 77
soul-mysticism (*Seelenmystik*) 93, 94, 95, 96, 119, 120
of unifying vision (*Einheitsschau*) 93, 94, 119, 120
Zen mysticism 43
Mysticism East and West 26, 29, 38, 169 n.24
see *West-östliche Mystik*
mystikos 86
mystocentrism 88
mythologia (the knowledge of myth) 76
mythological apperception 65
mythological foundation 76
mythos 76

Nakamura, Hajime 92, 171 n.49
Nakayama, Shōzen 160 n.21
narrative 5, 21, 39, 74, 75, 78
National Liberal Party 17
natural (*natürlich*) 64, 66, 137, 138, 139, 148
naturalism 17, 58, 69, 73
Naturalistische und religiöse Weltansicht (*Naturalism and Religion*) 17, 58, 73
Nelson, Leonald 17
Neo-Friesianism (*Neufriesianismus*) 25
Neo-Kantian philosophy 13, 17, 24
nescience (*avidyā*) 101, 125
New Testament 16, 20, 40, 41, 139
Nicholson, Hugh 26, 50, 158 n.42, 162 n.36, 169 n.24
nirguṇa-brahman (non-qualified Brahman) 6
nirvāṇa 93, 119
no soul (*an-ātman*) 93
Nobel Peace Prize 49
noble man (*homo nobilis*) 135
non-Christian religions 2, 4, 20, 27, 29, 30, 44, 45, 48, 49, 50, 52, 53, 72, 74, 86
non-mediate psychological phenomenon 21
non-rational x, 6, 7, 20, 40, 41, 43, 54, 58–64, 66–9, 73, 77, 82, 86, 88, 91, 93, 104, 105, 110, 111, 118, 119, 121–3, 132–6, 137–44, 147, 148, 174 n.8
non-rational aspect of *the holy* 54, 64, 142, 147
see rational
"not this, not that" (*neti neti*) 92
nothingness (*wu*; *mu*) 137
numen 7, 58, 60, 66, 67
numinous, the (*das Numinose*) vii, x, xi, 1, 6, 10, 11, 26, 40, 43, 52–65, 66–9, 74, 75, 79, 81, 82, 85, 88, 91, 93, 103, 105, 106, 110, 111, 112, 117, 119, 121, 123, 133, 134, 135, 141–5, 147, 148, 149, 154 n.15, 165 n.45
numinous experience 40, 138, 145
numinous feeling 65, 66, 69, 79, 112, 137, 143, 165 n.45
numinous aspect of *the holy* 59
"Numinous Experience in Zazen" ("Numinoses Erlebnis im Zazen") 43

"object outside me" (*ein Objekt außer mir*) 61
objective transcendent reality 61
"objective" or value-free discipline 128
Obscurantism 86
Ochsner, Heinrich 54
Ōhazama, Shūei 43–4
Olaus Petri Lectures 29, 35
Oldenberg, Hermann 107
"one only, without the second" (*ekam eva advitīyam*) 6

"On *Zazen* as the Extreme of the Numinous Non-rational" 43
original feeling (*Urgefühl*) 67
Orsi, Robert A. vii, 13, 135, 175 n.20
Ottmer, Ernst 158 n.5
Ottmer, Johanne 18, 32, 158 n.5, 167 n.25
Ottmer, Margarete 80, 159 n.5, 167 n.25
Otto Renaissance 9
Otto, Wilhelm 14

paṅḍit (*paṇḍita*) ix
Parakāla Maṭha 81
Parakāla Svāmī 81
parallel 3, 5, 6, 38, 59, 72, 74, 75, 77, 78, 89, 100, 104–5, 107, 108, 109, 111, 115, 116, 121, 122, 134
parallelism 33, 42, 74, 76, 79, 85ff., 104–5, 116, 117, 134
"Parallelisms in the Development of Religion East and West" 33, 42, 79, 116, 134
Parish General Assembly in Kassel 80
Paul 124, 131
Penner, Hans H. 87, 88
phenomenological (*phänomenologisch*) xi, 11, 46, 54, 55, 56, 57, 69, 72, 131, 132, 135, 147, 163 n.16
phenomenological intuition 55, 148
phenomenology of religion 11, 13, 51, 54, 55, 57, 58, 71, 75, 85, 131, 132, 133, 139, 147, 148, 163 n.6
phenomenology of the sacred 139, 175 n.26
phenomenon of "meaning" 101
Philosophical Association of Japan, the 42
philosophical reflection 76, 121, 123
philosophy (*Filosofie*) 56, 76, 91, 108, 123, 131, 134
philosophy of religion vii, 3, 7, 8, 10, 16, 17, 19, 23, 30, 33, 38, 57, 73, 82, 83, 107, 115, 128, 132, 149
piety (*Frömmigkeit*) 73
"pious Lutheran adherent" (*pietistischer Lutheraner*) vii, 19
pneuma 77
polytheism 4, 78, 103
polytheistic characteristics of Hinduism 72
popular religiousness 21
post-Eliade studies of religion 148
post-Schleiermacher era 73
power 19, 26, 40, 42, 48, 88, 89, 97, 111, 132, 139
prapatti (self-surrender) 74
Prayer (*Das Gebet*) 7
pre-religion (*Vorreligion*) 75, 78
pre-verbal vocalization 65
primitive monotheistic doctrine (*Urmonotheismus*) 75
process of ethical interpretation of *the numinous* 75
profane 8, 26, 51, 59, 62, 138, 148
prototype 38
Proudfoot, Wayne 87
Prussian Landtag (State Legislature) 17
psychology of religion 19, 41, 129, 131
Pye, Michael 165 n.45

Qādosch (*Qādôsh*) vii, 60, 66
Quakers 151 n.2
Quellen der Religionsgeschichte 45, 46

Rade, Martin 31
Radhakrishnan, S. 87, 159 n.11
Rāmānuja xi, 3, 5, 6, 11, 38, 77, 81, 83, 96–8, 100, 109, 110, 120, 122, 123, 125, 134, 167–8 n.28
  qualified non-dual Vedānta philosophy 3, 81
Rāmānuja School (Vadagarai School) 81
  Rāmānuja College in Mysore 81
  Rāmānujan monastery in Melkote 123
Raphael, Melissa 9, 10
rational vii, x, 6, 13, 17, 19, 20, 21, 24, 40, 41, 53, 58–9, 60, 62, 66–9, 73, 77, 104, 111, 121–3, 133, 135, 136, 137, 138, 139, 141, 142, 144, 145, 147, 148, 174 n.8
  see non-rational
rational speculation 60, 111, 141
rationalism 58, 61, 73, 86
rationalization 86, 121, 133, 135
recognition (*Erkenntnis*) 24, 25, 45, 62, 89, 130
reductionist explanation 87

reflection of feelings 63
Reformation, the 18
Reich Gottes und Menschensohn (*The Kingdom of God and the Son of Man*) 16
religion
  development of xi, 4, 5, 33, 42, 51, 60, 66, 75, 79, 104, 107, 115ff., 131
  of grace (*Gnadenreligion*) 3, 11, 29, 38, 77, 78, 83, 108, 109, 123, 125
  reconstructed religion 82, 84
  of the Vedas 76
  uniqueness and non-rationality of 148
Religionsgeschichte (the history of religions) 23
Religionsgeschichtliche Schule 13, 14, 16, 71–84, 165–6 n.2
  see History-of-Religions School
religionskundlich 41, 46, 47, 72
Religionsurkunden der Völker 46, 160–1 n.24
Religionswissenschaft vi, viii, 2, 7, 20, 22, 23, 46, 56, 73, 79, 103, 128, 129, 130
  see History of Religions
religionswissenschaftlich 46
Religiöser Menschheitsbund 10, 17, 44, 47, 48, 49, 80, 149
  see Religious League of Humanity
religious
  "protected area" of religious experience 87
  religious *a priori* (*Religiöses Apriori*) 17
  religious awe (*religiöse Scheu*) 65
  religious evolution 4, 51
  religious experience (*religiöse Erlebnis*) 73
  religious life (*vita religiosa*) 76
  religious reality 5, 61, 88
Religious Essays: A Supplement to 'The Idea of the Holy' 19, 52
Religious League of Humanity 10, 17, 44, 47, 48, 80, 149
  see Religiöser Menschheitsbund
religious phenomena 40, 75, 76, 78, 85, 88, 93, 99, 108, 116, 117, 119, 127, 129, 130, 131, 132, 133, 134, 140, 141, 145, 148, 170 n.33
religious pluralism 69, 128, 129, 131, 134, 141, 145
Religious Studies of Understanding (*Religionswissenschaft des Verstehens*) 7
rescue of the lost 98
rescue and release from the 'bonds' 98
revelation (*Offenbarung*) 19, 21, 22, 26, 89, 116
Ricoeur, Paul 138–9, 141, 175 n.26
Ritschl, Albrecht Benjamin 15, 53, 98
Ritsema, Rudolf 152 n.4
rival (*Konkurrent*) 77, 82, 109, 120
Roku-dai shinpō ("Six Great News") newspaper 42, 160 n.15, n.16
Rollmann, Hans 3
Rosenhagen, Ulrich 9
Rudolf-Otto-Archives of Marburg University 11
Rudolph, Kurt 21, 56

sacré 51
sacred 8, 42, 44, 51, 59, 62, 132, 138, 139, 140, 148, 175 n.26
Sacred Books of the East, The 2, 45
saguṇa-brahman (qualified Brahman) 6
salvation 3, 77, 78, 80, 81, 82, 84, 91, 92, 93, 94, 95, 97, 98, 99, 101, 108, 109, 113, 121–5, 133, 134, 138
  attainment of 95, 97
  concept of 97
  enlightenment 75, 76
  of the soul 93, 123, 124
  teacher of (*Heilslehrer*) 91, 123
  way to 92, 122, 134
Sāṃkhya philosophy 39
saṃsāra (transmigration) 38, 98, 99
sanctus 31, 60
Śaṅkara 3, 6, 10, 26, 27, 32, 33, 38, 77, 81, 82, 85, 87, 91–101, 107, 119–25, 134, 135, 169 n.24, 173 n.18
  Śaṅkarācārya 81
Śaṅkaran Maṭha 81, 82, 95
  Śrī Śāradā pīṭha (the throne of Śrī Śāradā) 95
  Śṛṅgeri Maṭha 81, 82, 95
Śaṅkaran religious tradition 81, 94, 95, 170 n.36

Saussure, Ferdinand de 143
Scheler, Max 42, 54–5, 72, 147, 163 n.6
schematization (*Schematisierung*) 66–9, 74, 75, 121, 133, 165 n.47
Schinzer, Reinhard 30
Schlegel brothers 2
Schleiermacher, Friedrich Daniel Ernst 13, 15, 16, 21, 24, 25, 26, 53, 57, 60, 63, 72, 73, 75, 87, 97
Schmidt, Leigh Eric 86, 87
Schmidt, Wilhelm 75
Scholem, Gershom viii
Schüz, Peter 9
scripture (spoken, written) ix
Scriptural studies 83
Second Vatican Council, the 127
secret (*Geheimnis*) 110
self-abandonment (*Sich-verjagen*) 112
semantic perspective of religion 136, 138, 142
  semantic dimensions 136
  semantic interpretation of Otto's "holiness" 101
  semantic understanding of religion x, 101
semantics x
Semitic religions 60
sensus numinis 61, 65, 68, 73, 78, 110, 111, 143
Shaku, Sōen 44
Shaku, Sōkatsu 44
shamanistic possession 76
Sharpe, Eric 13, 39
Shin Buddhist monk 48
Siddhānta des Rāmānuja 5, 77, 116
signifier (*signifiant*); signified (*signifié*) 143
"Silent Worship" (*Schweigender Dienst*) 151 n.2
"silent worship" of Quakers 151 n.2
sin 52, 68, 98, 99, 113, 133
Śiva 80, 81, 95
Smart, Ninian 87, 131
Smith, Jonathan Z. 5, 88, 129
Smith, Wilfred C. xii, 84, 125, 130
sociology of religion 129, 131
Söderblom, Nathan 1, 23, 25, 26, 49, 75, 80
Sōsan's *Shinjin-mei* 44
soteriology (*Heilslehre*) 122, 134
soul (*Seele*) 110
  ground of the soul (*Seelengrund*) 112
  inner "wonder" of the soul 112
  salvation of the soul 93, 123, 124
Spieth, Jakob 161
spirit (*Geist*) 110
  of India 117
  of Palestine 117
spirituality 87
Stace, W.T. 87, 88
subjective state (*subjektive Zuständlichkeit*) 61
sudden inspiration (*plötzliches Aperçu*) 112
sui generis 15, 54, 57, 60, 72, 132, 141
superiority of Christianity 8, 11, 40, 62, 74, 75, 104, 124, 129
surplus (*Überschuß*) 60, 61
Suzuki, Daisetsu 44, 48, 160 n.18
symbol 58, 84, 111, 130, 137, 139, 140, 175 n.26
symbolic language 139, 141
sympathetic attitude of understanding religion 130
  sympathetic understanding xii, 130
sympathy 72
synagogue 31, 52, 80, 140

Tagore, Rabindranath 37, 38
Takeda, Ekijū 160 n.18
Takeda, Mokurai 160 n.18
Tamaru, Noriyoshi 23, 57, 75, 132, 171 n.10
Tao 76
Taoist philosophy 143, 144
tat tvam asi (That thou art) 94, 105, 135
temple of idols (*Götzentempel*) 47
Tenrikyo xii, 160 n.21
  Tenri University xii, xiii
  Tenri University Sankōkan Museum 160 n.21
  Tenrikyo theology xii
thāteron 65, 105
The Idea of the Holy 19, 52, 53, 58, 61, 139, 163 n.16
theism 4, 10, 27, 39, 62, 75, 78, 81, 91, 94, 95, 103, 105, 107, 118, 120, 124
theologia (knowledge of divinity) 76
theological (*theologisch*) 72, 147

theology vi, vii, viii, ix, xi, xii, 1, 3, 4, 5, 6, 7, 8, 10, 11, 13–27, 30, 31, 38, 39, 40, 41, 43, 45, 46, 47, 49, 50, 52–66, 71, 72, 73, 78, 83, 86, 93, 95, 96, 97, 98, 115, 117, 122, 125, 127, 128, 129, 131, 132, 133, 134, 140, 147, 149, 153 n.6, 155 n.8, 162 n.36, 167 n.28, 171 n.10
  Glaubenslehre 122, 125, 134
  Theologie 20, 21
theory of transformation as the realistic development (*pariṇāma-vāda*) 124
theory that the effect pre-exists in the cause (*satkārya-vāda*) 124
"Towards the Reform of Divine Service" 18, 156 n.12
traditional philological research 21
transcendence 87, 90, 139
transcendental idealism 69, 73
tremor 64
Triplett, Katja xiii
Troeltsch, Ernst 4, 13, 16, 20, 53, 71, 73, 153 n.6, 155 n.8, 165 n.45, 166 n.8

Über die Religion 15, 24, 25, 53, 60, 73
Underhill, Evelyn 88
ultimate principle of the world 76
understanding (*Verstand*) 25
[unspeakable] marvel (*āścaryam*) 6
unio mystica 90, 117, 119
union 40, 87, 90, 91, 93, 110, 117, 118, 119
  with the divine 87
  mystical union (with God) 91, 93, 110, 117
  of the self with the transcendent 90
uniqueness of religion, the 7, 57, 72, 73, 85, 132, 148
  see sui generis
  uniqueness of religious experience 55
'unity' with the Highest (*die 'Einung' mit dem Höchsten*) 96, 97
Universal Religious Peace Conference 80
University of Uppsala 80
Upaniṣad 6, 38, 39, 49, 76, 94, 96, 104, 105, 106, 107, 112, 120, 135, 173 n.18
  Chāndogya Upaniṣad 6
  Classical Upaniṣad thought 76
  Katha Upaniṣad 37, 38
  Kena Upaniṣad 112

Vaikuṇṭha (Heaven; the land of bliss) 122
Vaiṣṇava tradition (Vaiṣṇavism) 3, 37, 38, 77, 78, 81, 83, 97, 98, 107, 109, 125
Vallabha 109
  Vaiṣṇava Vedāntin 109
  Śuddhādvaita (pure non-dual) Vedānta philosophy 109
van der Leeuw, Gerardus 55, 75, 132
Varuṇa 76
Vaughan, Robert Alfred 87
Vedānta-Mystik 77
Vedānta philosophy xi, 3, 6, 33, 37, 39, 81, 82, 90, 95, 96, 98, 100, 101, 107, 115-N25, 131, 134
Vischnu-Nārāyana 3, 5, 20, 41, 116
Viśiṣṭādvaita (qualified non-dual) Vedānta philosophy 3, 81
Viṣṇu 122

Wach, Joachim vi, 4, 8, 16, 26, 68, 75, 153 n.11
Wang Yang-ming 131
Warashina, Chie 11, 163 n.5
Warneck, Johannes 161
Wasserstrom, Steven 88
way
  of devotion (*bhakti-mārga*) 96, 122
  of introspection (*Weg der inneren Schau*) 94
  of knowledge (*jñāna-mārga*) 94, 96
  of unifying vision (*Weg der Einheitsschau*) 94
Weltanschauung x
Western concepts of religion 83
Western mystics 112
West-östliche Mystik 3, 6, 11, 16, 33, 38, 49, 57, 75, 85, 90, 91, 96, 100, 107, 116, 117, 169 n.16
wholly non-rational, the (*das ganz Irrationale*) 111, 118, 139
wholly other, the (*das ganz Andere*) vii, x, xi, 5, 6, 8, 65, 66, 83, 91, 101, 103–13, 118, 119, 121, 133, 137, 139, 143
Wiefel-Jenner, Katharina 151–2 n.2
Wilkins, Charles ix, 2
Wissen, Glaube, und Ahnung 24, 25
wonder (*Wunder, āścarya, mirum*) 64, 91, 110, 111, 112, 118, 119, 137, 139

World Congress for the Progress of Free Christianity and Religion (Weltkongreβ für freies Christentum und religiösen Fortschritt) 47–8
World Congress of Faiths 49
World Congress of Religions 48
world conscience (Weltgewissen) 48
World Religious Peace Conference 81
world-affirming (*weltbejahend*) 96
world-denial 96
  world-denying (*weltverneinend*) 96
wrath (*orgḗ*) 68, 139
Wrede, W. 20, 73

Yoga 32, 39, 93, 94, 119, 120
  theistic and atheistic Yoga 119
  Yogic methods 93
Yōka's *Shōdō-ka* 44
Younghusband, Sir Francis Edward 49

Zaehner, R.C. 87, 88
zazen 43, 160 n.17
  zazen practice 43
Zen 11, 43, 44, 100, 56, 160 n.17, n.18
  experience 43
  master 43, 160 n.18
  meditation 43
  monk 43
  Zen Buddhist temple 42, 43, 160 n.17
  Zen Buddhist thought 41–3, 56
Zen: Der lebendige Buddhismus in Japan 44
zero-point of Being or consciousness 142
Zur Erneuerung und Ausgestaltung des Gottesdienstes (*For the Renewal and Reformation of Divine Service*) 17, 156 n.12

www.ingramcontent.com/pod-product-compliance
Lightning Source LLC
Chambersburg PA
CBHW061827300426
44115CB00013B/2278